IF THESE HALLS
COULD TALK

IF THESE HALLS COULD TALK

THE DANIEL MENDEZ STORY

ANNA MENDEZ

TATE PUBLISHING
AND ENTERPRISES, LLC

Published by Tate Publishing & Enterprises, LLC
127 E. Trade Center Terrace | Mustang, Oklahoma 73064 USA
1.888.361.9473 | www.tatepublishing.com

Tate Publishing is committed to excellence in the publishing industry. The company reflects the philosophy established by the founders, based on Psalm 68:11,
"The Lord gave the word and great was the company of those who published it."

Published in the United States of America

ISBN: 978-1-62510-201-0
1. Biography & Autobiography / Personal Memoirs
2. Social Science / Violence in Society
13.04.01

Dedicated to our big guy.

ABOUT THIS BOOK

This book is inspired by a true story of a young teenage boy who had everything to live for. He had a family who loved and supported him, a love for life and humanity that was unshakeable, and a bright future to look forward to, but the bullies at his school had something else in mind.

The bullying/suicide phenomenon has become a social epidemic. This book is written from an insider's perspective of what is believed to have happened either from actual experience or inspired by written or verbal accounts. With the exception of those of the immediate family, all names have been changed and characters composited or fictionalized. This book is not written with the intent to accuse or place blame, but rather to educate and expose all of the dynamics that surround this tragic social epidemic in order for society to gain awareness and help bring about positive change as we work together toward a resolution.

Much cultural change is needed to adequately address this social issue. This story is intended to inspire us to make certain that no one ever has to go through the torture that this young man was forced to endure. And it isn't just hell for the children. This unfortunate phenomenon has affected people of all ages, ethnicities, orientation, and in every level of socio-economic status. It is a malignant disease that has fewer biases than one may think. It affects children regardless of race, color, creed, national origin, religion, or sexual orientation. But there is hope for a cure. Although there are countless antagonizers spreading the disease and even more victims, there are also heroes who are willing to sacrifice everything for change.

PROLOGUE

"Children who are victims of bullying can have serious health effects, including physical injuries and emotional problems such as depression, low self-esteem, anxiety, and suicidal thoughts and actions," says Matthew Davis, MD, director of the C.S. Mott Children's Hospital National Poll on Children's Health and associate professor of pediatrics and internal medicine at the University of Michigan Medical School.

In the United States, an estimated 160,000 children miss school every day out of fear of attack or intimidation by other students, according to the National Education Association.[1]

Victims of bullying—and the bullies themselves—are at increased risk of suicidal thinking and are also more likely to attempt suicide than their peers who aren't involved in bullying, according to a systematic review of thirty-seven studies conducted in sixteen different countries by Dr. Young Shin Kim of Yale University School of Medicine in New Haven, Connecticut and Dr. Bennett Leventhal of the University of Illinois College of Medicine in Chicago."[2]

Over time, the symptoms (of bullying) result in psychiatric injury, which is not a mental illness. Despite superficial similarity, and comments, both direct and implied, there are many distinct differences between psychiatric injury and mental illness.[3]

You do not have to identify as gay to be attacked with anti-lgbt language. From their earliest years on the school playground, students learn to use anti-lgbt language as the ultimate weapon to degrade their peers. In many cases, schools and teachers either ignore the behavior or don't know how to intervene, according to Dr. Eliza Byard.[4]

Far from being isolated events, bullying is frighteningly commonplace across the country. In the largest survey of its kind to look at the issue, a Clemson University study released October, 2010, researchers surveyed 524,054 students at 1,593 schools across the nation over the last two years to get a better picture of bullying in grades three through twelve. They found that 17 percent of kids reported on anonymous questionnaires that they are being bullied two to three times a month or more. Of those bullied, nearly 40 percent of the girls and 45 percent of boys, say it's been going on in some form—verbally, physically, or online—for more than a year.

The survey found that the kids who were bullied in high school were the ones who had been tormented for years on end. According to the survey, many kids don't believe there's a system in place to protect them, especially as they get older. For example, 30 percent of boys in grades three through five said their teacher had done little or nothing to reduce bullying as compared to almost 60 percent of boys in grades nine through twelve that said their schools had done little or nothing to reduce bullying.

What is more disturbing is that much of the bullying takes place in classrooms even when a teacher is present. The result seems to be that kids become increasingly closed mouthed to discuss bullying as they get older. The survey found that the older the kids were, the less likely they were to talk to parents or teachers about the bullying.

According to William Pollack, associate clinical professor in the department of psychiatry at the Harvard medical school, "Kids can't take the lead in the fight against bullying. They're too vulnerable to stand up on their own." In his own studies, Pollack has found that while many youthful bystanders would like to step in and help bullied kids, they don't feel safe doing so.

Pollack explained, "They just didn't feel there was an adult at the school who they could come forward to who would be capable of making a change or who could protect them from retaliation."[5]

In 2005, Nishina, Juvonen, and Witkow of UCLA conducted a study and reported on their findings regarding the effects of bullying on middle school children. The UCLA research shows that middle school students who are bullied are more likely to feel depressed, lonely, miserable which in turn makes them more vulnerable to further bullying incidents.

The damage to victims of bullying may be physical, emotional, and psychological, and the resulting trauma can last a lifetime. Educator responsibility to provide a safe school environment for students has been upheld by the courts in numerous illegal harassment cases and is now shaping the court's response to bullying litigation.

There are three types of bullying:

1. Physical bullying: harm to another's person or property
2. Emotional bullying: harm to another's self concept
3. Relational bullying: harm to another through damage (and or the threat of damage) to relationships or to feelings of acceptance, friendship, or group inclusion.

The victims of bullying respond in many ways; some suffer self-doubt and a drop in self-esteem and confidence, and others become bullies themselves in an attempt to compensate for their suffering[6]. Bullying is particularly harmful because it is a series of repeated acts. The effects are cumulative, and in extreme cases bullying is life threatening, driving the victim to suicide.[6]

David Kinchin's 2004 book, *Post Traumatic Stress Disorder: The Invisible Injury*, states that worldwide research proves that bullying causes post-traumatic stress syndrome.[7]

Experts classify bullying as chronic trauma. This is distinct from time-limited events that result in trauma such as rape or car accidents. Chronic trauma is a repetitive and insidious accumulation of everyday insults to one's integrity and sense of safety as a human being. The more a person is bullied and threatened, the more he or she is traumatized. (Author's Note: the bullying may not necessarily be extreme on the surface but only a repetitive accumulation of everyday insults.)

According to Dr. Herbert Gravitz, clinical psychologist, one of the most pernicious parts of being bullied is the inculcation of shame, which may show up later in addictions, compulsive behaviors, depression, and anxiety.

Trauma causes the victim to view life through a distorted lens, resulting in a loss of self-esteem, misdirection of life, lack of a purpose, an inability to adapt to stress, and/or a disconnection from other people. The eventual cost of cumulative trauma can be a loss of self.[8]

CHAPTER
ONE

Kindness to children, love for children, goodness to children—these are the only investments that never fail.

—Henry David Thoreau

It was the first day of May, and the spring sun was pouring in through the kitchen bay window as twelve-year-old Victoria and her sixteen-year-old brother, Daniel, prepared for breakfast.

Victoria, a striking girl with dark hair and dark eyes, couldn't wait for the weekend to begin. Her brother was also happy to finish up this Friday morning because he and his friends had the perfect weekend ahead of them. They were looking forward to seeing the latest action movie that had just hit theatres and playing football on the greenbelt the next day, so the sooner breakfast was over, the closer Daniel was to his weekend of events.

Sprawled out on the breakfast table was the usual morning feast—pancakes, bacon, toast, eggs over hard, and Nonna's breakfast potatoes just the way Daniel liked them. The day couldn't really start until Nonna, Victoria and Daniel's doting Italian grandmother, had kicked things off with a breakfast banquet. Having lived with the family since Daniel was born, it was her mission in life to make certain those two bellies were kept full at all times.

Nonna was an immigrant from her homeland in Italy and knew all too well about the realities of hunger and going without. So she was committed to making sure that her two grandchildren never did. Meals weren't just food to Nonna; it was her way of giving something to her grandkids that she never had. Although the kids probably didn't realize the significance that the home cooked spreads had for their grandmother, they did always leave the table, even if a little hurried, with a good feeling. Nonna's love warmed them as much as her pancakes did.

As the kids filled up on breakfast, their parents were upstairs preparing themselves for a much needed weekend anniversary getaway to Palm Springs. Unlike most Friday mornings when Danny and Anna would be rushing around their master bedroom, getting ready for their commutes to work, the two found themselves leisurely packing their suitcases with facials and fine dining on their minds.

The couple rarely ever went away without the rest of the family. Although Danny might throw out suggestions of couple's retreats and weekends away for just the two of them, Anna would usually decline.

"The kids will only be young once," she would tell her husband. "One day they'll be off on their own, living their own busy lives. Until then, I want to enjoy as much time as I possibly can with them."

But May was a big month for the couple, and Danny had finally talked his wife into a short getaway for just the two of them. May 5, just a few days away, would commemorate their twentieth wedding anniversary, and Danny wanted to mark the occasion by something a little more romantic than the traditional china. Just a week after that was Mother's Day, followed by Anna's fiftieth birthday on May 20th; it was going to be a May to remember.

With a mouthful of potatoes, Daniel double stepped the stairs and rushed into his parents' room.

"Mom," he mumbled with his mouth still full. "Can you give me that check for the summer program to Washington, DC, before you and Dad leave?"

Anna looked up to see her son standing in the doorway. It struck her how handsome he had become. He wasn't a boy anymore. He was a young man. His child's body had been replaced by a strong, muscular one; his cute, puppy eyes with the striking dark brown eyes of a young man. *Where have the years gone,* she thought as she looked at the budding adult standing in her doorway.

Danny stopped packing and turned to his son. "Are you sure you want to go back again so soon, Son? Why don't you skip one summer, and you can go back during your junior year?"

"I'd really like to go, Dad," replied Daniel. "I know we have to be more careful these days because of the economy and all, and if I can't go this time, I understand, but I really, really want to do this. I had an awesome time last year, and I learned a lot. I learned how to write a business plan and how to put together a strategic plan. I was able to search for my ancestors on Ellis Island, and I met a lot of really cool people. And anyway it will look really great on my college applications." Daniel swallowed the last of his food and flashed a toothy smile, proud of how persuasive he thought he must have sounded. His father grinned. He knew right then he'd be writing out the check.

Daniel was a driven sixteen-year-old. He knew what he wanted in life, and he did everything in his power to make sure he would get it. He had spent two weeks in New York City the previous summer studying as part of a young congressional leadership conference. He had thoroughly enjoyed the highly rigorous academic program and had been hounding his parents for the last few weeks to go again this coming summer, this time choosing the law series in Washington, DC. He'd recently informed his parents that he wanted to study law in college because he could help others, and anyway, "I can debate with the best of them."

As her son stood making his compelling case point by point, Anna recalled just how much she missed him that summer and how she had looked forward to his phone calls. She hated the thought of him being so far away for two entire weeks, but she hated even more to disappoint him.

"Daniel, love, I promise we'll give you that check when we get back on Sunday night, okay?"

Daniel gave her his trademark smile as he spoke. "But next week is the deadline, and I don't want to miss it," he pointed out. He was right; he could debate with the best of them.

"I promise you won't miss the deadline, love."

He hugged his mother and bounced away in his classic stride that always allowed her to pick him out of any crowd. It seemed to tell everyone that he had not a care in the world. *What a kid*, thought Anna, smiling.

She zipped up her small weekender and hurried downstairs for her much needed first cup of coffee. She was pouring her espresso when Nonna turned to her.

"Daniel wants me to pick him up from school two times today. He wants to skip class. I don't mind, but I want to check with you first," she said in her thick Italian accent.

That's odd, Anna thought. Daniel almost never missed school.

"That's fine, Mom." Anna took her coffee and headed up the stairs just as Daniel came bounding down toward her.

"Mom, is it okay if Nonna picks me up from school today before lunch and Italian class and then drives me back for my last period class? I have a trig test I don't want to miss."

"Why do you want to miss lunch and Italian but go back for only one last class?" Anna was confused.

"I just don't feel well." She placed her hand on her son's forehead. He felt fine.

"What's wrong, love? What hurts?"

"Nothing serious, Mom. I just don't feel very well today."

"Should I make a doctor's appointment for you?"

"No, Mom. Nothing that serious. I would just miss lunch and Italian."

"Well, if that's what you want, Nonna certainly doesn't mind. But if you go to school, why not just stay for lunch and

Italian? You're already there, and it's just lunch and Italian." Anna shrugged. "But whatever you think, Daniel."

"Okay, thanks, Mom."

She watched as he began organizing his books. *Hope he doesn't start to feel worse*, she thought.

The house was in typical family style chaos as everyone prepared to rush out the front door. Nonna, with car keys in hand, stood in the doorway to help direct traffic. Danny and Anna hurriedly kissed the kids and said they'd call later. Victoria gave her mom a hug as Danny placed his hand on Daniel's shoulder.

"You're the man in charge of the household while I'm gone, Daniel. I love you, Son."

"Love you too, Dad. Hear that, Victoria? I'm in charge." Daniel elbowed his sister with a mischievous smile. Victoria rolled her eyes. The parents watched as the kids jumped into the car and disappeared down the street. The weekend was almost upon them.

CHAPTER
TWO

The worst thing about prejudice is that while you feel hurt and angry, it feeds your self-doubt…you start thinking, perhaps I am not good enough.

—Nina Simone

Well, that's how my story begins. But what's really important is how it's going to end. See, my mom and dad had no way of knowing on that Friday morning that school had become a lot like a war zone for me. The thing is, for somebody like me, just a guy who doesn't believe that violence should be met with more violence, the system didn't work. I guess if I would have had a more get-even-and-fight-back attitude—at least that's what my best friend, Aiden, would always say—then maybe more attention might have been drawn to my specific situation, which was that I was being terrorized every single day I went to school. But that just wasn't my nature, so my hell was looked right over by teachers and principals, and I was on my own.

I know Dr. T was trying to help me, but he didn't get it. Nobody did. And how could they? They just saw a young kid with a perfect life who sometimes got depressed. To them, I was the typical teenager who was going through typical teenage stuff. But no one wants to wake up every day wondering how many times they're going to get kicked, shoved up against a locker or punched. How many times they're going to hear the word faggot and loser and half-breed yelled at them. I did, though. Some kids wake up dreading a math test, but I woke up dreading my life.

My goal was to make those guys at school like me. That might sound a little naïve, but I really believed I could do it. I thought that if I could just get them to know me a bit better, they might think, Wow, this guy isn't so bad after all. But I didn't know that bullies don't really work that way. So I was on a mission: mission impossible.

I was a black belt in Tae Kwon Do and was taking karate, so I could have taken any of those kids down. But I didn't want to resort to violence. Plus there were too many of them. I thought I should've been able to reason with them, win them over. My Tae Kwon Do training had taught me that we have to have strong courage in the face of danger and personal dignity in the face of adversity. Every time I was pushed, shoved and shouted hateful names at while other people stood by laughing, my personal dignity was stripped from me. I had none left. It had been destroyed. So I must be a failure, right? And anyway, would I have to fight my way through my whole life? We lived in suburban America, for crying out loud. Why did I have to live a life of violence just to get by? No, I wanted people to get to know me a little better, maybe even like me. I wanted to be accepted. That's all.

Well, that never happened. Not only did it not happen, I wasn't able to hold out the way I had planned. I know my parents were doing everything they knew to help me, but this wasn't something they could fix. And anyway, I didn't want their help. Running to Mom and Dad only made matters worse for a kid who might as well be walking around with a "bully me, I'll take it" sign hanging around his neck.

Besides, who wants to admit that they're such a loser that everyone's bullying them? I hated admitting it to myself. See, it's like bullying is the perfect crime because the victim doesn't want to admit that they're being bullied. The bullies have their fun, and all people see is a depressed kid who thinks he's worthless. And they wonder why. When it got really bad, I told my doctors about it, but they never really figured it out. Sometimes I even talked to my uncle or even my friend's dad. They all had advice, but none of it was working. So I eventually stopped talking about it. No, I had to figure this out on my own.

The kids that talked crap to me at school were the cool kids, and they had a lot of friends. It seemed like if you were popular, you could treat anyone like crap, and if you were a nobody, you just had to take it. Yeah, everyone liked them, and I was the nobody. That's just how life had dealt the cards. So I needed to get them to like me or go through life being treated like trash.

One of the things that always confused me was how the teachers looked the other way. I know they saw what was going on. I even went to them sometimes and asked for help, but nothing changed. That really got to me. Even the system was turning its back on me. Sometimes I got the feeling that they blamed me for bringing it on myself, or maybe they just didn't know what to do. Whichever, the torture continued day after day, year after year, and it was wearing me down.

A couple of my friends would tell me to blow it off, that everyone gets bullied, so what's the problem? What they couldn't understand is that, yeah, everyone may get bullied at some point, but not like I was. Oh, they might go through a week or so of some kid picking on them, but for me it was almost everyone at school all the time for years and years nonstop.

So I thought if I could just change who I was, these guys might leave me alone, and I'd fit in better. Maybe if I was just a bit more careful about the things I said and did, they would leave me alone. Maybe I did sound stupid when I talked. Or maybe I wasn't wearing the right kind of clothes. The bullying had to be my fault, not theirs.

I even changed my name from Daniel to Dan but that didn't work either. I started becoming so obsessed with not sounding dumb that the simple act of speaking made me panic. I found my heart racing every time I attempted a conversation with someone at school. Great, I thought, now I've got panic attacks to deal with. Wait until Sal and his friends realize this. I started to hate that my mom and dad had raised me like this. Why was I so weak? Maybe if I'd grown up less protected things would have been different. Maybe if I would've grown up in a ghetto, I would be tougher, know how to fight dirty, how to make quick comebacks every time someone insulted me. If only one of my parents had a drinking problem or treated me like crap and told me what a screw up I was, then I'd have toughened up and I'd have high school in the bag. I mean, we didn't even cuss at home.

Everyone at school cussed, and maybe if I talked like that, I'd blend in more.

One doctor even tried to convince me that I was imagining things. Examine the evidence, he would say. Maybe I just needed to learn to cope better. That really made me hate myself. I was sure it had to be me. I mean, a doctor was telling me, right?

I asked God for help a lot. We went to church all the time, and my mom had taught us to pray from when we were really young. I prayed all the time for God to help me, to stop the bullies, to give me strength, to show me the path, to just give me a normal life. But it seemed like He wasn't listening to me either. Even He was turning away from me. Maybe He wanted me to have a crappy life. Maybe I did deserve what I was getting. I started getting angry with God.

Coming to the conclusion that I was unfit for life, I figured that what was happening to me in high school would surely follow me to college. And what about after college? What about when I got a job? Would I be that loser who everyone sent emails about and laughed at behind his back? I began blaming my family, my friends, God, the very people who loved me. Maybe everybody hated me, but they just didn't know how to tell me.

I went off to school that Friday morning like I always did. I was excited because my mom and dad had agreed to give me a check for the summer program I had been looking forward to all year. Plus me and my friends were going to the movies later. All I had to do was get through this one Friday. This would end up being the worst day of my life; the worst day of a lot of people's lives.

Sal had been giving me crap as usual, and I decided that I wouldn't do his homework anymore. There's only so much a guy can take, right? Well, that sent him into a rage. He warned me if the homework wasn't done by Friday, there'd be hell to pay.

I hardly ever missed school, but on that day I just didn't want to deal with the whole frickin' situation anymore. Maybe if I asked my grandma to pick me up before lunch and drive me back after Italian class, I could avoid the whole thing. I really needed it to just go away.

I had to find a way to avoid Sal, and I would deal with the fallout on Monday. It was getting really old. I could feel something slowly bending inside me and it was about to break.

I had told my friend Aiden that I wasn't sure how much more of the crap I could take. I asked my parents if they would be mad at me if I got suspended from school for fighting. Funny, my dad told me violence wasn't the answer, but my mom said that I should pick the biggest guy and punch him right in the nose. She isn't generally a scrappy person, but she could see what I was going through, and she finally had had it. She told my dad that the bullies needed to know that I was willing to fight back and then they would back off.

So the day arrived, and, just like I expected, Sal was ready to show the whole school what a big man he was. And what a loser I was. This time, though, I didn't just sit back. I did what my mom told me to do. When the time came, I punched him right in the face. But my punch didn't exactly do what I had hoped. It was my final option, and it hadn't worked. No, it sure didn't happen the way my mom said it would.

CHAPTER

THREE

There are moments when even to the sober eye of reason, the world of our sad humanity may assume the semblance of hell.

—Edgar Allan Poe

The lunch bell screeched through the halls. Daniel was the last one out of his classroom. While other kids had been staring at the clock waiting for the bell to ring so they could go hang out with their friends and grab some Chipotle, Daniel was fighting back panic. He knew that Sal would be waiting for him and that there'd be hell to pay. One thing about Sal, he was definitely a man (or boy) of his word. But Daniel had decided that he couldn't take the crap anymore.

He slipped down the halls furtively, his eyes darting from one face to the next as he searched for signs of trouble. He felt like a character in an action movie, the target trying to get out of enemy territory, as he maneuvered through the giant campus. He weaved in and out of groups of kids laughing and talking as they headed off to the cafeteria or the parking lot. As he got closer to the hallway leading out to the lunch tables, he started to feel a little more relaxed. He was close now, almost out of the danger zone, when he heard it. He knew the moment he'd been dreading had arrived.

"Hey, Mendez, did you do the homework?" The words echoed in Daniel's ears. Sal could tell by Daniel's expression that there was no homework.

"You're a dead man," Sal grinned menacingly. Daniel turned and headed off in the other direction. He reached the lunch tables where his friends were sitting. They were laughing about some joke that Aiden had just cracked, but Daniel was in no mood for jokes. He sat quietly through lunch and watched for the sharks.

The second bell rang, and lunch was officially over. As the other guys headed for class thinking about how boring it was going to be to listen to their history teacher drone on about propaganda used by the Nazis in World War II, he was trying to keep himself from having an all-out panic attack. He scanned the crowd looking for the enemies. Once he saw they were nowhere near, he began his trek to Italian class.

Please, God. Let me make it on time. He walked quickly down the hallway toward the classroom, his heart pumping and eyes shooting in every direction. His legs felt heavy with the numbness of panic. He looked more like a terrified witness to a mob murder than a kid going to take a quiz on subjunctive verbs. He could feel sweat starting to soak the collar of his shirt. Just a little bit farther and he'd be there, just a little bit farther. He tried not to look too obvious; it was just around the corner now. Seconds, just seconds, and he'd be home free. *Please God. Stay with me.*

Daniel began to let his breath out. He was going to make it—going to get through Italian, Trig, and then go home and get on with his weekend. Things were going to be fine. As he turned the last corner, he froze. There was Sal, waiting for him with his sidekick, Allen Carter.

"What's the big rush, faggot?" Sal hissed at Daniel and threw himself in front of his victim. Allen Carter eyed Daniel up and down with a threatening smirk on his face.

It's now or never, Daniel thought. With his teeth clenched and fists balled tightly, he summoned every ounce of courage that he had and let loose.

"Leave me alone! I'm sick of this!" Daniel's own words caught him off guard. With years of built-up anger swelling in his chest and burning in his mind, he lunged forward and put his entire weight into punching Sal directly in the jaw. He wanted every faggot, idiot, half-breed, dirty Mexican, and loser to come out of his fist and meet Sal's face. He wanted to make him feel, if just for that moment, the way he had felt three thousand times before.

Daniel's fist slammed into the side of the punk's jaw, and Sal was jolted backward by the force. He was stunned. What was this kid doing? Stepping out of line, that's what, and Sal wasn't about to have some peace-loving half-breed wimp get an unanswered shot on him. Especially with other kids watching. He couldn't let the power tables be turned. Before Daniel could even think to move, Sal and Allen had doubled up on him.

"You're dead now, half-breed," Sal howled as Allen grabbed Daniel's arms.

Allen braced Daniel's arms back while Sal unloaded on him. Every insecurity Sal had landed right in Daniel's abdomen as Allen kept Daniel still so his buddy wouldn't have to work too hard. Daniel kicked his legs, trying to get free.

"Let me go! Let me go!"

But the two guys who spent more time shoving kids around than going to class were really fired up now. And not only were they more experienced at beating another kid to a pulp than Daniel was at escaping, it was two against one.

He tried to block out the people that were just standing by watching as Allen held him back and Sal jack hammered his fists into him. It was beyond humiliating. Some kids were actually laughing. It was incomprehensible to think that not one person would step in, that not one person had enough empathy or courage to tell the bullies to stop or to go get a teacher. Maybe it was Genovese Syndrome—you know, where everyone just assumes someone else'll do something in an emergency situation so no one does anything, or maybe it was that humanity really hadn't made it as far as we like to think from the days of throwing gladiators in the pit and watching them fight to the death for entertainment. The reason didn't really matter to Daniel. All he knew was he was getting his insides pounded and no one was doing anything to stop it, as usual. The second bell echoed through the halls like a bell going off at a boxing match. Sal and Allen released their victim and began walking away, leaving Daniel to crumple to the ground.

"We'll finish you off later," Sal promised as he rubbed his swelling jaw.

Daniel stood up and straightened his shirt as if smoothing the creases from it would undo the blinding humiliation he had just endured in front of a gawking crowd. His face burned hot from adrenaline, anger, and embarrassment. He stood for a second trying to regroup, trying to push the event to the back of his mind, and then slowly made his way to Italian class. As he walked, he could feel the tension in his muscles; his chest was clenched tight around his lungs, and he felt sick to his stomach. It wasn't so much the physical pain that hurt as much as the total humiliation of it all. He wanted nothing more than to just leave, to disappear, or maybe to scream, "F*** you!" to all the kids who stood and watched him get pounded, but instead he walked slowly down the hall to Italian class where he would have to sit an excruciating hour with Sal, Allen, and all the other kids who thought that Daniel's public humiliation had been a source of entertainment.

He made it to class and slumped into his desk while Sal and Allen continued to eye him. *Don't dwell on it*, thought Daniel. *Let it go.* Any time he let his eyes move from his textbook, he could see Sal at the edge of his peripheral vision, glaring at him, pumping his fist into his open hand and sliding his thumb across his throat. Daniel tried to ignore him. He looked around the room. Mrs. Conti was looking right at him. Why didn't the teacher do anything? His only goal was to finish his test as fast as he could and get the hell out of there.

He watched the clock like an inmate on death row. Austin, another kid in class who had watched Sal and his cronies harass

Daniel all year long and had just gotten a glimpse of Sal playing Mike Tyson in the hall earlier, noticed that Daniel was still shaking and flushed.

"Hey, Daniel, you okay?" Austin leaned forward to whisper as Daniel finished the test and stood up to leave with his eyes fixed on the door. Daniel only nodded and quickly left the classroom.

It had taken Danny and Anna longer to get on the road than they had expected. The long weekend had begun, and the fact that their tires didn't meet the open road until after noon wasn't of any concern to either of them. Anna had just completed her submission of accomplishments to be used for her annual review at work. She felt good about the progress she had made for her company. The kids were safe with Nonna, and now it was time for a little rest and relaxation with her husband. The sky was aquamarine blue with swollen white clouds hovering over the distant mountaintops. The desert wildflowers were in full bloom and the air was clean and warm. It was going to be the perfect way to end a hectic week.

Just before they approached the resort city, Anna looked down at the time display on her cell phone and realized that Daniel would be just getting out of school by now. She remembered that he hadn't felt good that morning and had asked to skip a couple of classes. She texted her son. "Hi, love. Are you okay? How was school?" No reply. *It must be the mountains blocking the reception*, she thought.

The couple arrived at the desert resort a little later than anticipated. It was almost three thirty. They had just enough time for a rest before they would head off to dinner. The place looked like a paradise with its tall palm trees reaching up toward the beautiful, clear sky on either side of the drive, standing one after the other all the way to the resort entrance.

They breathed in the floral scented air, took in the postcard picture that lay before them, and made their way to the grand entrance. They walked hand in hand into the sun-filled lobby to check in. As her husband stood at the registration desk and filled out forms, Anna suddenly froze. A harsh, cold chill had enveloped her body. The lobby was open air, and she thought it must be a cold breeze that swept in from the desert, but that made no sense. It was May in Palm Springs and almost ninety degrees outside. Something was unsettling her. The paralyzing cold swept through her body, and she started to feel as though she couldn't move her limbs. The sensation settled in the pit of her stomach, a sense of doom with it. Anna said nothing to her husband.

The two made the short trip to their room, and Danny threw the suitcases on the bed.

"We're finally here. Let's unpack." As he looked around to check out where they would be spending their next few restful days, his eyes fell on his wife, and he noticed the somber look on her face.

"What's wrong? Don't you like the view?"

"No, it's fine," replied Anna, not wanting to put a damper on the trip already. But Danny knew his wife too well, and this sudden mood change wasn't fine.

"Are you sure? Let's see what else they have available." He wanted everything to be perfect that weekend.

Anna smiled at her husband who was so eager to please.

"No, the room's great. I'm just getting this feeling. I just suddenly feel worried about the kids. Something doesn't feel right." Anna looked at her husband for affirmation.

Danny grinned. *Here she goes again*, he thought.

"Love, you know how you get whenever we're away from the kids for more than a few hours. They're fine. Nonna's picking them up as we speak. They'll be home from school soon, and we'll call them in a few minutes just to make sure everything's okay.

Now come join me on the terrace." Danny walked outside with a bottle of wine. "It's beautiful out here."

"I just want to wash up a bit first." Anna walked into the bathroom and stared into the mirror. What was this complete and utter feeling of dread that had suddenly consumed her? It was true that she would worry about the children whenever she was away from them for any extended period of time, but this was different. She decided to try to push it out of her mind. She knew that once she spoke to the kids, everything would be fine.

She splashed water on her face and had begun washing her hands when she heard it. The phone rang. She listened to her husband's voice escalate from calm to panic as the day's chain of life-altering events began.

She rushed out of the bathroom and saw the terror on his face. He was yelling. She had never seen him like this.

"You have to calm down! I don't understand. Nonna, calm down! I need to understand what you're saying!" Danny was screaming into his cell phone.

"Danny, what's happening? Are the kids okay? You're scaring me. Just tell me they're okay!"

His face tightened as he struggled to understand the frantic voice on the other end of the phone line.

"Nonna, calm down. Speak slowly," he urged as he listened to the words that would change both their lives forever. The color drained from his face, and Anna watched her husband age ten years before her eyes.

"Danny!" she screamed. "Please, just tell me the kids are all right!"

He hung up the phone and stared into his wife's unblinking eyes.

"Danny! Are they all right?"

"No." His voice cracked, and tears began to run down his cheeks. "Daniel broke into the gun cabinet and took off in his car. Nobody knows what's going on."

In that very moment, her sense of doom was validated. Everything spun around her. Danny's words—*gun cabinet, Daniel, car, no one knows*—they all collided in her head. Her mind wanted to slow everything down to try to make sense of what she had just heard. Nothing did. If her instincts hadn't told her she had to move and move fast, she would have collapsed. But she couldn't. They flew into high gear, making frantic calls to 911, calls to family, packing, and rushed to the car.

CHAPTER
FOUR

Death and life are in the power of the tongue.

Proverbs 18:21 (KJV)

The drive back to the house was excruciating. It seemed to last forever as Danny pressed his foot against the pedal, breaking every speed limit posted. The parents were silent but thinking the same thing. *How did this happen?* Daniel was so responsible, so well behaved. He never gave them any problems. He had never done anything even close to this before. What was going on?

Between the tears, Danny kept nodding his head. "He's going to be fine. He'll come back home. He always does the right thing. Everything's going to be fine." Through her own terror, Anna could sense his.

She texted her son, "Daniel, it's Mom. I love you. Please come home." But there was no reply—and she knew. No matter how much she wanted to believe otherwise, how much she wanted to believe what her husband kept repeating, something deep down inside her told her that this was the bone chilling doom she had felt in the hotel lobby. A mother knows when her child has left this earth. She just knows.

As they weaved in and out of traffic, Anna called her neighbor to ask for help. "Terry, please go to the house. My mom is there with Victoria, and they need support. Please. Stay with them until we arrive." Anna's words ran together as she tried to get them out in one breath.

Danny dialed his brother-in-law Roger and struggled through telling him the unfathomable news.

"Call the relatives. Tell them what's happening." Danny had to find some control in the chaos. "And Roger, Daniel's not picking up his cell phone. We're driving back from Palm Springs. Can you try to call him? He may pick up for you."

Through his panic, he realized that in his earlier call to the police he had not given them his son's license plate number. That would be critical if they were going to find him fast. He dialed Terry back, who was now at the house.

"Terry, look in the file cabinet. Daniel's license plate number is there. Can you tell me what it is?"

The neighbor found the number and read it to him. He hung up and called the police department again. His voice shook with fear.

"This is Danny Mendez. I'm calling about my son, Daniel. You're trying to locate him. I have his license plate number now. It's…"

"Sir, can you please hold?"

Danny and Anna listened as hold music began to play. Why had they been put on hold? The police officer came back on the phone.

"Sir, how far away are you now?"

"What? I told you before we're on our way back from Palm Springs. We should be there in a couple of hours. Why?"

"Sir, drive carefully, but just come back as soon as you can."

"Of course. But I want to give you his license plate number so you can find him faster." Danny's voice was irritated.

"Yes," said the voice on the other end. "Okay. Go ahead and give it to me."

Danny provided the number and hung up. Why hadn't they been more eager for the license plate number? Where was their sense of urgency?

Their phone rang, and the caller ID showed that it was Anna's sister, Lilly. She grabbed the phone, hoping against hope that they had heard from Daniel.

"Has he called you yet?" Lilly was sobbing into the phone.

"Not yet," Anna's heart sank. "Please call Mom and Victoria. Try to calm them."

After what seemed like an eternity, the two distraught parents finally made it home and ran inside the house. Danny grabbed his keys.

"I'm going to Michael's house."

Michael and Sean Harrison were good friends of Daniel's, and their house was where the neighborhood kids always hung out.

Daniel, Aiden, Michael, and Michael's younger brother, Sean, spent many sun-filled afternoons skateboarding in front of Michael's house and countless evenings playing video games in their game room. The Harrisons had a video game collection that rivaled that of any Blockbuster, and the kids in the neighborhood were always welcome there. Maybe, maybe that's where he was.

Anna couldn't sit idly by. But she couldn't leave Victoria behind either. Nonna was hysterical, and she knew she couldn't leave her little girl with her mother any longer. She grabbed her daughter by the hand.

"We're going to look for him too," she said firmly, trying to keep her voice steady for her daughter's sake.

Danny jumped into his car, slammed his keys in the ignition, and sped off toward Michael's house. As he turned the corner, his heart stopped. Flashing lights and police cars were everywhere. Yellow police tape roped off a whole block immediately in front of the house. Then he saw it. His son's car was parked on the curb. The shiny black car, the surprise sixteenth birthday present from just a few short weeks ago. A towel was draped over the license plate. Seeing your child's car surrounded by flashing lights and yellow police tape is what pure horror feels like. It's the way a nightmare feels at its climax when your blood runs cold, right before your body jerks itself awake. Danny leaped from his car and ran toward the officers.

"Where is he? Where is he?" the distraught father yelled as he ducked under the police tape.

"Sir, you have to go around. Please drive around," police officers instructed Danny as they motioned him to go around. He had to find the strength to put himself back behind the wheel of the car and drive around the block to the other side of the yellow police tape. He rushed out of his car where detectives met him.

"Please, tell me where he is. I'm his father," Danny begged. "Please, just tell me where my son is."

One of the detectives looked at him and shifted his eyes down to the ground.

"I'm sorry, sir. He's with the coroner."

Danny looked the detective in the eyes. *Coroner…* The word didn't register. It couldn't.

"What do you mean? Please, just tell me. Tell me! Is my son alive?"

The detective looked at the father with tears in his eyes. "I'm sorry, sir. Your son is dead."

The father collapsed to his knees, face to the sky, and began screaming. He felt his mouth open and knew that air was escaping, but he had no idea if any sound was coming out. In that second that the detective said "dead," his life had changed forever. His mind tried to grapple with the words he had just heard. They were the most permanent words that could ever be spoken—the most permanent and the most heartbreaking to a parent. Now he had to get back in his car without his son. He had to find a way to tell his wife and daughter what had happened—tell them the lie he had just been told. His son could not be dead. He couldn't be. Not Daniel. Not their child.

Anna and Victoria had driven only a few blocks before a call came in from Danny.

"Where are you? You have to come home. You have to come home." He sounded weak, exhausted.

As Anna and Victoria drove up to the house, a bizarre sight greeted them. Strangers were crawling all over their front lawn. Their front door was wide open. It was a frightening scene. Anna instinctively put her arm around her young daughter as they cautiously approached the doorway, determined to protect her from whatever terror awaited them inside. They stepped into their home, and she heard screams coming from somewhere inside. Was that her mother? They were the kind of screams you hear in movies when mothers are handed the golden star or when doctors say, "We did all we could." People were sobbing, and there were hushed whispers. Danny made his way to his wife and daughter in the foyer, barely able to walk. He stumbled toward them, knowing he had just received the worst news a parent can ever receive and now he was going to have to tell his wife and daughter. How was he going to tell them?

Please God, don't let him speak the words, Anna prayed. *As long as I haven't heard them, I can hope.*

Danny put his hands on their arms and choked out in a broken voice, "Our boy is gone. He's gone. He shot himself."

Anna and Victoria began to scream, collapsing in what seemed to be slow motion to the floor, arms wrapped around one another. Their screams filled the house; they rose above the other cries and tore at the hearts and souls of anyone in earshot. They were the kind of screams that burn into a person's mind and never go away. They wanted their screams to pierce reality and reach all the way up to the heavens.

Danny helped them up and led them to the sofa. Mother and daughter kept their arms tightly wrapped around each other. They held on to each other as though if one let go, the other would float away and be lost forever, just like Daniel. As soon as little Victoria could catch her breath, she looked up at her mother and, with her arms still wrapped around her, said in a suddenly strong and rational voice, "Why did he do it, Mom? His life was perfect."

And that would be the ultimate question.

His life was perfect. The words reverberated in her brain. That's what his family saw. What had happened? Why? Daniel was a great kid. Never got into trouble. A consistent honor roll student. In advanced placement classes. A Boy Scout. An athlete. Loved God. Hated violence. He was always respectful, engaged, the love of their lives, well behaved. How could this be happening to their family?

In the midst of her excruciating sorrow for her family, for her son, she was overwhelmed with anger toward him. Her emotions collided. She was angry, but he was gone. How could he do this to them? He had never done anything before that didn't have them bursting with pride. He knew how devoted they all were to him, and he loved them more than anything else in the world.

Anna's mind flashed back to bits of the past. Aiden had once told her that Daniel never wanted to do anything wrong, that he would even refuse to let his friends play the ding dong ditch game whenever he was with them. "Come on guys, it's not nice," Daniel would say. The elderly widow living alone in the neighborhood marveled at how he would always insist on taking her trash cans in for her when he was out walking his dog. Other neighbors would often comment on how happy he looked when he waved to them during those walks. So what had happened?

What could possibly have been happening in his life that was so powerful it overshadowed all of his family's love and devotion? What demons had haunted him? What would make such a responsible kid do something so inconceivable, so out of character, and so permanently irreversible?

This simply did not fit the profile that the experts tell parents to watch for. Teens who are at high risk of suicide will display feelings of anger, detachment, grades will suffer, and social life will decline. Obviously not since none of those things applied to Daniel. Danny and Anna knew in that moment that they would stop at nothing to find the answer.

Aiden was on his way home from school in the car with his father driving.

"I love you, Aiden. Don't ever forget that."

"I love you too, Dad." Aiden started to wonder what the heck was going on because that was the third time his dad had told him he loved him since they left the school. *Kinda weird*, thought Aiden.

As their car turned the corner to their street, Aiden saw the flashing lights and police cars. The car stopped, and he jumped out. His father called out for him to stop, but he didn't listen. Aiden ran toward the flashing lights and police tape toward a scene that would leave an imprint on his soul forever. Something inside him told him his life was never going to be the same, and his legs carried him, almost on autopilot, toward the chaos. He tried to pass the yellow lines, but the officers stopped him. Then he saw his friend's car.

"Aiden, a boy died, but they haven't told us yet who it is." Aiden's father tried to remain calm.

"No way that's Daniel's car. No way in hell. That's not him!" Aiden was screaming now, angry and fighting with the universe because there was no one else to be angry at. Maybe if he said it loud enough or with enough conviction he could undo what had been done. Maybe if he showed the world how unfair this was, time would move the other way. Maybe if he just refused to believe his own eyes, reality would reshape itself. He spent the rest of that evening trying to call and text his best friend, hoping beyond hope that Daniel would text back.

"Hey, man. They say you're dead, but I don't believe it. Text me. We're gonna hang out tonight, right?"

No reply came. It never would.

Austin was driving home with his mom when they passed the scene of flashing lights, police cars, and fire trucks. His mind flashed back to the scene he had witnessed at school just hours before. He remembered how upset his friend had been after the most recent attack. His ears had turned bright red, for God's sake. He remembered the months of harassment he had witnessed Daniel endure. *Man, I sure hope that's not Daniel,* he thought to himself. *Maybe I should have done something. Maybe I should have stepped in. If it's not too late, I'm gonna stop the goons from now on. If that's not Daniel, I swear I'm gonna do something now. Please God, don't let it be too late.*

The evening was a nightmarish blur for the family. Time had stopped for them. They were unaware of the moments before or the moments after they took each breath. They were unaware of what hour of day or night it was. Anna called a friend who had lost a young daughter years earlier to a traffic accident. Her parents were good friends with the family, and they made the seventy mile drive to be with them that night. They knew what many don't. When a parent loses a child, they don't want to hear words of great wisdom or prophetic revelations. They just want to be held and be allowed to cry.

The following days were filled with a flurry of activity around funeral plans. Funeral plans for a happy, healthy sixteen-year-old boy who, just days earlier, had the world at his feet. One moment it was all about the college plans, and in the next, the question of Harvard or Princeton was replaced by where the burial plot would be. How life can turn on a dime.

The house was filled with helping hands, when there was a knock on the door. Anna's sister Lilly answered. She called her sister over.

"You need to hear this."

Mary, a neighbor down the street, stood in the doorway with a young girl named Mindy. She introduced the girl as her son Kevin's girlfriend. Both attended Daniel's high school, but as far as Anna knew, neither were close friends of Daniel's.

"She has something to tell you. Go ahead," Mary encouraged.

"He was being bullied." The young girl kept her eyes fixed on her sandals as she spoke.

"The school has started a bullying investigation. Everyone knew he was being bullied."

The words hit Anna like a brick as she absorbed what the young stranger was telling her. *Bully*—the word that had haunted her family for the last several years. Her son, the nice guy, the kid who would go out of his way to help anyone, was being bullied. Anna began recalling the past incidences of Daniel being bullied and her suspicions that he still was. A little clarity began to set in.

"No. Not bullied…" She moaned. She didn't want to believe it. Her son had been being bullied, and she had been unable to save him. Something she had known about, had continued to suspect, had fought against, and thought she had handled. She had lost the most important battle of her life, defeated in the worst possible way, with her precious child as the ultimate sacrifice. He was being bullied, so much so that the school knew and had already begun an investigation, still while making no contact with the parents. The bullying had started up again, and he had done his best to hide it from his parents this time. Why? Why had she been so ineffective when her child had needed her the most? She had taught her son to be wary of strangers, to wear his helmet when he rode his skateboard, to say no to drugs and alcohol, but she had failed to protect him from people who could steal his soul.

She stepped back from the door with vacant eyes, stunned and defeated, as she began to recall back to normal times. At which point exactly had she gone wrong?

CHAPTER
FIVE

The ache for home lives in all of us, the safe place where we can go as we are and not be questioned.

—Maya Angelou

Daniel's elementary years had been idyllic. He was a smart, happy child, and his friends were all good kids. Daniel and Victoria were raised with the loving influence of two doting grandparents in their household. Before Anna's dad passed away, he was a major part of the kids' lives, taking them to parks, teaching them to garden, and telling them stories about the old country. Having lived with the family for several years prior to his death, he and his grandson would spend hours tending to the figs and tomatoes in the garden while Daniel listened to stories about history, Mussolini, Hitler, and who invented the telephone. Well, his grandpa's version of history anyway. According to him, all good things had come from Italy. Daniel's grandpa even helped him with his elementary school homework, but when Daniel began getting answers wrong (no, it wasn't an Italian who invented electricity), Grandpa was banned from helping with any more assignments.

Stable finances allowed the family to take regular vacations together and visit faraway places: Mexico, the Bahamas, Hawaii, Park City, Mammoth, even Europe.

Their cruise to the Virgin Islands had been particularly splendid. Anna had decided to stay in for the morning for some spa time while Danny took the kids out to explore the port. She had carried out her platter of fruit and coffee to the balcony and sat looking out onto the colorful horizon. She looked down and spotted the three people she cherished most in the world walking together toward the shore. She waved at her trio and called out to them. She knew her voice had no power. The ship was too big, and they couldn't possibly hear her. But she called anyway.

Daniel suddenly stopped. He turned back and looked up at the very spot where his mom was standing, just a pinpoint on the massive ship that was their backdrop. It was as though instinct told him she was calling to him. He smiled at her and stopped his dad and sister so they could all wave good-bye before they were off for their morning adventures. She waved and thought about the special connection that she and her son had always had – a bond between them that couldn't be explained by words. They both looked at life in much the same way, and sometimes it was as though they could read each other's minds. He was her firstborn, her pride and joy, the one who had first granted her the honor of being a mother, her most important role in life.

She watched her family disappear into the throngs of tourists. She felt a sense of gratitude. *No one can take this away from me*, she thought.

Daniel and his sister were inseparable during their trips. They hiked, swam, snorkeled, rode horse back, fished, and golfed together. Although four years separated the two, Victoria was able to easily keep up with her big brother. The constant competition made her a force to be reckoned with at an early age. Their parents were grateful that they were close. Neither Danny nor Anna had been part of a large family and were comforted to know that at least their son and daughter would have each other growing up.

Daniel helped his sister with her homework and took pride in knowing that she was ahead of her class because of his mentoring. He had also helped her get over her fear of ghosts. One night as she had laid in her bed and he knew she was scared, he had shined a light on her wall and, hiding behind a closet door, began speaking in as friendly a voice as he could imagine for a ghost.

"Hi, Victoria. I'm a ghost. But I'm a friendly ghost. I'm here to protect you. Just close your eyes and go to sleep."

"Okay," replied little Victoria. "But what about the little dots of light I see when I close my eyes?"

"Oh, those are my friends. They're friendly ghosts too," replied her brother from his secret hiding place.

He had silently slipped away and bound into his mom's room.

"Mom! I cured Victoria of her fear of ghosts! I pretended to be one with a flashlight in the dark!" he had exclaimed proudly as his mother listened on in horror.

When Daniel wasn't helping Victoria with her fear of ghosts or hanging out with the guys, he was busy with Boy Scouts. He had reached his star level and was hoping to make it to Eagle. He loved scouting, white-water rafting, camping trips and rock climbing. Anything that was about the outdoors would do.

CHAPTER

SIX

We will have to give an account on the day of judgment for every careless word spoken.

Matthew 12:36 (CEV)

It was the first week of middle school and Daniel was ready to take on this new chapter in his life. He found his way around the school, got his new locker in order, and started getting familiar with how middle school worked. It seemed simple enough, and changing classes was pretty cool. Yeah, he was going to breeze through this.

He was carrying his lunch out to the tables when he noticed a boy sitting alone. He hated to see another kid without anyone to eat lunch with, so he walked up and sat next to him.

"Hey, I'm Daniel." He smiled at the kid.

The Asian boy looked up slowly from his sandwich. "Hi. I'm Aiden. Why are you talking to me?" The kid was genuinely surprised.

"Why not?" Daniel shrugged.

"Well, everyone's been pretty much dissing me all week," Aiden went on to explain. "I'm new around here and I don't really have any friends."

Aiden Kai had found the kids a little cold since he had moved to town, and he was grateful for Daniel's welcome, knowing that most kids had already labeled him as an outsider. Lucky for Aiden, Daniel wasn't the easily influenced type, so instead of walking away when Aiden asked why Daniel was talking to him, he saw it as an opportunity to give a kid the chance to fit in somewhere.

"Well, not anymore." His new friend laughed. "You like basketball? Let's play after school."

The next day, Daniel was looking forward to hanging out with Aiden again. *What luck*, he thought, *to meet such a cool guy my very first week.*

As he found a seat at the back of the room, a large foot came out of nowhere and kicked at his chair.

"I don't want a faggot half-breed sitting next to me," a kid with a nasty grin on his face barked at Daniel.

The boy's name was Phil Jensen, and he was one of the school's biggest bullies. This kid had made a name for himself by terrorizing others for no reason beyond entertaining himself, and now he had chosen a new target. Without realizing how or why he had been drafted by the bully to be a whipping boy for everything that had gone wrong in this kid's life, Daniel had been picked out, and his life was going to get real tough if Phil had anything to do with it.

Daniel moved around to the other side of Aiden and took that desk instead, thinking that if he just didn't rile the unexplainably nasty kid then he would leave them alone. As Daniel slipped into the new seat, he and Aiden exchanged quick glances.

Phil had a lot of family problems going on at home. His dad had left his mom for his young, attractive secretary, and Phil felt that he had chosen to leave him, too. He never saw his dad any more. He was refusing to pay alimony or child support, so money was really tight. His parents had been fighting since Phil could remember, probably since the day he was born, and it just kept getting worse. Phil thought it would get better when his dad finally moved out, but it didn't. The fights between his parents only got worse. He had to listen as his dad called his mom a fat slob and complained about how useless she was. His mom would hurdle back her own accusations, yelling that he was sleeping with whores. It just went on and on.

The night before Phil had chosen Daniel from his peers to be the new victim to his pent-up hate, their neighbors had called the cops on his parents. That had been a really bad scene. While watching his home life turn into a season of *Cops*, Phil Jensen was mad at the world and looking for an easy target to take his anger out on. In walked Daniel who was quiet, kind, and, best of all, didn't fight back—just what he was looking for. And just like that, Daniel became his new personal target. Talk about bad timing.

———•◦•———

The Tae Kwon Do studio was solemn as preparations began for Daniel's black belt presentation. He had been studying the art for six years. It had helped him not only with his physical training but also his mental awareness, discipline, and self-confidence. Tae Kwon Do focused on developing spiritual strength, strong courage to face danger, to help the weak, and to be a good person. One of its major tenets focused on honor, one's dignity in the face of adversity. Daniel admired not just the physical aspect of Tae Kwon Do but also the spiritual part. When he was very young, Daniel was the first of the students who had memorized his student oath in full; he was able to recite it at a moment's notice. They weren't just words for him; he felt the message in his heart. He had received his master's praise for that. Today, his hard work would once again be recognized.

The candles were lit over bowls of water, the lights were dimmed, and the ceremony began. Daniel took his bow, removed his red belt, and his master handed him his new black belt. After helping Daniel put on the belt, his master stepped aside. Daniel turned to the audience, bowed solemnly, and began his speech of thanks and gratitude. At the end of his speech, he turned to his grandfather. Grandson and grandfather locked eyes as Daniel said, "I thank God my grandfather is alive to see me receive this honor." Daniel's grandfather had suffered several heart attacks, and the family knew it was only a matter of time before his heart would eventually fail him completely.

Tears welled up in the old man's eyes. He nodded in appreciation. How he loved that boy. Only a few short days later, Daniel's grandfather passed away. On his deathbed, he had whispered to his daughter, "Take care of my grandchildren." They were the most important thing in this physical world to him.

———•◦•———

Science class was one of Daniel's favorites. He basically pulled straight A's in all of his classes, but science was one he really liked. He also liked the dark-haired girl who sat a couple of seats away from him. She was a Hispanic girl named Louisa, and she always made sure to smile at him.

With the help of her friends, he had decided to buy her a stuffed teddy bear with chocolates in its pocket for her birthday; you couldn't go wrong with stuffed animals and chocolate for girls, he figured. And her friends were going to open her locker so he could sneak in the teddy bear to surprise her.

Daniel sat in his classroom, looking around to see who else was filing in. Maybe he'd be lucky and Phil Jensen would be absent today. Phil had begun ramping up the harassment against Daniel and enlisting a number of other kids to join in. Some of the kids seemed uncomfortable with it, but they did it anyway. They were just happy that Phil wasn't bothering them. If you can't beat 'em, join 'em, right?

Steve Wright was a good friend of Phil's and ran a close race with him for the school's worst bully. Steve's parents had been split for years. His mom had left his dad because of a drinking problem, and the family was having trouble making ends meet. Steve himself had been messing around with drugs and alcohol in the wake of his family falling apart. Funny how that happens. A kid sees that kind of destructive behavior and he's either going to avoid it like the plague or fall into it himself. Steve did the latter. It somehow made things easier for him to bear.

Steve hated his dad; *hate* is a strong word, but that's exactly what Steve felt for his father. His old, drunk dad had always told him he'd amount to nothing. He often thought he should just prove his dad right, really be the loser his drunk of a dad said he was. So beating up on kids who didn't have the loser gene was a great way for him to get revenge on the world, maybe be like his old man, and he sought out anyone he thought would take it. Any kid who didn't want to fight back, who didn't have enough hate in them to call names back or use their fists to defend themselves would do.

Steve could tell that Daniel didn't have to go home to the same kind of crap he did, so he got a real kick out of seeing the kid squirm whenever they harassed him. This kid was just too easy a target. He didn't know what tough was, didn't have a dad at home telling him he'd amount to squat. Steve thought he would level the playing field a little by giving this honor roll kid whose parents weren't just scraping by a taste of the hard life. Why should he be the only one to suffer?

Daniel noticed Phil coming into the classroom with Steve strutting at his side. *No luck*, thought Daniel. *I have to deal with them again.* The harassment had begun to take hold. At first it was just every so often. Daniel tried hard to shrug it off, but these guys were as relentless as their lives were bad. The bell finally rang, and Daniel gathered his books. *Good*, he thought. *No crap from either of them today.* As he walked toward his history class, he was suddenly shoved hard into the lockers. His head ricocheted off the locker doors. He looked up to see Phil Jensen, Steve Wright, and two of Phil's other buddies. This was not going to end well.

"Hey, Daniel, was that you we saw getting into the school golf van?" Phil asked with a mocking smile planted on his face as everyone else snickered.

"What a faggot. Don't you know only faggots play golf?" Steve laughed. *So that was the punch line. When all else fails, pick out whatever a guy does and make a homophobic reference. Genius.*

Daniel felt the sting of the word *faggot* every time they said it. Who gave them the right to decide what he was or wasn't? Why was it that these guys—who never took the time to get to know anybody and hated everything and everyone that wasn't as messed up as them—were given the authority to define him as a person? Why did people just accept what the dullest guys in school were doling out? Maybe they figured they had no choice if they didn't want the bullies to turn on them. It seemed strange to him that a bunch of teenage punks were granted so much power in the school world. This was not at all what he had expected from middle school. Why hadn't anyone prepared him for this? Daniel rubbed his shoulder and walked away. At least it was Friday.

CHAPTER
SEVEN

Thou shalt not be a victim, thou shalt not be a perpetrator, but above all, thou shalt not be a bystander.

—Yehuda Bauer

It was a dark tunnel, but it was leading down a new path. The two friends walked together in the blackness. Aiden and Daniel had come upon the opening to a sewer line. They found that the gate to the entrance was not completely hinged shut. They figured out that if they swung it really hard and ran fast, they could make it through the opening before the gate swung back the other way. Nothing was as inviting as the unsecure opening into a city storm sewer (to teenage boys, anyway).

"Where do you think this'll end up?" Aiden asked.

"I don't know. Let's just keep walking," Daniel replied. "Maybe we should've brought a flashlight. At least we have the light from our phones."

"Phil and Steve are really on your back, Daniel." Aiden was worried about his friend.

"Yeah, they won't let up."

"Are you going to do something about it?"

"I don't know. They're getting a ton of other kids to harass me too now. It's like the whole school is thinking I'm a loser. They're making fun of the way I talk, the way I walk, everything. Is there something wrong with the way I walk?"

"No, dude. They're just jerks. You need to tell someone."

"I did. The teacher's not doing anything. I'm not sure who can help. Life's getting pretty complicated."

"Yeah, I know what you mean."

Without being able to see where they were going or what they might be wading through, the boys talked and walked in the darkness, hardly concerned that there could be God knows what lurking around the corner or hanging out below the city's surface. It didn't matter to either of them. It was a long stretch of calm that allowed them to face life's questions in a new paradigm. They felt at peace walking in total dark and quiet. They had no idea what was ahead of them, but the two friends figured they could handle it as it came to them. Walking around in the tunnel became a common pastime when they just felt like it. When the world above them just didn't make much sense. They eventually showed their other friends the secret tunnel. As long as they had their close knit group and good conversation, there was nothing they couldn't handle.

The gym floor was shining with its new coat of varnish. They were in PE class, and Phil Jensen was in a particularly sour mood. He looked over at Daniel. He noticed that Daniel could do more pushups and run faster and longer than any other kid in that class. *Gotta make sure that kid's kept in his place*, Phil thought. He walked up behind Daniel, pushed him hard against the wall, and laughed demonically as Daniel rubbed his shoulder in pain.

"Look at those hairy legs. Those are the legs of a dirty Mexican for sure," Phil mocked. "A dirty Mexican who's a rat. You gonna go crying to your mommy now, little faggot, 'cause I said you have hairy legs?" Phil taunted.

Other kids started laughing. Daniel tried to keep himself calm so no one could see that he was about to throw up from the humiliation. *Just ignore them, and they'll get bored. Show no emotion.*

The PE teacher waved at them as he walked by. Daniel was mortified. Why did the teacher stand by and let it happen? He knew he saw what was going on. Daniel couldn't understand. The bell rang, and he waited until everyone left before approaching the PE teacher.

"Mr. Raymond, do you have a minute?"

"Sure, Daniel, what's up?" The teacher looked up from gathering the balls.

"Can you ask Phil Jensen to leave me alone? He's really bothering me really bad, and I can't stand it anymore. You saw what happened today. Please. Ask him to stop."

"Sure, Son. I think he's just playing around. Aren't you two friends?" The teacher picked up his last ball, getting ready to leave.

"No." Daniel couldn't imagine why anyone would think that. "I've tried, but he's constantly on my back. I don't know what I've ever done to him. He pushes me around and calls me names, and other kids just laugh. Please tell him to stop. I just want him to leave me alone."

"Sure, Son. No problem."

There. He didn't have to hate himself anymore for not speaking up for himself. With the promise from his teacher, Daniel was hopeful. Maybe they were going to get somewhere. Maybe he wouldn't have to dread school every day anymore.

———◆·◆·◆———

"I say we golf tomorrow." The steaming bowl of pasta with shrimp and broccoli was on the dinner table and Danny was getting ready to dig in. He looked around to see if everyone else was on board.

"Yeah!" Victoria was in.

But Daniel wasn't as excited as the rest of them this time. "No. I don't wanna go." His eyes were fixed on his dinner plate.

"What's the matter, Son?" Danny looked up from his plate. "Do you have other plans?"

"No. I just don't want to play golf anymore. Golf sucks," Daniel snapped.

"What are you talking about?" Anna was concerned with her son's sudden moodiness. "You love the game. You can drive two hundred and twenty yards right down the middle of the fairway. You just got a new set of Taylormades for your birthday."

"People are making fun of me for playing, Mom," Daniel suddenly blurted as he tried to keep his voice from shaking. "They saw me in the golf van, and they're making fun of me now. I'm not playing anymore. Ever again."

Danny and Anna glanced across the table at one another with troubled expressions on their faces.

"Hey, Daniel"—Victoria smiled at her brother—" I bet I can finish faster than you!" Both kids doubled up on their forkfuls of pasta.

As soon as the kids had finished dinner and run upstairs, Anna looked over at her husband.

"I cannot believe this," Anna fumed after the kids were out of earshot.

"These troublemakers at school are having such a profound effect on his life choices. I don't get it. Why do they harass him? There's nothing about him that I would think would attract it." Her husband was also at a loss for an explanation.

Daniel thought he had it figured out though. If he stopped playing golf, the harassment would stop. He was almost relieved he had a solution. But to his dismay, it didn't work that way. Several days later, the harassment continued, and so he decided to take action.

"Don't worry, Mom," Daniel said in his self-assured manner. "Everyone has enemies at some point in their lives. It's normal. There's a process at school to handle this."

"What do you mean, 'a process'?"

"There's a form I fill out and hand in to the administration office, and then they take care of it. That's all. I'm going to do that tomorrow."

Anna hugged her son and smiled.

"Yes, that's the right thing to do, love."

She was proud of how he handled adversity. He was being level-headed and confident. He wasn't taking it personally. This kind of stuff happened in life, and he was just going to use the established channels to handle it.

"Daniel, don't react when the kids are mean to you. The more you react, the funnier they think it is. If you show it doesn't bother you, they'll get tired and leave you alone. Show no emotion."

"I know, Mom. Don't worry. I have it handled."

Still, she was worried. As they got ready to turn in for the evening, Anna looked at her husband with uncertainty nestled in her furrowed brow. She wasn't going to let go of this easily.

"Danny, he's being bullied. Our son is being bullied."

"Don't worry, love." Danny put his hands on his wife's shoulders. "You sound like he has a terminal illness. He seems to have it under control. I'm proud of our big guy. I don't want this to make you crazy."

Maybe he's right, Anna thought. *Maybe I'm being overprotective and not letting my son grow up.* She tried to allow herself to let go of the fear and relax enough to get to sleep. *Every kid hits rough patches, right?*

CHAPTER
EIGHT

All anyone asks for is a chance to work with pride.

—W. Edwards Deming

The rain was coming down hard outside Anna's office window. She sat at her desk, looking out onto the city skyline, index finger pressed to her lips. Daniel was being bullied. Should she worry? Was she overreacting like everyone said? Perhaps. Her phone rang, jolting her out of her deep thoughts. Someone needed a special loan approval. Anna worked for a major financial institution and held the position of chief lending officer. It was a high ranking position that carried with it major responsibilities. She invited the credit analyst upstairs to discuss the loan conditions. Moments later, her e-mail pinged and notified her of an urgent incoming message. The board meeting was taking place in a few days, and Dean Hathaway, the CEO of the savings bank, needed additional information from her. It was going to be a precarious board meeting. The institution had suffered major loan losses in the years past, and Anna had recently been recruited by the company to turn the savings bank's loan portfolio performance around. In just a few short days, they were going to have to deliver the unpleasant news to the board of directors that, although Anna had instituted more sophisticated credit analysis systems when she came on board, the savings bank's portfolio was still riddled with legacy problem loans. In an effort to lend to more customers and meet their organizational income goals, the savings bank had taken more risk than they realized when they granted the loans a few years back. They were paying for it dearly now in escalated loan losses. More losses were on the horizon, and Dean Hathaway was going to have to break the news to the board members. But the senior executives at the savings bank had faith in him. He was a charismatic man, and the board was charmed by him. They had total trust in him. He had the gift of gab and could speak easily on difficult topics, explaining them in such a way that would leave the listener impressed and convinced, even if still a little confused—a quality very useful among successful financial institution CEO's these days.

"Please, come in." Anna waved the manager into her office. She was a middle-aged woman with a slight build and a perpetual frown on her forehead. She had been with the savings bank for many years.

"I'm worried about this one," Christy began. "The applicant says he knows our CEO personally. Says Dean's a good friend of his, even is godfather to one of his kids."

"Okay. Tell me about the loan request." Anna knew that just a few short years ago, the savings bank would have been granting the loan request with no questions asked, but the regulatory environment had changed significantly. Now, they had to be more prudent. But the personal relationship with the CEO bothered Christy, and she was worried about turning down someone with such close ties to her boss's boss.

"We can't do this." Anna spoke without emotion after hearing the loan particulars. "The borrower doesn't qualify. We have to handle it the way we would any other loan request."

Christy looked worried. "Can you call him with the bad news then?"

Anna felt a twinge of pity for the poor woman. She had worked for the institution for a long time. She knew the dynamics of the corporate culture and the players there. She was also divorced and had three kids to support without the benefit of an additional income. She knew that, in order to survive at this place, you had to play the politics. Sometimes, you had to do things that you didn't necessarily agree with. Years ago, when Christy had first been hired, the accounting manager had put an arm around her and advised, "In order to survive here, you have to be willing to throw yourself in front of a bus for Dean Hathaway." And that's exactly what Christy had done. She had three little mouths to feed and a roof to keep over their heads. Her family took priority. If anyone wanted to criticize her for that, let them. She would do anything to keep the powers-that-be contented with her. But Anna was on a different page than the rest of them. Christy felt like she was caught between a rock and a hard place. She had warned her new boss of the corporate environment but she just wouldn't listen.

"Christy, I don't mind speaking with the borrower. But only after you place your call to him. We need to follow stand-ard protocol."

Christy was about to make another appeal to her boss when Anna's e-mail system pinged her again. Dean really needed the information from her, and the board meeting was quickly approaching. She apologized to Christy and indicated their meeting was over.

She swiveled her chair toward her computer and pulled up the e-mail. Dean needed her best estimates as to specifically what reasons had caused the borrowers to charge off their loans this past month. Was it lack of income, loss of employment, or dete-rioration in home value? What had their original credit scores been at the time the loans were granted? Had they been deficient to begin with, or had they deteriorated over time? Dean was also requesting another estimate of what their anticipated loan losses would be for the next twelve-month period.

I've already given him that, thought Anna. *He doesn't like my answer, and by asking again, he's sending me a very clear message that he would like a different one.*

Anna began hammering away on her keyboard. Just because he asked the same question over and over again did not mean she was going to change her answer. The data spoke for itself. Like it or not, loan losses would be increasing. The institution had put borrowers in homes that they never qualified for to begin with, and there was no changing that. She was estimating that loan losses would reach $260 million by the end of the year. This number would put the savings bank's financial position in a hazardous situation. If she was right, the institution would fall below their regulatory net worth requirement and would allow the regulators the option to take conservatorship at any time. Effectively shut them down. Even if she wasn't right, the confirmation of the fact that the institution had taken an inordinate amount of risk in the past could cause the board to lose faith in their CEO. So, even if the savings bank did survive, Dean Hathaway might not. Anna completely understood the gravity of the news she was communicating. She just couldn't compromise the integrity of the data or what it was telling them. She hit the send button.

◆◦◆

"Daniel! Victoria!" Anna called upstairs. "Is anyone coming to join us for the Clue game? We're all ready!" The dinner dishes were cleared, and the game board was spread out on the family room ottoman. Victoria's door flew open, and she came racing down the stairs. "I want to be Professor Plum this time!"

What was taking Daniel so long? Anna walked upstairs and opened her son's bedroom door. He was lying in bed, sobbing. He saw his mother and quickly sat up, trying to hide his tears, but his red, swollen eyes betrayed him.

"Love, what's the matter?" She was alarmed by his uncharacteristic behavior.

"Everyone hates me, Mom. They all know I reported the bullies, and now even the kids I don't know, even kids two years older than me, are passing me in the hallway and laughing. They're calling me a loser and saying I'm a snitch and that I'll never have any more friends." Daniel choked back tears that threatened to start again.

"It's so much worse now, Mom. I wish I'd never reported them. One kid came up to me and said, 'Daniel, what did you turn us in for? You're going to be sorry.'"

Anna was devastated.

"Love, you know it was the right thing to do. I really think this will all blow over. This is one of those life lessons that you'll learn from. It's sometimes hard for people to accept punishment."

"Everyone hates me." Daniel wiped his eyes. "They're all calling me gay. Mom, how do you know if you're gay?"

"Is that something you've been wondering?" Anna rubbed her son's back. "It's very common for boys your age to ask these questions."

Daniel thought for a minute.

"Well, it's just that everyone's calling me gay, and maybe they see something I don't."

"Love, don't label yourself. You're very young. Just live your life, and be true to yourself. Whatever you determine makes you happy, we will always love and support you."

Daniel paused for a moment. "And they call me wetback and spic. Mom, why is there so much hate in the world?"

"Sometimes people are intolerant of anyone who's different than they are." *He's just beginning to understand enough of life to grasp how pervasive bigotry and hatred are in the world*, Anna thought as she felt her heart breaking.

Daniel sniffled and then paused again. "I think they're just mad at me for reporting the bullies. Mom, reporting those kids was the worst mistake of my life."

"Everything's going to be fine. You did the right thing and in time, they'll realize it too."

She heard her own words but wasn't convinced herself, and the whole situation left her stomach in knots. Was she overreacting? She talked her son into joining the rest of the family downstairs for the board game.

"Daniel, the school dance is coming up. Are you going to invite Louisa?" asked his mom, after rolling the dice, attempting to lighten his mood.

Daniel didn't look up from his cards. "Louisa and I broke up."

"Sorry, Son. What happened?" His dad was curious.

"The Mexican guys told me to stay away from her. They said I'm not a real Mexican."

"What?" Anna put her cards down. She couldn't believe what she was hearing. "What do they mean by that?" She could feel her pulse rising.

"They said I'm a Mexican wannabe, only part Mexican, and Louisa deserves a real Mexican. They said, 'You live in that neighborhood? You're not one of us.'" Daniel shrugged.

"Daniel, that's deplorable. Those kids have no right to tell either you or Louisa what you can or can't do." Anna was dismayed that her son was so easily accepting defeat.

"Louisa says it's for the best. I just want to drop it," Daniel insisted without much emotion. "Besides, all of us guys are going together. No one's bringing a girl."

After the game board had been put away and the kids were in bed, Anna turned to her husband. "Danny, it's gotten worse for him. I'm so angry with these kids. Why can't they just leave him alone? It isn't just one group now. It's everyone. White kids, Mexican kids, everyone. And to attack him more when he finally stands up for himself—it's unconscionable."

"This kind of thing happens. Really. Let him work it out. It'll all blow over," Danny tried to reason with his wife.

"Why am I the one who always has to fight for him? Why aren't you as angry as I am?" Anna could feel her frustration rising inside of her.

"Love, don't get angry with me about this. Calm down. Sometimes you overreact when it comes to the kids."

"I'm not overreacting. He's in pain and I'm the only one worried about him."

"Things will be just fine. You'll see. Daniel's a tough kid. He'll work it all out." Danny drew his wife close to him and tried to hug her but she pulled away.

"Danny, this isn't going away by itself. In fact, it's gotten worse, and I want it stopped now." Anna's teeth were clenched as she spoke to her husband. "I want you to do something."

"Okay. Calm down. I promise I'll go talk to the school authorities."

"When?" Anna pressed. "This can't go on much longer. Our son is being traumatized. He's going to need therapy just to get over everything he's experienced so far."

Danny sat in the school principal's office. He had promised his wife he would address the situation and so here he was. Mrs. Pajot, a staunch older woman with thick glasses and a faded bun, was the principal of the middle school. She had held the position for many years and was very proud of her school. She sat, listened with a sympathetic ear, and reassured the concerned dad that she would look into the situation immediately. She convinced him that after her involvement, his son's harassment would stop. Danny felt satisfied with the principal's promises.

"The principal assured me she would handle it." Danny was relieved as he reported back to his wife. *There.* He hung up. *Mission accomplished.*

Daniel walked into his band class looking forward to his lessons. He enjoyed music and had decided to take up the trumpet this time. Unfortunately for him, Phil Jensen was also into music, but not so much so that he would be distracted from his primary goal of humiliating another kid at every opportunity.

The class had just gotten started when Daniel heard snickering behind him. He looked up nervously to see several students holding up two fingers in a peace sign and staring directly at him. One by one, other kids followed, trying to muffle their laughs. The band teacher turned around to look at his class but said nothing. Daniel couldn't get what the heck was going on. Why were they doing this, and what did it mean? Why was everyone staring at him that way?

"Hey, loser," whispered Phil, "it means 'Daniel's gay!' The whole class knows!"

As Daniel watched the domino effect take place around him, one easily influenced kid after another throwing up two fingers, he slunk down further and further into his seat until the entire class was roaring with laughter. *Why me? Maybe if I just ignore it, like Mom said. God, please make them stop. Please make the teacher do something. Why won't the teacher do anything?*

Mr. Cooper turned reluctantly, asked everyone to quiet down, and went on with his lecture.

Band practice had ended, and Aiden had had enough. He waited purposefully until the other kids had left the room and then approached the band teacher.

"It hasn't stopped yet, Mr. Cooper." Aiden's voice was low with determination.

"What hasn't stopped, Aiden?"

"What I told you about last week and the week before that and the week before that. It hasn't stopped. Phil Jensen is still doing it. He's got the whole class making fun of Daniel every day. He calls him faggot and makes fun of the way he walks, talks, and even the way he sits. I've told you this before, sir," Aiden tried to keep his temper in check.

"I've been watching. It's just kid stuff. Boys will be boys."

"It's not just kid stuff." Aiden's voice was no longer quiet; he was getting fed up with the teacher's apathy. "It's major harassment. Phil is a bully. You have to make it stop, Mr. Cooper. It's not right."

"I'll keep a look out, Aiden."

But Aiden had heard that promise before. He left the classroom, hoping that this time, things would be different.

———•◦•———

The sun hadn't set yet and Danny could tell by the color of the sky that it was going to be a beautiful one. He was home from work early, loosening his tie and looking foward to enjoying a rare opportunity to watch the sunset with his family when he heard voices in the family room. He walked over to join his wife and son, and noticed Daniel was particularly upset.

"What's going on?" he asked, sitting back on the couch.

"Kids in band class are holding up their fingers in a peace sign, which means, 'Daniel is gay.' Then they all laugh. It's not a big deal. Mom, please don't do anything. The school won't listen, and it'll just get worse for me. Dad, tell her not to."

Anna promised she wouldn't take any action. She didn't want to upset her son any more than he already was. But it was getting way out of hand, and she was disgusted by everything that was happening to her child right under the school's nose. It was time to get aggressive. Who would want to hurt her son? And why?

Anna went into their home office and sat at her desk. Danny followed her.

"Why are the school administrators not in more control of their classroom environments?" She almost screamed out the words in emphasis. She turned to her keyboard and hammered out a pointed e-mail to the band teacher:

> Mr. Cooper, we are very concerned that our son is being harassed in your classroom. Apparently, kids are holding up two fingers that symbolizes the message "Daniel is gay." Then they all join in laughter. This has been going on for several weeks and is very upsetting to our son. Can you

> please make sure that this behavior stops as soon as pos-
> sible? Please do not let Daniel know we have contacted
> you. He is very concerned about repercussions from being
> known as a snitch.

After hitting the send button, she also e-mailed Daniel's pastor, letting him know about the school incidences and asking for
his support. She knew that a lot of the kids in band class also
attended the parish and that the pastor would be in a good position to help.

The band teacher's e-mail reply was cordial.

> Yes, I have noticed something odd happening with the
> kids holding up their fingers and laughing, and now I
> understand what it means. I'm sorry this has been hap-
> pening and promise to take care of it.

Anna felt some relief. She only hoped her son wouldn't suffer
any kind of backlash by the bullies because of her complaints.
God, please protect my son, Anna prayed. It seemed that lately her
prayers had all been focused on Daniel's protection.

Each day that went by without incident was a godsend to
her. She was encouraged that Daniel hadn't complained about
any harassment for several weeks now. Things at school must
have been taken care of and another chapter of childhood was
behind them.

CHAPTER
NINE

There is no deeper wound than humiliation. The momentary glory we may feel in humiliating someone is short-lived compared to the damage we cause.

—Irwin Katsof

Saturday morning was upon them and the start of a new weekend. The sun was out in full force as Daniel, Aiden, and Michael skateboarded in front of Michael's house. Michael and Aiden lived only a block away from each other, and Daniel always wished he lived right next door rather than a whole mile away. He really liked that neighborhood. It was always full of kids hanging out and having fun.

Aiden was the best skateboarder of the three and showing the other two how to do kick flips. After a few spills and some tears in their jeans, the three decided to skateboard up to Daniel's house.

"Hey, Mom! Aiden and Michael are here!" Daniel and his two buddies busted through the front door.

"Are you guys hungry?"

"No, Mom, we're just gonna hang out front and skateboard on our street. It has a different slope than at Michael's."

Nonna heard her grandson's voice. "You must be hungry. I gonna make you boys pasta. Don't go far. It will be ready in two hours."

"Sure, Nonna. But I don't know where we'll be in two hours." Daniel laughed as he slammed the front door behind him.

"Pasta is ready!" Nonna had set a steaming bowl in the middle of the table as Anna walked outside to round up the boys. She noticed their skateboards were in the front yard, but they were nowhere to be seen.

"I wonder where they went," she wondered aloud to her husband. Suddenly their front door opened, and Michael walked in. He was flushed, and his hair was soaked with sweat.

"Michael, where are Aiden and Daniel?"

"We went for a run, Mrs. Mendez, but when we got to the street behind yours, Aiden and Daniel were tired and decided to climb up the slope rather than go around the block. I told them they were nuts, and I walked around. Aren't they up here yet?"

The Mendez house was elevated, and the backyard was fairly high above the street below. The steep slope leading up to their backyard was overgrown with tall, tangled shrubs and thick groundcover over six feet tall in some sections. They all hurried outside and looked down the slope.

Daniel and Aiden were struggling to climb up, their bodies almost disappearing into the ground cover and shrubs. The boys were red faced and looked like they had been caught in a downpour they were so drenched with sweat. Daniel was almost at the top, but Aiden was lagging behind. Michael couldn't help breaking out into laughter at the sight of the two. As Daniel approached, he had to clear a six-foot fence before he would be in his back yard. His father carefully coached him over to the other side.

"Man, that was harder than it looked." Daniel was winded as he brushed leaves out of his hair. They all turned around to see what progress Aiden was making. He was still far from the top. He was also, unfortunately, far from the bottom.

"I have an idea." Daniel ran off and came back a few seconds later with his dad's ladder. He stuck it through the fence posts and laid the ladder down on the slope.

"Daniel, the ladder may slip down the slope," his father cautioned.

"Come on, Aiden. I'll hold the ladder. You can do it. Just hang in there a bit longer."

"I'm gonna turn and go back," Aiden called back. "I can't make it."

"No, man. Don't give up. Just trust me. Hang on a bit longer. I'll help you."

Aiden struggled hard a few more feet. He grabbed a hold of the bottom rung and began painfully pulling his way up to the top while Daniel held the ladder steady. Nearing the top, Aiden stretched his hand out and after what seemed like forever, finally grabbed onto Daniel's extended one. With his friend's help, he emerged. There were thorns in his hair, dirt on his face, and his clothes had been ripped apart by the brush. Staring at Aiden, who looked like he'd had a run-in with a mountain lion, the three boys broke out into laughter.

"Told you guys you were nuts!" Michael rolled his eyes.

"Man, it looked like a shortcut." Aiden tried to brush himself off. "Whose idea was it, anyway?"

"Yours." Daniel laughed so hard his sides hurt.

"The pasta is cold now!" They heard Nonna's disapproving calls from inside the house.

"Hurry, boys. Come eat." Anna turned to go in. "We need to get ready soon for your band concert tonight."

———◆•◆•◆———

Parents and students had crowded into the noisy multi-purpose room as they each maneuvered for the best seats. Anna and Danny settled into theirs, excited to watch their son perform. The boys in the band, all dressed in their crisply starched white dress shirts and dark suit pants, filed down the aisle next to them to take their places up front. As Daniel passed by, a proud mama nudged Danny's arm.

"There's our son! Isn't he handsome?"

She turned as she heard Daniel's name being shouted out from a few rows back. Who was it that was so insistent on getting her son's attention? To her dismay, she realized they were not friendly calls. She noticed the ringleader was a young boy with blond hair and bright-green eyes. The shouts that she heard turned her stomach.

"Hey, Daniel! Moron! What an idiot!" The boy's friends had joined in.

"He's deaf!"

"What a loser!"

Anna silently prayed. *Please, God, don't let him hear*, but no such luck. She saw her son's head turning toward the bullies' shouts.

When he first heard his name, Daniel had turned his head and peered out, gladly looking for a friendly face. Was one of his buddies trying to get his attention? As he searched the crowd, his eyes locked with the kid who was leading the tirade of insults. He heard the scathing remarks and realized he was being made fun of, and worse, in front of his parents and everybody else there.

These guys never took a break. His shoulders sank low, and his head dropped. He felt more ashamed than ever.

His posture deteriorated with the visible confusion of innocence and pain. He sat down and slumped as low in his seat as possible. He wanted to just disappear, to float away, or sink into the tile beneath him. His mother watched as her son's body language went from excited anticipation to shame and fear. Her heart hurt, and her muscles tightened. She felt the blood pulsating in her temples. She could not restrain herself another second. It was more than a mother could bear. She stood up from her seat and tripped over parents' feet as she barreled toward the bullies. She was just about to grab the little blond monster by his shirt collar and ask him what the hell he thought he was doing when she felt her husband's hand on her arm, pulling her back.

"What are you doing? Come back to your seat."

She paused for a second, took a breath, and realized her husband was probably right. She would later come to regret that she hadn't at least gotten the names of the hostile kids, but their mocking faces would be etched in her mind forever.

———◆◆◆———

The sound of the gavel hitting its base was the first thing she heard. The chairman of the board was calling the meeting to order as Anna hurried into the boardroom. It was frowned upon to be late to the board meeting, but Anna had been talking to her son about his day at school and didn't want to cut the conversation short. She quickly took a seat at the end of the table and flipped open her laptop. She needed to be prepared for whatever questions were directed her way. The chairman was a wise, grandfatherly man in his late sixties. He smiled at Anna as she took her seat. He had a particular admiration for her skill sets and her accomplishments in cutting the savings bank's loan losses after having been with them only a few short years. Most of all, he admired her spunk.

The board meeting began, and her mind wandered to her recent conversation with Daniel about how his school day had gone. He seemed happy enough with his classes. But there was something missing. Why didn't he open up to her the way he used to do? He just didn't give his mother very many details anymore. They had always been so close, so open about everything. *Should I worry?* thought Anna. *Maybe I'm just being paranoid again.* Suddenly, she noticed all eyes in the room were directed on her. A question must have been asked of her area of responsibility, but she hadn't heard it.

"I'm so sorry," Anna stuttered. "Can you please repeat the question?"

"We're asking how confident you are in these estimates of future loan losses," repeated the chairman of the board patiently.

"Very confident," replied Anna. "If you will notice on page twenty-two, we have spread the losses and the recoveries, and you will find the net loss ratio at the bottom of the page." As she directed the board members to the appropriate section in the board report, her heart sank. The loan loss number was not at all what she had provided. In fact, it was significantly less. She was stunned. Her report had been changed.

"Excuse me. I'm sorry, but I think there's a slight mix up," Anna began mumbling. She was interrupted by her CEO.

"Yes, the numbers Ms. Mendez refers to have also been reduced to reflect residual values of the collateral securing the loans," Dean Hathaway explained. He looked directly at the chairman of the board, refusing to meet Anna's questioning stare.

But he knows the number I had provided already took collateral value into consideration, thought Anna. *It's in my e-mail. He knows this. It's always been part of the process. My numbers have never been altered like this before.*

The board meeting continued. The voices were excited with the good news. The forecasts were positive, and the board members were happy. A lavish dinner of steak, shrimp, and wine was brought in for the dinner reception. Anna watched the clock. She just wanted to get home to her family.

The meeting was finally over, and a frustrated Anna went back to her office to pack up her belongings for the long drive home. Just as she was about to leave, someone entered the room. She looked up to see Gabby, the Senior Vice President of Finance.

"I know you're upset," Gabby began.

"Gabby, those aren't my numbers." Anna looked her directly in the eyes. "Who changed them? Your area produces the reports, so you must know."

"Don't worry," reassured Gabby. "Dean has promised me that he'll straighten it out with the board during their executive session. They're in there right now. I'm sure he's telling them what the adjusted numbers are."

"How do you know all of this? Why didn't Dean just do it in the regular session, with all of us present? Why didn't I know my numbers would be changed?" Anna pressed on.

Was that pity she noticed on Gabby's face or humor? She couldn't tell.

"Don't worry," Gabby repeated. "Dean asked me to let you know that he would straighten everything out with the board. And I believe him. You should too. Now go home to your beautiful children before they're both asleep."

The flickering freeway lights were bright against a dark sky as Anna drove.

Was Gabby placating me? Anna wondered. *Are they manipulating my numbers and don't want me to know?*

But she couldn't worry about it right then. She needed to get home to her children. They were her priority and had to remain so. She would talk to Dean Hathaway herself in the morning.

<hr />

"Hut! Hut!" Daniel grabbed the ball and took advantage of the man coverage as he threw it deep to the receiver. It was lunchtime, and the four friends were playing a quick game on the school field. Just as Daniel wound up and released the ball, a group of boys walked onto the field. Three of them shoved him hard, and he slammed to the ground. Daniel got up, brushed himself off, and looked at the kid who was obviously the guy in charge.

"Hey, what's the problem?" He rubbed his chin that had hit the ground first when he had gone face down.

"Problem? You're our problem, dirty Mexican half-breed. You don't belong here." The thug and his groupies gave Daniel the death stare.

Daniel looked away. *Please God, make them leave me alone.*

Out of the corner of his eye, he noticed Aiden approaching.

"What do you think you're doing, dude?" Aiden's eyes fixed on the head bully in charge.

"Come on, Aiden. Let's get out of here." Daniel pulled his friend away.

The bullies were coming out of the woodwork now. They didn't belong to any particular group or race.

There were the Mexican bullies. "Hey, half-breed! You're not a real Mexican! You're mama's little Italian boy! What a Mexican wannabe!"

Then there were the jock bullies. "There's the wetback! Hey, greaser! You mowin' lawns this weekend?"

And then the hostile groups led by Phil Jensen and Steve Wright.

"Loser!"

"Idiot!"

"Gay boy!"

"Spic!"

"No one would care if you died!"

Daniel couldn't understand how people could be so cruel and why he was targeted the way he was. He knew that harassment and bullying were part of life and that it would happen to people from time to time, but he just couldn't figure out why it was happening to him *all the time*. Why couldn't he just stay under the radar? What was wrong with him? If only he knew how to be more like the tough guys at his school. If only his parents hadn't overprotected him and taught him to be kind, maybe then he would know how to make those stinging comebacks whenever the bullies were throwing slurs and insults or punches at him. Why had everyone else figured out how to get along in the world, but he couldn't?

The boys were spread out on Michael's couch playing video games and polishing off burgers.

"What are you guys wearing to the dance?" Daniel licked ketchup from his fingers.

"I'm wearing skate shorts, a dress shirt, and a tie." Aiden smiled big.

"Aiden, you can't wear skate shorts to the dance." Michael shook his head. "I'm wearing a white suit."

"Okay, so you guys are all over the place. Whatever I wear will be something in between you two." Daniel laughed.

"Hey, anybody wanna go to youth group later?" Aiden asked.

The three friends had really gotten into the local youth group at their community parish. They went whenever they could. It was a good way for them to get together, talk about God, and just hang. After the sermons, most of them would stick around to play football or shoot hoops. Phil Jensen also enjoyed hanging around the parish.

Today Phil was, as usual, mad at the world and had decided to take it out on his favorite target. Who did this Daniel kid think he was anyway? Yeah, he may have parents who didn't get the cops called on them, and he lived in his privileged little neighborhood, but he didn't fight back, and Phil would be sure to take full advantage of that.

Daniel and Aiden were shooting hoops when Phil approached.

"Hey, half-breed!" Phil shouted out in Daniel's direction. "Why do you pretend to be Mexican when you're not? Do you want people to think you're tough? Come on, dirty half-breed. Show me how tough you are!"

"Leave me alone, Phil." Daniel threw his shot and missed.

"Why don't you make me, wimp?" Phil walked closer to Daniel as he was about to take another shot and pushed him hard. Daniel tripped and fell. Hiding the scrapes and bruises from his parents was becoming difficult, and he hoped he didn't have a new one from the fall. He had found a way to hide the emotional scars, but the physical ones were getting kinda hard to cover up.

"What are you, anyway? Are you Mexican, or are you white? Do you even know what you are, wimp? Maybe you don't even know. Maybe your mama doesn't even know." Phil was getting worked up now. Other kids had gathered behind Phil, laughing at Daniel.

Daniel turned and walked off the court. *Please, God. Don't let them follow me. Please, make them go away.*

Aiden stood, shaking his head at Phil.

"Why do you have to do this to him?" Aiden's eyes were burning, and his fists were ready. "Why do you pick on him so much?"

Phil loved seeing Aiden fired up like this. He shrugged his shoulders. "He's just the kid to pick on." He casually flicked Aiden on his shoulder with his index finger and his thumb, as if he was swatting a flea, and smiled.

Aiden wanted to level the kid right there, but he remembered what Daniel always told him. "We shouldn't fight them, Aiden. That will make us just as bad as they are."

Aiden ran and caught up to Daniel who was walking off with his shoulders slumped.

"Do your parents know about what's going on?" Aiden could hardly contain himself.

"Please, Aiden. Promise me you won't tell them. I told them about it once, and that was a disaster. They complained to the school, and things got worse. And telling them didn't do any good anyway. I mean, if my parents can't force the school to do anything about it, who can?"

Aiden thought about that for a second. "We can. We can fight back, Daniel. Teach them a lesson." Aiden pumped his fist into an open hand.

Daniel just shook his head. "We can't, Aiden. If we do that, they win. We become like them. Anyway, with our luck, we'll be the ones who get expelled."

The two friends stopped for a moment and laughed, but Aiden knew that something had to be done.

"Well, at least talk to Pastor Marks about it."

"Yeah, I already did. Nothing changed. Not even adults can do anything about it."

CHAPTER
TEN

We loved with a love that was more than love.

—Edgar Allen Poe

"Nobody bother me. I'm all packed." Daniel announced as he sat back on his heels on his bedroom floor in front of his big screen with the Nintendo control in his hands. Clothes were strewn about everywhere, some on hangers suspended from the top rafter of his bunk bed, others lying on his desk, his chest of drawers, and his floor.

"Daniel, you're nowhere near ready." His mother peeked her head in his bedroom and hurried off to help Victoria. "Get everything into your suitcase."

"Mom, that part only takes two minutes. It's no big deal."

The family was embarking on their summer vacation. This time the destination was Italy, Anna's birthplace. Anna's side of the family was Italian, and both kids always enjoyed connecting with that part of their heritage. Once on the plane, they could relax. The couple looked back on the school year behind them. They were hopeful that Daniel's high school experience would be better than his middle school one. God willing, things would be different in high school and middle school would be just a bad memory. Maybe middle school was just a right of passage for their son, and now that he had made it through, it would be smooth sailing for him without having to deal with the Steves and Phils of middle school anymore.

After the ten-hour flight from California, they had a short layover in Amsterdam before going on to Venice, their first destination. The kids had read up on the history and poured over pictures, but even then, they weren't quite prepared for the splendor that was now laid out before them—waterways everywhere, brightly colored buildings lined both sides of the canals. In place of automobiles, they saw gondolas floating down the watery streets. They were whisked away in a water taxi to their hotel on the Grand Canal and felt as if they'd been transported to another world.

They enjoyed local pizzerias and the sounds of the sidewalk musicians who poured their hearts out through the instruments. Daniel and Victoria spent the days soaking in the local people's customs.

"Daniel, why does everyone ride around on a little motorcycle?" Victoria asked her big brother as they strolled down a narrow side street off the Grand Canal. She always looked to him for her life answers.

"It's more fun that way." Daniel was watching the passersby. "Besides, the streets are too small. These people really know how to enjoy life. No one needs big cars here. I love it here, Mom. I think I want to move here after college."

"I'm coming with you!" His mother agreed.

From their hotel balcony, they could see the historic Rialto Bridge, the largest bridge that crossed the Grand Canal. Merchants were selling their colorful wares on both sides of the bridge as visitors sauntered by. They could almost see the Venetians of the sixteenth century selling their spices and silks from the Orient. Did they have to ever go back to the states?

St. Mark's Basilica became a personal favorite of Daniel's. The family sipped espressos and had rich, silky gelato, not the makeshift ice cream they called gelato in the states, as they listened to the coos of the pigeons and the sounds of the musicians. Although the kids understood that the pigeons were destroying the ancient ruins, they couldn't help but enjoy them. The pigeons seemed to be as much a part of Venice as the ruins were.

They visited Verona, the setting for many of Shakespeare's plays, where they took in a Giuseppe Verdi opera in the grand Verona amphitheatre. Danny had splurged on great seats to be sure they were padded for comfort for the kids. Maybe they were too comfortable. Just before the end of Act 3, when Rigoletto's beautiful daughter Gilda dies, both kids had fallen asleep. Daniel's head was slumped on Anna's shoulder, and Victoria's head was in her lap.

Danny smiled at his wife. "They lasted a long time. Are they too heavy for you?" She shook her head. She couldn't have been happier with both her children asleep on top of her. They could always see the rest of *Rigoletto* at a later time in their lives.

They took a train down the eastern coast of Italy and made a stop for lunch in Padua for a local meal of paduan hen with risotto and asparagus. The seating area was outdoors, and chickens strutted around the diners' feet as they feasted. Daniel and Victoria thought free wandering chickens in a restaurant was one of the funniest things they had ever seen. You'd never see anything like this in the states. They finally arrived in Roccamorice, Anna's hometown. The area seemed to be a million miles from anything in a scantily populated part of Eastern Italy on the Adriatic Sea. The little mountainside village was peppered with shepherds and their flocks, which they tended to daily, just as shepherds had done for as many generations as the mountainside itself could remember. Anna's family still had a house there, a modest home that was large and rustic, where she had been born. The main house had two bedrooms, and the back of the home, which years ago had housed sheep, had been refurbished into two one-bedroom units by Anna's sister Lilly. After much negotiating with his parents, Daniel had convinced them he was old enough to stay in one of the one-bedroom units by himself. He threw his suitcase on the bed, opened it up, and took out a poster of Led Zeppelin he had brought all the way from the states. He taped it up to the stone wall and sat back to admire it. He finally had his bachelor pad.

Anna and Danny stayed in the second unit right next to Daniel's, while Nonna and Victoria shared the main quarters. The house was remotely located, and neither of the kids knew the area or the locals well.

"I don't want you kids walking around the property by yourselves," their mother advised. "There are animals that run loose around here, and we don't know the locals well."

"Mom, you're just being paranoid." Both kids laughed.

Maybe so, she thought, *but I'm from the states*.

It was early their first morning when the tired parents were awakened by a knock on their heavy wooden door. Anna stumbled out of bed bleary eyed and opened it to find her son standing before her with an amused look on his face. *I told him not to walk around the property by himself*, she thought.

"Mom, umm, I went up to the main house and was having breakfast with Nonna and Victoria when we heard a knock on the door, and when I opened it, there was an old woman with no teeth dressed in black standing there. When she saw me, she screamed my name, grabbed my face, and kissed me." Daniel tried hard not to laugh.

"What? You opened the door to a stranger? Where's the woman now?" Anna belted her bathrobe.

"Umm, she's right behind me. She followed me." Daniel shifted his eyes sideways and covered his mouth to muffle his laughter.

Just as he had described, an old woman with a weathered face and a toothless grin appeared in the doorway. She shouted Anna's name before wrapping her fragile arms around her and squeezed tightly. Anna had no clue who she was. This sweet, old woman was a villager who had heard the Mendez family had returned from America to visit relatives. She had gotten up at the crack of dawn and walked from the neighboring town to be one of the first to greet them in proper Roccamorice style.

Anna invited the woman in for coffee and pastries. The conversation centered on what life was like in America, a land these people could only dream of. For them, America represented opportunity and hope along with a better life for younger generations. They wanted to hear all about it. Even this old grandmother had traveled far on foot to hear the tales of the enchanted land. Daniel and Victoria were happy to entertain her with stories of what schools and the promise of a good education meant in America, the land of hope and freedom.

After helping themselves to cornettos, espresso, and more conversation, the elderly villager was ready to begin her long journey back and would not hear of accepting a ride home. She kissed the children one last time, made an eloquent motion to bless them in God's love, and waved empathically as she began her trek home. *No wonder they live so long*, thought Anna.

The family took mountain hikes, stopped to buy fresh cheese from the shepherds, and visited relatives they hadn't seen in years, meeting some for the very first time. Anna's great aunt Filomena, the matriarch of the family, had taken a particular fondness to Daniel. A firstborn male was especially cherished in an Italian household. She kissed his forehead and firmly told him when he got older, if he moved to Italy and married an Italian girl, she would assign her pension to him, and he could live with her forever.

"You'll never have to work again!" Aunt Filomena would often say to him in her thick Italian dialect as she pinched his cheeks. She said it with so much passion that no one could tell whether or not she was actually serious, or was she just trying to make her granddaughters jealous so they would obey her more?

"See, Mom"—Daniel smiled at his mom—"I'm going to move here!"

Their trek to a particularly dense part of the region to visit a hermitage of a saint still revered in the small town became the highlight of their trip. The townspeople still celebrated the Festa

Di San Bartolomeo annually in honor of him. The terrain was rugged, with overgrown brush and foliage, so the family was forced to park their vehicle. They would need to continue the rest of the way on foot.

The hermitage led to an old mission, which was hundreds of years old. When they finally arrived, they stood back to absorb the holy scene before them. It was a beautiful place, a hollowed-out sanctuary against a mountainside, secluded and peaceful. Inside, the original altar from hundreds of years earlier was still standing. A rambling brook ran just outside, and the water was said by the locals to be holy water; the townspeople believed that anyone who drank from the brook would be protected from worldly evils. Anna watched as her children lay on their bellies and strained to take a drink from the blessed waters. *We can use all of the protection from evil that we can get*, thought Anna.

They reflectively returned to their vehicle to start the ride home when Danny realized he had inadvertently parked with one of the tires more elevated than the others. The car wasn't getting enough traction to move. He would need more weight on one side of the vehicle. It was a narrow path with a drop off of about three feet on either side—not dangerous but certainly inconvenient. Danny got into the car; he had a plan.

"Daniel, get in. I need your weight on the passenger side."

The rest of the family waited outside and watched. Daniel started to get into the passenger seat, when he turned to his mother with a big smile. "Remember, Mom, if I die, I love you."

Everyone laughed as he jumped in the car. His weight had been enough to help the tire gain traction, and they were off again.

Their next stop was Rome where they toured St. Peter's Basilica, the Sistine Chapel, and the Coliseum. Although prohibited, Daniel had been unable to keep from touching the relics, the artifacts, the monuments, still so full of life. They took a horse-drawn carriage to the Spanish steps where they eventually settled into the most quaint restaurant for a dinner of pasta, mussels, and dandelion flowers. Then they were off to Florence before leaving this amazing part of the world chock full of history and life, to head back to America.

As their plane was touching down, Daniel turned to his mom.

"Europe was great, Mom. Next year we should choose another continent. I want to travel the whole world just like Aunt Lilly and Uncle Pierre." Somehow, Anna knew he would.

CHAPTER
ELEVEN

If we are to teach real peace in this world, and if we are to carry on a real war against war, we shall have to begin with the children.

—Mahatma Gandhi

The crowd was thick as churchgoers walked orderly out of the grand old church. It was Sunday and the Mendez family practiced the Catholic faith. Keeping with tradition, both Daniel and Victoria were baptized and celebrated their first holy communion there. As they exited the beautiful mission, Anna put her arm around her son and asked him if he wanted to be confirmed in Christ.

"The decision is completely yours, love. Your dad and I made the decision for your baptism and first communion, but the confirmation is completely up to you. If you do want to move forward, we need to be signing you up for the classes now."

Daniel enjoyed his religious studies and all the discussions he had with his friends at the local youth group about faith. And he was committed to Christ, so it was an easy decision for him.

"Yes, Mom, I want to."

"Okay." Anna looked at him. "There's only one problem. The Catholic Church requires that you have a qualified sponsor, and that person can't be a parent. The sponsor needs to be Catholic and has to have been confirmed in Christ as well."

Daniel looked at his mom. The Mendezes had no local relatives that they could rely on for such a huge commitment, and none of their immediate friends were Catholic.

"I've decided who my sponsor is going to be," Daniel announced on the drive home.

"Who?" His father was surprised that he had such a quick solution.

"I'm going to ask Terry."

Terry was a sweet, elderly neighbor who was still quite spunky and had taken an immediate liking to Daniel from the moment they met. Daniel would often stop to chat with the animated little lady whenever he walked his dog. Anna wasn't sure asking her was such a good idea.

"Daniel, we don't know Terry very well, and that's a big commitment you would be asking her to undertake."

"That's okay, Mom. I know Terry. She and I talk all the time, and sometimes she joins me when I take Sasha for a walk. Terry loves me. I know she'll do it."

Anna loved how her son could so easily relate with everyone, regardless of what generation or walk of life they came from.

Daniel pulled out his cell phone and dialed Terry.

"Hello? Terry, it's me, your neighbor, Daniel. I was just wondering, I'm going to start my religious confirmation process, and it's a really big deal for me, and, well, I need a sponsor, and I was wondering if you would do that for me."

After a short pause, Daniel's parents heard him exclaim, "Okay, great! Oh, and just one more question, are you a Christian? Okay, great."

Pleased with himself, Daniel turned to his parents and shrugged.

"See, guys, problem solved. I'm gonna go meet up with the guys for football on the greenbelt now."

Sunday afternoons were always the best for the boys when they were playing football. They all agreed the prime time to play was just after a rain. That way when they got tackled, the mud would fly everywhere.

The four friends had rounded up several other guys to make their football game on the greenbelt really great; the more players, the more slinging of the mud and the pigskin.

"Just pass the ball to Daniel." Aiden was going over their game plan. "He'll score every time."

One of the guys threw a long pass down the greenbelt. Daniel caught it and took off down the field. Once Daniel had the ball in his hands, you could bet not many were going to stop him. As he made his way to the end zone, Jeff Schaeffer, a shy kid who knew he wasn't going to be drafted by the NFL anytime soon, was running alongside him to block anybody from the other team from getting to Daniel. The two were coming up on a touchdown when Daniel noticed out of the corner of his eye that Jeff had disappeared. He looked over to see that his friend had lost his footing and slammed down into the shrubs that marked the boundaries of their makeshift football field. Daniel knew Schaeffer well enough to know that this would be embarrassing for the shy kid, so instead of making his way to an easy touchdown, he stopped in his tracks.

"Hey, dude. You okay?" Daniel extended his hand.

"Thanks, man." Jeff quietly accepted the outstretched hand. "I don't think this game's for me."

"No, you were great, dude." Daniel helped Jeff to his feet. "Don't be hard on yourself. You've just started playing. Everyone falls every once in a while. We just have to keep getting up again."

Jeff smiled at his friend, and the two stepped back onto the muddy field.

Daniel's cell phone rang, and he walked away from the group to answer. The boys began discussing how to burn the rest of the afternoon. They kicked around all their options: skate boarding, pizza, the movies. Daniel hung up and turned back to his friends.

"That was Audra. She and Brittany and Julia are going to the beach tonight for a bonfire, and she wants us all to go join them."

"Hey, why did she call you? Does she like you or something? Yeah, I think Audra likes Daniel!" The guys started ribbing him.

"We're just friends." Daniel laughed. "Seriously, though, let's go to the bonfire tonight."

They spent the evening around the fire, telling jokes and stories, some true, some not, and talking about how easy school was or how bad it sucked while the waves foamed and bubbled on the shore and the fire burned hot on their faces.

———◆———

Anna and Danny sat at the fire pit in their backyard with blankets in their laps. Summer was ending, and the evenings on the coast could get cool. The change of weather had come early this year. Daniel had just returned from a bonfire and was inside, helping Victoria gather the making for s'mores. Anna took the rare opportunity to have a private conversation with her husband.

"After our experience with the culture at middle school, I'm worried about sending Daniel to a large public school. I think I want to enroll him in the Catholic high school. It'll give him a fresh start. It's a smaller school, and I think they're more in control of the classroom environments there. I'm going to call them and see if I can get him on the list."

"I agree." Danny looked into the flickering flames. "It'll also be a different group of kids than those that have been harassing him. No more history that will follow him."

The kids emerged with their arms full of marshmallows, Hershey's chocolate bars, and graham crackers. Victoria thought s'mores were the best dessert ever. Daniel was content with just the marshmallow. He happily accommodated his sister by eating her burnt ones.

"Daniel," began his mom, "I think it would be a great idea for us to check out the Catholic high school for you."

"No. I want to go to SV High." His quick reply had a tone of finality.

"But you'll have a completely different experience at the Catholic high school. They have great sports teams. And their academic programs are among the best in the state. Let's just check it out."

Daniel knew exactly what his mom was trying to fix.

"Mom, you don't understand. What's happening to me will happen to me wherever I go. At least at SV High I'll have my friends around me. If you put me at a different school, it'll be worse for me because I won't have any friends there. No, I won't go."

Anna's heart sank. *If I push him to do something he doesn't want to do, it may be worse for him*, she thought.

"But I do want to take up martial arts again." Daniel announced as he licked his fingers of the sticky marshmallow.

"I'm glad to see you interested in taking it up again," said his dad. "After the black belt in Tae Kwon Do, we weren't sure if you had just lost interest in the art."

"Yeah. I need to be able to know that I can physically defend myself." Daniel's voice had calmed as he stared into the fire. "I think I want to take karate this time." He pulled another burnt marshmallow off Victoria's skewer. Lucky for him, she wasn't a very good cook.

CHAPTER
TWELVE

Bullies thrive wherever authority is weak.

—Tim Field

His freshman year in high school began and with it, renewed hope. Although he was in advanced placement classes, Daniel breezed through his workload with ease and still had plenty of time left for his karate and guitar. He had begun playing guitar a couple of years back and had recently talked his parents into arranging private lessons for him. His uncle Pierre had given him a shiny, new electric guitar for his birthday, and it had become one of his most prized possessions. As soon as he would burst in through the front door from school, Daniel would throw his books on the counter, bound up the stairs to his room, and the sounds of "Stairway to Heaven" soon filled the house.

"Dinner!" Nonna yelled as she brought out a giant bowl of hand-cut pasta alla chitarra.

"What do you guys think about me joining the football team?" Daniel pulled out his chair and scooped a big helping of the pasta onto his plate.

"It's a big commitment, Son. But I think it's a great idea." His father was enthusiastic.

His mother liked the idea too. "You've always loved the game from the day you could crawl. Remember when you were three and you would watch the games on TV. You would stand in front of the screen with your hands on your knees, and you would run around in little circles, then you would throw yourself on the ground with your legs straight up in the air and roll around. I have to find those videos."

———•◦•———

Daniel joined the SV High football team. He really did love the sport and worked out as often as he could. Writing was another one of his hobbies, and when combined with football, well, there was no stopping him then. He registered as a writer for an online sports blog. The administrators of the blog didn't know he was only fifteen. He assumed a penn name and wrote several football articles that won awards for the number of readers they garnered. His mother swore he knew more football facts and trivia than some of the football commentators on the major networks.

It was a balmy Thursday afternoon, and the family sat in the bleachers as they cheered and shouted. Daniel had caught a long pass and ran it thirty yards to score a touchdown. Victoria screamed as she saw her big brother running for the goal line and heard people around her say, "That was Mendez! Great play!"

"That's my brother!" Victoria made sure the people within ear-shot knew that.

The game ended, and although they lost, Daniel came off the field to a crowd applauding him. "Hey, Mom, can Jeremy and Aiden join us at the restaurant? Let's go have sushi."

"That was such a great play, Daniel." His mother was still con-gratulating him when they were shown to their table.

"It was really no big deal, Mom," Daniel replied in his humble way. "I just happened to be standing there and caught the ball and just ran. That's all I did."

His parents chatted about the day's events, while the boys started their own side conversation—out of earshot of the adults.

"You're owning football, Daniel," began Jeremy.

"Yeah, it's all good if you can forget about Phil Jensen and Sal Gutierrez. They never let up. Jeremy, Phil bothered you a lot in middle school, too. How is it now for you?"

Jeremy thought a minute. "Ya know, he really kinda leaves me alone now. I see him once in a while, but he doesn't bother me anymore. It's like my life is completely different now that he's not around."

"That's good to know. Happy for you, dude." Daniel couldn't help feeling a little unsettled.

Man, he thought, *it really is only me. This will follow me forever.*

———◆•◆———

The bullies from his middle school had followed him into high school. But high school had also unleashed vicious, new ones of its own. Sal Gutierrez, the Mike Tyson knock off from Italian class, had already spotted Daniel as an ideal new target. Daniel decided to be proactive and reach out to the guy. Maybe they could like each other.

"Hey, Sal, how's it going?" Daniel waved as they both walked in the same direction to class.

"What's it to you, dirty Mexican half-breed?" Sal mocked. "Heeey, Saaal, how's it going?'" Sal imitated Daniel in an exaggerated voice and contorted face. "What an a—hole."

Other kids laughed as Sal tore into him. Even his football teammates had begun taking jabs at him on and off the field.

"Hey, Mendez! What an idiot! Hey, Mendez! Are these your new cleats? Not anymore." He watched as his new cleats were tossed up on top the roof of the school. When would it ever stop?

He was getting ready to turn in for the night and resigned himself to tell his parents he had lost his cleats. He would need new ones if he was going to continue playing.

"What do you mean you lost them? Where did you lose them?" Danny was frustrated. "Those were expensive, Son. Have you looked everywhere?"

"Yeah, Dad. Just don't worry about it. I'll pay for new ones." Daniel walked off to his room.

The campus was crowded the next morning as Daniel made his way from PE down the hall to English class. Then it happened. He was waylaid by three bullies from the football team, led by Sal Gutierrez. They grabbed his arms and lifted him up off the ground.

"Hey, let me go! Let me go!" Daniel was shouting now.

The delinquents threw him into a nearby trash can. They began rolling the trash can around and slammed it against the side of a building. Daniel grimaced as the can slammed into the brick wall.

"That's what we do with faggot half-breeds around here," one of the bullies growled as they walked away.

"That's right!" The other boy laughed.

"You might as well just stay there 'cause we'll just throw you right back in."

The three boys walked away, laughing and shouting.

"Hey, guys! Look at the trash in the trash can," one of the jocks mocked as other kids walked by. Heads were turning toward a crumbled and mortified Daniel as they passed by. He slowly pulled himself out of the trash with half-eaten food and garbage sticking to his clothes. The humiliation was unbearable.

Look what Jesus had to bear, thought Daniel. *If this is the worst I have to bear, I can take it.*

As he pulled himself out of the trash can for the second time that week, the bullies decided they needed to up the ante. "On the ground, wetback! Told you to stay there!" A kid pushed Daniel to the ground, where he crouched on his knees, head down, barely able to hold back his tears. One of the most insecure bullies that had to prove himself to the others kicked him in the back. *God, please don't let me start crying in front of them. I don't want them to see me cry. Please, God. Make them go away.*

He tried taking different routes to class, hoping to avoid his assailants, but somehow they always seemed to find him. What was this pleasure they took in tormenting him? And what purpose did others have in watching it? To watch it as though waiting for it to break his endurance.

Why can't I just throw a punch? Why don't I just get more aggressive? Why does this keep happening to me?

"Aiden, they just won't leave me alone. I don't know what's wrong with me."

"It's not you. It's them. They're just jerks." Aiden was disgusted by what was happening.

Daniel had finally had enough. "Aiden, I don't want to get you in the middle of this, but if Sal challenges me to fight him, will you back me?"

"Yeah, of course I will! I'll crush 'em." Aiden was already getting worked up at the mere thought of an opportunity to finally have a turn at the bullies.

"I don't want to start anything, though." Daniel calmed his friend down. "Maybe they'll just stop. I keep telling my teachers about it, but they don't do anything. I just don't get it."

It had been a great football game. Daniel had scored another touchdown, and his family was beaming.

"Daniel, that was a great touchdown," his dad began.

"It wasn't anything really. I just happened to catch the ball and just happened to run it to the end zone. That's it. No big deal." Daniel was almost irritated at the compliments. "And I don't want to go to dinner either. Just take me home."

Why isn't he happier? Anna thought as she sat in the car on the ride home. *He should be pleased with himself. Why the moodiness?* She had a suspicion.

"Daniel, are the kids still bothering you at school?"

The question angered him. "No, Mom. No one's bothering me. I really don't need your help."

"Daniel, why are you acting like this? What don't you want me to know? What's wrong?"

"Nothing, Mom. Okay, let me just say that in middle school when you convinced me to report the bullies, that was the biggest mistake of my life. That was bad advice you gave me. I need to solve my problems on my own from now on."

"Daniel, sometimes kids at your age can get jealous. They may be jealous of you, and that's why they say mean things sometimes," Anna tried to reason.

"Believe me, Mom. No one's jealous of me. And no one's bothering me." His voice was angry with rebellion against pity. He shut down the conversation.

"I'm worried about him, Danny. I think the bullying is picking up again and he's not telling us," Anna began when she and her husband were finally alone.

"Love, I don't think anything major is happening."

"I do. Didn't you notice how moody he was in the car? And I'm not sure why I'm the only one worrying about him all the time. I wish you would get more concerned about this whole bullying thing. We can't just ignore it and hope it all goes away. I'm going to call the school in the morning."

Anna woke up the next morning with the conversation still heavy on her mind. She picked up the phone and dialed Daniel's English teacher, his guidance counselor, and the school principal. The conversation was the same with all three.

"I'm worried about my son. I think he's being harassed by other kids. Can you please keep an eye on him for me?"

"Why do you think he'd be harassed?"

"I don't know. He's a little shy. I think sometimes he talks in a hurried manner. I have no idea why, really." They were all looking for a high risk factor that would potentially make him a target, and not having one, Anna realized she sounded paranoid.

"He's a great student," his English teacher had told her. "The kind of student teachers pray for more of. Quiet, respectful, smart, reserved."

Each school administrator assured her they had noticed nothing out of the ordinary and promised to keep an eye out for her son. When she spoke with the principal, he took it a step further. Mr. Sacker had been the principal at SV High for many years and prided himself on his status.

"He has a good group of friends he hangs out with, so we know he'll be fine. It's the loners you have to worry about. Not kids like Daniel," the principal touted.

"If he was involved in more clubs, he wouldn't have these issues," he continued. "Believe me. I've run into this many times. I've forced kids to join multiple clubs, and everything gets better for them when they do as I say. And when I talk, kids listen." This principal seemed very assured of himself.

More clubs. Okay, let's try that strategy, Anna thought.

CHAPTER
THIRTEEN

Our lives begin to end the day we become silent about things that matter.

—Dr. Martin Luther King Jr.

She sat on the couch in her bedroom changing from her work clothes, her mind trying to focus on a relaxed weekend ahead. It had been another grueling week at the office. *I need to let go of the stress from work*, she thought. Maybe a nice, long bath after dinner would do the trick. Anna looked up to see her husband walking in with a strained expression on his face.

"Love, I don't want to frighten you with what I'm going to tell you, but this is pretty serious." Her muscles tightened back up as she prepared for whatever it was he was about to say.

"Daniel's upset. He told me that he has been having thoughts of…"

"Go on," Anna prodded, anxious to hear the rest. "Thoughts of what?"

Danny took a deep breath. "Well, thoughts of hurting himself."

She was stunned.

"Hurting himself? What do you mean, hurting himself? How?" She sat on the bed with an absent stare. Danny tried to get the words out.

"He said he's been having thoughts of…ending his life. Not often, but it's happened a few times. He's terrified. He burst out crying when he told me. He's in tears now."

She stood up, not willing to accept what she had just heard her husband say.

"No." She couldn't believe it. "It just can't be. Not Daniel. Why? Why?"

Both parents knew only one thing for sure. Their son needed help, and he needed it immediately. Danny ran through every option they had. He called his health insurance carrier and spoke with a counselor who advised him that they might want to take their son to the nearest hospital just to be safe.

They took a deep breath and walked out of the bedroom together toward their son's room to tell him it was time to go.

Neither parent wanted to alarm their young daughter, so they explained to Victoria that Daniel had a stomachache, and they needed to take him to the doctor. The three loaded up into the car and drove to the nearest emergency room.

The hospital was cold and gray. The admitting nurses took Daniel's vital signs and quickly hooked him up to an IV. They placed him in a bed located in the IC unit. The parents were told they would have to wait until the psychiatrist on staff could visit with the frightened boy. It was probably going to be a while. It was obvious by just looking at Daniel that the entire experience had unnerved him; his eyes were shrink-wrapped with tears, and he bit his bottom lip as he stared wide eyed at everything around him. Seeing her son so terrified made Anna feel sick to her stomach.

"Love, it's going to be a while. Why don't you go home? I'll call you when the doctor gets here," Danny tried to convince his wife to leave so she could get some rest.

She took his advice, but after only a few minutes at home, she got back into her car and drove back to the hospital. She couldn't leave her son's side. She had to be with him.

The three sat in the chilly room beneath the dingy fluorescent lights holding hands and listening to the sounds of passersby's footsteps on the linoleum floors, just waiting for the footsteps to make their way to their room for what seemed like forever. Both parents each held on to one of their child's hands.

"Everything's going to be just fine, love." Anna wasn't convinced of her words but kept repeating them for her son's sake. Finally, in the wee hours of the next morning, the psychiatrist appeared. She warmly greeted the parents and got their background information before politely asking them to leave. Danny and Anna sat nervously in the waiting room while the doctor examined their son. After several more hours, they were finally called back in. At this point, Anna was ready to be admitted herself.

"We've done a full psychiatric workup," began the doctor. The optimism in her voice seemed misplaced for the occasion but immediately provided some relief to the worried parents.

"Your son is fine. Yes, he has had some visions of ending his life, but the thoughts he's had are normal for a boy his age. He does not have a plan, and it is my professional opinion that there is no real or immediate danger. In our profession, we call the thoughts he's had 'ideations,' and they are very common. We've examined him and have concluded that he is not suicidal. He's quite rational and lucid and understands the consequences of his actions."

As the psychiatrist finished stating her diagnosis, Anna couldn't contain herself any longer and broke out into tears of relief.

"What do we do now?" Danny needed to hear next steps.

"Well, you can follow up with his regular doctor on Monday, but believe me it's very normal for these thoughts to occur, especially in teens. We see it often. Sometimes medication helps. And you may want to get him started with therapy. A lot of kids his age see a therapist. It just seems to help with all of these normal teenage issues. And whatever you do, don't overreact to this. Believe me. It is very normal. Your son is fine."

The doctor shook their hands and left the room.

As they made the trip back home with their son safe in the back seat, Danny and Anna were baffled. The initial relief of the psychiatrist's assurances began to wear off, and the worry had begun creeping in again. Were they overreacting? A full psychiatric workup had been done, and Daniel was fine. The doctor had been certain in her diagnosis. She was the expert, right? They had been warned not to overreact. They both heard the doctor say it.

Sitting quietly in the back seat, Daniel seemed relieved that he was okay—a weight lifted off his shoulders. His expression was relaxed, and in his eyes a calm replaced the fear his mother had seen hours ago in the hospital room.

The parents were exhausted, changing out of the clothes they had been wearing since the day before when Daniel walked in.

"Hey, guys, can I ask you a question? Can I start seeing a therapist?"

Anna was relieved that the question was a good one and happy about his desire to see a counselor. "Of course you can, Daniel. And I'm very proud of you for wanting to see one."

"Mom, I know lots of kids who do. In California, everyone has a therapist! I think I want to."

The three hugged. That night, Anna's prayer was brief. It was the same one as it had always been lately. *Please God, protect my child.*

———————————

Over the next several months, life had settled back down to a happy normal. Anna had researched psychologists within their healthcare network and found one that she thought Daniel might relate to.

The initial meeting consisted of the three of them and the psychologist. After that, the meetings were strictly held between the doctor and Daniel only. Anna was not pleased with that arrangement but understood that it was the way the doctor said it needed to be, and, after all, he was the expert. At least whatever had been bothering Daniel would finally be shared with a professional who would provide a diagnosis and know what to do.

The dinner dishes had been cleared, and before they were getting ready to go downstairs to settle back with some popcorn and a movie with the kids, Anna turned to Danny.

"Why doesn't the doctor keep us more updated? Daniel has been seeing this doctor for several weeks now, and the doctor gives us no updates. I know it's supposed to be confidential, but he's a minor, for pete's sake, and we're his parents. I thought when we brought him to a doctor, we would finally have a diagnosis. But we have nothing."

"I agree." Danny looked at his wife. "I don't like it either. Let's call him in the morning and see if we can get more information. But you need to stop worrying about things so much. Daniel is just fine. If you don't believe me, believe the doctor."

He put his arm around his wife as the two went downstairs to spend the evening watching movies with the kids. Anna let herself relax so she might actually follow the plot this time. *This will all be fine*, she kept saying to herself. At least the school year was almost over, and summer was always a welcome relief.

CHAPTER
FOURTEEN

What's the use of a fine house if you haven't got a tolerable planet to put it on?

—Henry David Thoreau

Cancun was beautiful that summer. Anna's sister Dena and new brother-in-law, Roger, had joined them. The couple had married late in life, and, still childless, this was their first real vacation as a married couple. The Marriott resort was spectacular, with the luxuries of paradise and all the comforts of home. The weather was smoldering hot, but that's the way they liked it. Not like California, where it was always cool, even in the middle of summer. Daniel and Victoria spent their days swimming and snorkeling and even did some deep-sea fishing with their dad while their mom and aunt took the opportunity to get in plenty of spa time. Daniel discovered a new hobby–fishing in a Panga boat off the beach in front of their hotel with his dad and his uncle Roger. Daniel was the closest thing Roger had to a son of his own, so the two had a tight bond. Daniel, with the help of his uncle and his dad, practically filled the boat with fish, and the three made sure to get photographed documentation of their accomplishments at sea as soon as they made it back to shore. In the evenings, the family took advantage of being close to the ocean and feasted on fresh shrimp and snapper with the backdrop of the sounds of the ocean crashing back and forth against the beach. They laughed and talked and joked. They had found a place in which the demons that seemed so determined to attack their family back home couldn't follow them.

So why was Anna still worried about her son? Maybe her husband was right. Maybe she just needed to stop worrying so much. It was obvious to anyone who came into contact with him that Daniel was truly happy. It shone in his eyes, and you could hear it every time he laughed, sincerely laughed from a place that no sadness could exist. God was answering her prayers. Anna decided to make an oath to herself there in Cancun. She decided to put things into perspective before panicking when it came to her children. She was only making life harder by always assuming the worst and waiting for it at every turn. Life was too short for that.

It was a warm, gray afternoon, one of the last of their trip, and the family was hanging out by the pool. The clouds unexpectedly opened wide and started pouring rain. The adults were under a bamboo cover in an open-air bar area enjoying margaritas when Daniel and Victoria came running in for cover.

"Why are you coming under here?" Anna laughed. "We're in Mexico, not California! The rain is warm! Go have fun!"

The kids stood for a minute looking at her with water pooling at their feet and then turned and ran back to the pool. They rejoined their new vacation friends who were already in the pool while the rain pounded down on them.

"We'd be freezing in California right now," Daniel said to his new friend.

"Kids in Mexico sure have it good!" shouted Victoria.

At dinner, they watched a heritage dance production as they enjoyed agua frescas and tacos de barbacoa. Daniel and Victoria joined the performers on stage to close down the dance number. An awesome way to end their time in paradise, but the vacation was over, and it was time to go home. The kids were sad to say good-bye to Cancun and their new friends, but Daniel was already thinking about the next trip he was scheduled to take in just a few short weeks.

Because of his high academic scores, Daniel had been selected to attend a young global leaders' conference with other high achieving kids from all over the country. It was a two-week program that would be pretty intense academically and would earn him college credits. Daniel was excited about the entire experience, both the business and pleasure sides, and couldn't wait to attend.

"Mom, can I order room service when I'm in my hotel room?"

Oh, he thinks he'll be staying at a Marriott. Anna smiled to herself, sure that when he realized he was staying in a college dorm room, with all of its inconveniences, he would decide against it. But to her surprise, he was still up for it.

Anna read the dress code and thought surely this would change his mind. Boys were not permitted to wear jeans or T-shirts with prints of any kind or baseball caps, casual dress was khakis and polo shirts, and for classes and for dinners, they had to wear coats and ties. But Daniel was still game, blazers, ties, cafeteria food, and all.

The next two weeks without her son were a challenge for Anna. She had never been separated from him for so long, so she did what any other red-blooded mother would have done; she called him often. But at her husband's prompting, she limited herself to every other night. Nonna was having a pretty rough time not hearing her grandson's voice every day, and Anna had to threaten to take her cell phone away if she called him every day. When they did get the opportunity to speak with him, he sounded happy, excited, rambling on about everything they had done that day. He was enjoying himself so much that some nights he was too busy cracking jokes with his roommate to spend more than a few minutes on the phone with his mother. "Mom, gotta go! Love you!" He enjoyed the city and seemed to really be in his element.

He had gone to Ellis Island and was sure he had found some of his ancestors.

"I'm so stoked!" he told his parents during that evening's phone call. "I found my great-great-great grandpa."

He was fifteen years old when he had taken the long connecting flights from California to New York City all by himself. His parents had insisted that he travel as an unescorted minor so that airline personnel could help him. On the way back, however, he wouldn't hear of it; he was practically a pro by now. His mother imagined everything that could possibly go wrong. During his two hour layover, Daniel might get bored, he could fall asleep. He might even miss his flight, get on the wrong one, and end up in Chicago.

But in the end, she finally agreed to let Daniel fly unescorted. "Danny, if anything happens to him, I swear I'll never forgive myself."

Danny stood patiently at the crowded airport waiting for his son to arrive. When he spotted him, he was struck by how mature Daniel looked. It had only been a few weeks but he could see a difference. *My boy is really growing up*, Danny thought. He loaded up his son and his baggage in the car and called home.

"No, he didn't end up in Seattle. I have our boy with me," Danny said into his cell phone as soon as they were headed home.

"See, guys. I told you I could travel across the country all by myself," Daniel announced as he busted through the front door. His mom threw her arms around him and he held her tight. What would she do when he went away to college, got married, and maybe moved out of state? She wouldn't think about that right now. She was just grateful he was home.

"Hi Victoria!" Daniel had to pry himself loose after his little sister had come running down the stairs and thrown her arms tightly around his waist.

He smelled something good in the kitchen.

"Mmmm… Nonna's pasta. Nonna, this is just what I've been waiting for."

Nonna ran over to him, arms outstretched, and Daniel gave her the same bear hug he had given his mother. Nonna, being quite a bit smaller than Daniel now, pulled his forehead down toward her and kissed him on it over and over again. Daniel was finally back home. Now it was time for Nonna's famous rigatoni bolognese.

They all took their places at the table, and the stories from his trip began to spill out of him. He could barely keep up with himself there was so much to tell. The only breaks he took were to shovel more of Nonna's pasta into his mouth between words. Even Italian food in New York didn't compare to Nonna's.

"Mom, the kids there were so different than at my high school. No one beats each other down. They all help each other, and they listen to each other. No one calls anyone names. They don't have anything to prove. We had a blast. We always worked in teams on projects and stuff, and the field trips were awesome."

"That's exactly what we wanted you to experience, Daniel." His mother nodded. "High school is just a tiny piece of the amazing life ahead of you. Right now it seems like the whole world to you, but once you get out, it's very different. Kids in college are paying a lot of money to be there, so they're serious about their education, and they want a good experience from it, not like high school. Plus, they're more mature. We wanted you to get a glimpse of what the world outside of high school can really be like."

"Yeah, my roommate was a really cool dude from Brazil. He was hilarious. We're going to keep in touch. And I met a lot of other kids that I'm going to keep in touch with. I kinda miss them already."

"So glad you enjoyed yourself. I'm proud of you." Anna hugged her son. The trip had given him a new confidence. Although the two weeks without her son had felt like torture to her, she knew his experiences had been well worth it.

Just three short weeks later, Daniel was off for his last trip of the summer. He and Aiden had planned a week at a skateboard camp. This trip would be the polar opposite of the last; there would be no dress codes, no strict schedules, and no lectures to attend, nothing but hanging out with friends and skateboarding for an entire week. It sounded like a teenager's dream come true. The camp was out in a rural part of California hours away from their suburb. Daniel was stoked about the trip. New York was awesome in its own ways, but this was going to be all about having fun.

"Daniel, I'm going to be traveling while you're at the skate camp," his father reminded him the morning before he left. "Have a great time, Son. Remember to stay safe."

With both Daniel and Danny gone, the house was uncharacteristically quiet. "It's girl time!" Anna threw up her arms as she and Victoria embarked on their day of shopping, dinner, and a movie. They were tired as they entered their front door back home. Nonna heard the door open and rushed over to them.

"Daniel called. He said he has to come home. I don't know why."

There was no cell phone reception in the rural area the skate camp was located in, so Anna dialed the skate camp office and asked to speak to her son. Daniel's voice on the other end was shaky.

"I have to come home, Mom. I feel like I'm paralyzed. I can't move."

Worry gripped her. She wanted nothing more than to just have him home. But it was already dark outside, and Anna knew she would never be able to find the camp that was three hundred miles away in an unincorporated part of the state by herself.

"Mom, I'm sorry. I know we paid a lot of money."

"Don't worry, love. I don't care about the money. I care about you. Can Aunt Dena and I drive up to get you in the morning?"

"Yeah, that will be great. I love you, Mom."

Anna hung up and dialed Daniel's doctor, who promised to call him right away. She waited nervously until her phone rang again.

"Something happened up there, and he won't tell me what it is. He's saying he feels paralyzed. That's a fear response, a sign of anxiety. He said he felt like he was out of danger only when he knew you were driving up to get him in the morning," the therapist explained.

Anna hung up the phone and called her sister Dena who was ready to drop everything to help. Dena lived more than an hour away in Los Angeles, but it was on the way to the campsite, and Dena would be able to emotionally support her sister through the ordeal. Anna could barely think the entire drive up the next morning. When she arrived at Dena's house, her sister offered her a cup of coffee.

"I can't eat or drink." Anna put her hand to her stomach. "I'm sick to my stomach. I just want to get going."

"Eat this piece of toast," Dena encouraged. "You'll be no good to him if you pass out."

On the drive to the camp, Dena continued to reassure her sister it would all be fine, but Anna wasn't hearing a word. All she could wonder was why her son felt like he was paralyzed. It was a fear response the doctor said. Fear of what? This camp was supposed to be nothing but hanging out with friends and fun. What could cause so much anxiety that Daniel couldn't stay?

It was only when they had Daniel safely in the car with them that she felt like she could finally breathe again. Dena and Anna kept the conversation light for Daniel's sake.

"It's so hot out here, Daniel. I can see why you didn't want to stay," Dena empathized. "Good thing we live on the coast!"

"I'm so glad I won't have to wait a whole week to see you again," Anna followed her sister's lead.

Safe at home that evening, Anna went into her son's room to kiss him goodnight.

He turned to his mom. "Kids can be really mean, Mom."

"Daniel, did something happen there?"

"I don't want to talk about it. Please, Mom. I really don't. I'll talk to my doctor about it. He's a doctor. You're not."

The next morning, the prior day's events still weighed heavily on her. She called the skate camp. The camp guide had no idea why he left early. He had asked around, but none of the kids seemed to know either.

"Does anyone know if he was picked on at all?" asked Anna. The camp guide indicated they really didn't know anything.

The breakfast dishes had been cleared, and Anna made her way upstairs to her son's room.

"Daniel, you have your appointment with the doctor tomorrow. I had forgotten to cancel it. I want you to be sure to talk to him about what happened at the skate camp. How are the sessions going, anyway?"

Daniel looked up from his guitar he had been strumming.

"I'm not sure, Mom. I don't really think he gives very good advice."

That was all she needed to hear. Within a week, she had found another therapist for her son to see. At the final appointment with the doctor, Anna asked him why he thought Daniel had reacted the way he did to skate camp.

"I'm not sure," replied the doctor. "Perhaps he has social anxiety?"

"That makes no sense." Anna shook her head. "He just came back from two weeks in New York and had a fabulous time. He met people from all different walks of life. He didn't even want to take my phone calls on some nights. He was so happy that he wants to go back next year. Why would the two experiences have been so different for him?"

"I'm not sure," the doctor repeated. "He definitely had an anxiety attack. The feeling of paralysis is very symptomatic of one. Something in that environment must have been very threatening to him. Something that wasn't present in New York."

"Remember his history of being bullied," reminded Anna.

"He told me people looked at him like he was an idiot, he kept screwing up, saying stupid things, and people thought he was a jerk." The doctor could offer no other insights.

CHAPTER
FIFTEEN

Thoughtless words can wound as deeply as any sword, but wisely spoken words can heal.

Proverbs 12:18 TEV

Within days, Anna had chosen a new doctor. This one practiced something called cognitive behavior therapy. The doctor's fees were very expensive and he was not part of their health insurance network but both parents were willing to pay anything to help their son.

The new doctor listened carefully to the parents' concerns. The parents described in detail how Daniel had spoken about having thoughts of hurting himself a few months back and how the doctors had found that he was not a danger to himself. Anna talked about how Daniel had been bullied incessantly in middle school, and she suspected it was continuing in high school but that Daniel did not want her to get involved, so he kept it private.

"I practice what is referred to as cognitive behavior therapy. We focus on the reaction that patients have to negative stimulus. So, for example, if your child is afraid of heights, we begin by slowly exposing him to heights and graduate him progressively throughout the therapy. So an exercise might be to put a ladder against the house, climb up to the first rung, and so on, until he's at the very top of the ladder with no anxiety. In other words, we teach coping skills." The doctor asked the parents to leave while he had a private session with Daniel.

"You need to take a more pragmatic approach with your stressors," the doctor instructed his patient. "If someone tells you

you're worthless, consider the evidence. Ask yourself, 'Am I really worthless?' You'll find that the evidence proves otherwise. Deal only with the facts. This is the method we'll teach you to employ."

"But what if the facts are that people are treating me like crap every day of my life?" asked Daniel, genuinely interested in this new method.

"Then you question whether you really are being treated like crap. Or is it just your mind telling you that? Consider the empirical evidence and reconsider your premises. It could be just your mind telling you that. We'll teach you how to have a more positive reaction to negative stressors."

Before ending the appointment, the doctor met again with the parents.

"Do you think we should consider medication?" asked Anna.

"I would not recommend medication for him right now," he said.

"Why?" Anna was relieved but curious.

"Because I only recommend medication for the kids who come in completely uncooperative, arms folded, slumped in their chairs, defiant, and uninterested in life or therapy. Your son doesn't qualify. He comes in like this…"

The doctor scooted his chair up closer to the desk in imitation of Daniel. He folded his hands, put them on the desk, and held his head high, taking a position like the model student about to solve a tough calculus equation the teacher has written on the board.

"Okay, Doc. Here's what's happening in my life. Here are the thoughts and feelings I'm having. What are we going to do to fix it?"

"What does he say is wrong with his life?" Anna pressed on.

"Just teenage stuff. Nothing to be concerned about. I think your son is going to be just fine. He has so much going for him. A fine young man you're raising. I'm very impressed with him." The doctor rubbed his chin. "No, Daniel is very engaged, very interested in the next steps. I would absolutely not recommend medication at this time. What he's experiencing is very common for teenagers. Everything is such a big deal for them at this age. We'll teach him to put things more into perspective."

Daniel was energized on the drive home.

"I think this doctor is going to be really good, Mom. He's going to teach me how to not let things get to me so much."

Why is the doctor focused only on changing his response? Anna thought. *Why aren't we as a society focusing on the troublemakers changing their behavior?*

As she walked down the hallway to her son's room, she overheard him on the phone talking to one of his friends.

"Yeah, it's called cognitive behavior, and it's going to be really cool." She smiled, surprised at how much he shared with his friends. She hoped this new doctor would measure up to her son's expectations.

———— ◆ ————

"Breakfast is ready!" Nonna called out as the kids scrambled down the stairs. It was Sunday morning, and the family was preparing to go to Mass.

"Okay everyone, after church we'll have lunch and then go shopping. I hope neither of you have anything planned until later." Anna passed the waffles to Daniel.

"Is there anything you need for football this year?" Danny asked his son.

"Dad, I'm not going to play football this year."

Anna and Danny exchanged glances.

"Why not? You love the game, and you did really well last year." Anna was concerned.

"I just can't, Mom. I just can't. Let's just drop it, okay?"

His father pressed on. "Well, are you thinking of another sport? Maybe lacrosse, like Aiden?"

"No, Dad. No sports. I just can't." Daniel remained firm.

"But you should be involved in some sort of physical activity."

"I'll have my karate. That'll have to be enough." Daniel's voice grew agitated.

He wasn't budging. He could feel his dad's eyes burning into him, and he was just hoping he'd drop the conversation. No one was going to convince him that any sport was worth the crap he'd taken the last year. When he put those football cleats on, Daniel knew he was as good as done. He had tried that before, and he wasn't about to do it again. Why would he? Aiden always told him that lacrosse was different, but Daniel knew that it didn't matter what sport it was. As long as there were kids on the team, he was going to be a whipping boy for them. For some inexplicable reason, he just attracted it. No, he would just have to watch from the sidelines where no one could slam him into the ground or shove him into a field house locker.

———◆•◆•◆———

Anna stood at her desk, staring at her telephone receiver. She had just been notified by the vice president of human resources that she would no longer be reporting directly to the CEO.

"No need to worry," reassured Jeannie Walsh. "Your salary, grade level, title, nothing will change. You'll just now be reporting to Harold Bart. He's a great guy. You'll love him."

"Jeannie," Anna began, "I like Harold, but he has no experience in the lending and credit risk area at all. He's a property management guy. A good one at that, but still, no experience in lending. None. Not even the regulators will like that."

"He's a really great guy, and it's a necessary move as part of the restructure," continued Jeannie. "Dean has the utmost faith in him. Harold is very loyal to Dean. We should all be grateful we just have jobs."

"I'm grateful. I'm just not sure how this will benefit the organization." Anna shrugged her shoulders and hung up. Corporate ladder climbing was the last priority on her list right now. And she knew she could get along with anyone. She hammered out an e-mail to Harold, her new boss, congratulating him on his new appointment and inviting him to lunch so that she could brief him on her department priorities.

As she turned from her screen, Christy appeared at her door. Anna motioned her in.

"Word is that you're reporting to Harold now," began Christy tentatively. "I can't believe he's our new boss. He knows nothing about our business."

"How did you find out?" Anna began. Then she realized there may be a reason why she was the last one being told.

"Harold's a good guy, Christy. And whatever he doesn't know, we'll teach him. There are a lot of people who have invested their life savings with this organization. We need to think about them and support the corporate direction."

"Anna, wake up." Christy would not be hushed this time. "You're being effectively demoted. You no longer report to the CEO but to someone who knows nothing about our business. And word is, it's happening because you won't play the politics. Harold will. You're too vocal. You say things that Dean doesn't want to hear."

Christy ran her hand through her hair in frustration. "I've told you time and again, but you just won't listen to me. Don't think you're so smart. I've reported to others like you in your position. When they don't play the game, they're eliminated. Just like that." She snapped her fingers for emphasis.

"Christy, I'm really tired." Anna rubbed her forehead. "I appreciate your concern for my career, but I have to do what I think is best. And I really don't think there's a master conspiracy plan like you've been hinting at forever. Relax. Everything will be just fine. You'll see. By the way, have you gotten the federal examiners the information they're looking for?"

Because the institution had been suffering escalated loan losses, regulatory scrutiny had increased for them. When Anna first came on board, the scrutiny had been quite severe, but as losses declined, the regulators began feeling more comfortable and backed off a bit. Still, they weren't out of the woods yet, and Anna wanted to be sure all of the regulator requests were met swiftly.

Christy assured her she had taken care of it and turned to leave. At the door, she looked back at her boss.

"Keep it up and you may find yourself unemployed. Just saying... Think about it."

"I'd rather be on welfare than do something I don't believe is right." Anna smiled at her and waved good-bye.

She packed up her briefcase to start the long drive home. Christy was prone to drama, but she knew the woman also had some insights. Christy was right in one regard. Anna had been a bit too vocal for Dean's liking lately—not being tactful enough when speaking out at meetings and pointing out weaknesses in their management systems unabashedly. She always noticed Dean grimacing whenever she spoke up about a politically sensitive topic. And lately, it had been happening more often. She knew he didn't like it. But it had to be said. And she knew he respected her accomplishments. Loan losses had declined substantially under her leadership. Credit quality had significantly improved from where they had been. No, she couldn't worry about politics right now. She just had to hope that her contributions to the organization would outweigh any political sensitivities he had. She put it out of her mind, and her thoughts turned to her family at home waiting for her.

⎯⎯⎯⎯ ⋯•◆•⋯ ⎯⎯⎯⎯

Thanksgiving was approaching and plans for the big day had begun. Anna's sister, Dena, had recently relocated to California from Texas and had recruited several friends to make the move with her. Both sisters felt blessed to be able to spend holidays together without extensive travel. Anna found herself hoping that it would be only her sister that would be attending this time. On Easter, Dena had brought her friend Gigi with her for the family holiday, and Anna had felt it had taken away from the intimate family environment.

"I don't know if Dena's going to want to invite her friend again." Anna was concerned as she spoke to her husband. "I don't mind hosting her on other days, but the last time they came together, it changed the family dynamics. Dena felt a huge responsibility to entertain her friend, and that took away from her ability to interact with the kids or with us. The day was more about adult conversation and private jokes between Dena and Gigi rather than reconnecting with Daniel and Victoria. Even my mom was disappointed. The kids won't be young forever, and I want to make the most of every family moment with them. Do you think that's understandable?"

"Of course it is. Just explain it to Dena. She'll understand."

"You're right. I don't see my youngest daughter much. When I do, I want to spend time with her." Nonna agreed with the phone call that Anna should make to Dena.

Anna called her older sister, Lilly, for her opinion. Lilly lived in Canada and typically only flew in at Christmas time.

"I think it's perfectly understandable. Maybe if you explain to Dena that the kids really look forward to spending quality time with her, I'm sure she'll understand."

"It's not that I don't like her friend. She's a nice person. But I'd like the holidays to be about focusing on family. I want to create a few special family memories for my children while they're still young. And for some reason, it never happens when she and Gigi get together."

After getting Lilly's input, Anna took a deep breath and called Dena with the request. But Lilly was wrong. Dena didn't understand.

"I have to bring her. She's expecting it." Dena sounded perturbed. "You just don't like her."

That hurt.

"Dena, that's not fair. I don't dislike anyone. I'm just asking you to allow us to spend some precious family moments with each other. Please understand. It's important to all of us and it should be important to you too. We don't get to see you much, and when we do, we want to reconnect with you. That just doesn't happen when you and Gigi are together. Is that too much to ask?"

But Dena wasn't budging. Not wanting to upset her sister any further, Anna dropped it and later regretted having said anything at all. She called Lilly.

"I don't understand why she can't understand the importance of our family time. I just want to be sure we make the most of family time together while we have it. Especially during the holidays. These are our life memories we're creating, and we get only one chance at it."

"I know," replied Lilly sympathetically. "Very soon, Dena herself will be a mom. I think she'll share a deeper appreciation of what you're saying then."

———◆◆◆———

Thanksgiving had come to an end, and after Anna had kissed both kids goodnight, she found her husband in their room, preparing for bed. The day had gone well enough. The roast turkey was picture perfect; the scent of the baked cinnamon apples Daniel loved so much and the pumpkin pie still filled the air. Anna and her mother had worked tirelessly side by side in the kitchen. Daniel had been in charge of setting the table and of the cranberry sauce. He really liked cranberry sauce. He could have eaten it every day. He'd even worn a red shirt so he wouldn't have to be careful of any spills. Victoria had helped with the homemade pumpkin pie and was proud of her creation. Especially when her brother had thirds. She was sure it had made up for all of her burnt marshmallows. But any meaningful time Anna had hoped her family could spend with her sister had not happened. That part of the evening had gone just as Anna had feared. Dena had spent the bulk of her evening entertaining her friend. But interacting with family in only a way that family understands, reminiscing about younger years together, none of it had happened. Anna missed those moments with her sister. And she missed that her kids were missing out on them too.

"I'm not sure why Dena doesn't have the same sense of urgency I do to get in as much family time with the kids as possible," Anna said to her husband. *Maybe next holiday it will be different.*

CHAPTER
SIXTEEN

My God, my God, why have you forsaken me?

Matthew 27:46 (ESV)

The sun reflected off the blue pool tiles as Victoria cannonballed into the water. Dena, and her husband, Roger, were visiting with their new baby boy, Girard, who was floating in the pool in a plastic duck that his mother was holding firm. Daniel was hanging out with his friends but had promised to be back well before dinner to spend some time with his aunt, uncle, and his new baby cousin. He enjoyed hanging out with his uncle Roger and talking about football, school and girls.

Daniel sometimes discussed life issues with his dad too. He loved watching comedian impersonators like Frank Caliendo and Daniel had perfected an exaggerated impersonation of his dad giving him advice on girls that would have the whole family, including his dad, laughing uncontrollably. Daniel would hook his thumbs into his make believe belt loops and begin to slowly drawl, "Ya see, Son. When ah was yer age, back in Texas, ah was a real ladies mayan. See, Son, ya gotta be nahs to the girls. Ya gotta say 'Hey, lil' lady. Hows it goin'?'" Daniel himself could barely get through it without bursting out laughing.

"What do you need good grades for? Maybe you can become an impersonator," his dad would often laugh.

He really did appreciate his talks with his dad but talking with an uncle is just different. Plus his uncle was a Raiders fan, and Daniel was a Chargers fan. He really liked going head to head with him on game stats and was sure that he could talk his uncle into taking him to a Raiders/Chargers game in Oakland one day.

Anna was busy on the internet, searching for a new recipe that she wanted to make for dinner. She took a moment to check e-mail when she noticed something that caught her off guard. There, in their e-mail inbox, was a response e-mail from Daniel's doctor to Daniel. It had been written in reply to an e-mail Daniel had written the doctor days earlier. Daniel wasn't allowed to have his own e-mail address, so he shared one with his parents. She clicked on the e-mail and began to read, becoming more sickened with each word that sank in. Danny walked into the room and noticed his wife's agitation.

"What's the matter?"

"Read this." Anna pushed the laptop toward him.

The e-mail sent by Daniel to his doctor talked about how down he had been feeling lately. He had attached a letter he had written awhile back that would give the doctor an idea of how low he sometimes felt. The e-mail began,

> Dr. M, I know my appointment is tomorrow on Friday. The bad feelings of depression are beginning to come back to me. I have started to feel bad again, and I'm sick of it. This was written a few months ago, but one day I felt so bad, and I was on the computer, and I typed up a bunch of stuff explaining why my life sucks. I thought this would give you a better idea of what goes on in my head when I'm depressed, and it's all getting to me. I was hoping we could talk about this when I come in on Friday.
>
> —Dan Mendez

Anna opened the attachment. It was a dark letter. It expressed anger towards his parents and towards God. He talked about how weak he was, how he couldn't believe he had actually gone to his parents for advice when he was younger and people messed with him. How people would always mess with him and talk crap to him because they knew he wouldn't do anything about it. How he wished he could but he couldn't. How he knew that would never change. How he wanted to die to end the pain.

The parents sat together, horrified, as they read each of their child's words.

Nothing that the shocked parents read made any sense. It was like another kid had written it. Neither could wrap their minds around it. Even Danny was thrown for a loop.

"It doesn't sound like Daniel. It doesn't sound like him at all. The hopelessness, the self-loathing. He uses profanity. He never uses that language." Anna was devastated.

"What bothers me even more is that this e-mail was sent to his doctor over a week ago." Danny's eyes were still fixed on the screen on front of him. "The doctor replied to Daniel days ago but hasn't felt the need to tell us about any of this? Is this not important to him?"

Danny began to agree that his wife's concerns were not over-reactions, and the two decided to contact the doctor first thing in the morning. Upon hearing their worries, the doctor became very reassuring.

"Oh, you saw that e-mail. I didn't know if you would or not. Please don't worry about it. These are very normal things for kids to say," the doctor counseled, but Anna wasn't buying it.

"But what about the reference to school and people treating him like crap?" she asked. "What about the reference to his funeral? Remember, the reason he's in therapy was upon the recommendation of the psychiatrist who examined him after Daniel became terrified that he was having thoughts of hurting himself."

"I've already spoken to Daniel about this during our last session. It's very common for teens to have these types of thoughts. You notice, he wrote that attached document several months ago and was only letting me know how he sometimes feels. No need to worry right now," the doctor went on. "Do not let him know you read his e-mail, or he will stop communicating with me via that channel. We check regularly for suicidal risks, and he's absolutely not a danger to himself. Mark my words. Do not overreact."

"I'm telling you something is wrong. This doesn't sound like my child. He uses profanity. He's angry with God. I'm not saying he's perfect. I'm just saying that this absolutely is not him. It's a red flag." Anna wanted a better explanation.

"The majority of my clients are teens," continued the doctor. "They *all* talk like that. In general, Daniel is very respectful. More so than most teens I've met. Don't worry. It's very normal. I would recommend that he begin taking jiujitsu."

Jiujitsu? Is that his solution? "He's already taking karate. And he has a black belt in Tae Kwon Do." Anna struggled with the simplistic solution.

"He's very concerned about being able to defend himself," continued the therapist. "He said he wished he knew how to street fight. Not all martial arts disciplines are the same. I talked to him about considering jiujitsu. I think it would make a difference for him. I have a friend who runs a great studio. Let him know I referred you."

"Why is he concerned about defending himself, about needing to know how to street fight? What's going on in his life that he needs to defend himself?" Anna pressed on.

"Most boys are concerned about that at that age. Don't worry. It's normal. Consider jiujitsu."

"He's angry with himself. He's angry with us." Anna choked back tears.

"All kids say they hate their parents at some point in their lives. I've spoken to your son many times. He loves you both. Very much. If I didn't think so, we would be addressing that issue. But we're not. Because that's not the problem. He loves his family. He just gets frustrated when you try to help him. He thinks you overprotect him. He feels like you complained to the school when he came to you once and that made his life a mess. He gets angry with you when you try to press him for information now. Please don't worry about this. I know you want to help him. Eventually, he will come to you again for your input. But not right now. Let me be the one who counsels him. You're making this a bigger deal than you should be."

"But he does ask us for advice. He's always coming into our room and starting with 'Hey guys, can I ask you a question?' And it's about girls, school, peer pressures, everything. He comes to us with everything else he's thinking and feeling. Except when people harass him. I think that's what's making him hate himself, hate people who love him. He even says in his letter that the biggest mistake of his life was coming to us for advice when people messed with him." Anna was struggling to keep her voice steady. Why couldn't the doctor follow her logic?

"Really, you're making this a bigger deal than you should. Your son is fine. I'll see you in a few days. Get some rest. We're making good progress on the cognitive behavior action plan."

They hung up, still stunned. They wondered how exactly the psychiatric community checked for suicidal risk. Did they simply ask about it, and if the answer was no, all clear?

Anna and Danny weren't convinced, but this doctor was presumably one of the best. He was the expert, and he wasn't even fazed by the letter. This teenage thing was just completely new to them. If the doctor was in fact right, if jiujitsu a couple nights a week was the cure to all this, then the teenage years were more than either of them could comprehend.

⋅•⋅

Saturdays were always a welcome relief from the school week. The guys had gathered at Daniel's house and were tearing into their pulled pork sandwiches.

"I could eat a ton of these things," Aiden said with a mouth full of meat.

"You and me both," replied Daniel. "Hey, Aiden, we should have an eating contest."

131

"Sure, I'll annihilate you." Aiden laughed. "What should we use for the contest?"

"I know. *Arrosticini!*" Daniel blurted between bites. Aiden and Daniel loved the little lamb skewers that Nonna would often make.

"You're on!" Aiden said, accepting the challenge.

"Why would anyone want to eat until they get sick?" Michael just shook his head. He was always the most sensible of the group.

"Okay. Next Saturday," Daniel said, pushing his plate away and ready to take Aiden on.

"Yeah!" Aiden pumped his fist in the air. He knew he had this one in the bag.

"Let's go have brownies at the fire pit." The boys gathered around the fire as they waited for their rides home to arrive.

She was putting away the last of the dishes when Anna heard something. She stopped suddenly, with a dish still held mid-air.

"Listen." She put her hand on her husband's arm.

There was the sound of singing coming from outside. Anna recognized the song by Journey. The boys were belting out their rendition of "Don't Stop Believing." Daniel's voice was the loudest. Their boy was happy.

"Is that the most beautiful music you've ever heard in your life?"

CHAPTER
SEVENTEEN

A hundred years from now it will not matter what my bank account was, the sort of house I lived in, or the kind of car I drove, but the world may be different because I was important in the life of a child.

—Forest E. Witcraft

"Hurry and finish eating, sweetie. Your basketball ride will be here soon."

Victoria was dressed in her basketball uniform, hair pulled back in a neat ponytail, as she attempted to make a dent in the large plate of gnocchi with lamb ragu in front of her.

"Mom, the plate's bigger than she is!" Daniel snickered with his hand over his mouth.

"She has to eat all of it," Nonna said adamantly, nodding to Victoria. "Mangia!"

"Mom, why do we make such a big deal of dinners?" Daniel piped up again. "Michael and Sean's parents are so cool. You know what happened yesterday when I was at Michael's house? We were playing video games, and Sean came in and he had opened up a can of Spaghettios. And get this. He was eating right out of the can. And that was his dinner, Mom. And his parents allow that! They're so cool!"

"Maybe his mom and dad work full time and they don't have a Nonna to cook full course meals during the week."

"Could I do that one day, Mom?"

"Do what?"

"Can I just open a can of something in the pantry and just eat right out of the can? And that will be my dinner! Can I, Mom?"

Why is the grass always greener on the other side? Anna smiled to herself.

"Sure, Daniel. One day when Nonna's not home and we don't have to tie her down while you eat canned beans for dinner!"

Anna waved good-bye as she watched Victoria scramble into the carpool SUV. She turned to her son, who was still finishing his apple pie and ice cream.

"Daniel, is the doctor being very helpful?"

"Yeah, Mom, why?"

"I'm just wondering. I know that when you talk to him, you sometimes use bad language."

"Mom, it's no big deal. We're the only ones in the world who don't cuss. The doctor himself uses the same language when he talks with me. I only use those words when I'm talking to others who do. That's all. I'm just trying to fit in."

Anna remembered an email she had seen from her son to his guidance counselor at school. "I know you were trying to get in to talk to your school counselor today. Did they ever call you?"

"No."

"What are you going to do about it?" Anna was perturbed with the school for not responding to her son.

"No big deal, Mom. I'm handling it. The counselor didn't have time for me today."

Anna could sense the disappointment in her son's voice. It was Friday, and now he would have to go all weekend with his issues unaddressed.

"Okay, love. I'll let you handle it."

When he had left the table, Anna pulled her laptop toward her and began hammering out an e-mail.

> My son is having peer issues. He was supposed to meet with someone yesterday to discuss it, but no one called

him. Can you please let me know when he will be called? I would appreciate if this could be done ASAP.

"Is everyone present?" Dean was calling the meeting to order. It was their regular monthly strategy meeting, and the senior executives were seated around the conference table, binders and laptops in front of them. While the company's loan losses had greatly improved, they still needed to increase their sources of income. Each executive had been asked to be prepared to share their ideas at this meeting.

Dean looked at his management team sitting around the table. His eyes moved from one to the other and fell to his Vice President of Network Solutions.

"Chad, what do you have for me?"

"Well, I have some cost cutting ideas. We could limit the number of laptops a manager is allowed to have…"

"I didn't ask for cost cutting ideas." Dean rubbed his forehead and moved on to the Vice President of Branches. John Forbes had worked for the institution for many years. He knew what Dean wanted.

"We can run a loan promotion. Our customers come into our branches complaining that they're not getting approved for their loan requests. I see that as lost opportunities. We need to find a way to approve more members."

"I agree," chimed in the Vice President of Credit Cards. "And we hear from our customers that the lending department is asking them for things like income verification. Why would we ask for income verification just for a credit card application?" All eyes turned to Anna. She had to speak now as it was her department they were complaining about. Try as she may to the contrary, she sounded exasperated.

"We still have a lot of risk in all of our loan portfolios. There may come a time when we can once again rely strictly on a single risk indicator to approve loans. But right now, we don't have the systems in place, and we don't have room in our risk profile."

"So what would you suggest?" Dean looked her in the eye.

Anna continued. "While we're working toward that goal, we need to focus more on the opportunities that we lose every time we approve a customer for a loan request but don't call them to communicate the approval to them. Sometimes, it's taking weeks before our branches are finally getting around to calling the customer. By that time, the customer has already found the money elsewhere. We have reports that show we're losing a significant amount of loans, good loans, loans that the lending department has already approved because we aren't following up letting them know they're approved."

The Vice President of the Branch System held up his finger in protest.

"I haven't seen those reports. I know that we've talked about this problem in the past, but I need to see the reports before I can comment. And everyone should remember that our branch people are quite stretched. They have a lot on their plates."

"I agree," Anna continued. "But as a credit-granting organization, we have to find a way to capture more of the loans we do approve and bring them to a successful close rather than increase our risk parameters just to cast a wider net. If we improve our efficiencies, we can increase our loan production without taking more risk."

"I still don't think it's a good idea to ask for income verification just for a credit card application, especially when the customer has a good credit score." John Forbes wasn't letting up.

"Credit cards are completely unsecured, one of the riskiest products we have. We've all felt the effects the industry has suffered by relying on single indicators like credit scores and how ineffective that strategy has been." Anna was exhausted from having to make the same point over and over again.

"We have to open up credit again," Harold Bart, the Senior Vice President and Anna's new boss, piped in. "We have to stop inconveniencing our members with requests for paystubs or tax returns to verify income. It's ridiculous."

"And the branches need higher loan approval authority without the need to get the Lending Department's concurrence." John Forbes had been pushing for expanded loan approval authority for his branches for quite some time now.

Anna's pulse increased. "Please understand. If the loan portfolio goes south again, it's my position that the industry and the regulators will look to."

"Don't you think they'll look to mine?" Dean was clearly irritated with her now.

"Of course they will, Dean. They'll look first to you, and then they'll look to me." Anna met Dean's glare. Then she looked away. Dean adjourned the meeting. She returned to her office, dejected and tired as she began gathering her things to leave. Why was the organization headed in the same direction that it had taken in years past? The whole industry was, for that matter. Had no one learned? She looked up to see Jeannie in her doorway.

"I know you believe you're doing what needs to be done for the organization. But Dean's a very smart man. And it's not wise for you to go head to head with him like that, especially in a public forum."

Anna remembered the advice Christy had received when she had first come to work for the organization. *You have to be willing to throw yourself in front of a bus for Dean Hathaway.*

"Jeannie, I said what I had to say. I wasn't rude. I didn't make it personal. I stated facts. I offered reports to substantiate them. Perhaps this organization is simply going in a different direction than I want to go in. I'm not sure anymore." With that, she walked around Jeannie and headed for the elevators. She knew her conversation with Jeannie would be relayed to Dean, word by word.

———•◦•———

She stood in her kitchen, steak tongs in hand. Danny was beside her, slicing fennel for their salad as Anna began recounting her day's events.

"I'm speaking up at the office, but nobody's listening. Or else they don't like what they hear. We're not even through our worst loan losses, and already everyone wants to do exactly what they did that got them into the mess to begin with. And it's not just our institution. Our people just want to follow suit because all of our competitors are doing it."

"I can't believe it." Danny tossed the salad. "Haven't they learned yet from the financial disaster this country's in?"

She was cooking one of Daniel's favorite meals, steak au poivre, and giving Nonna the night off from the kitchen duties.

"Dinner!" Danny called out as the sizzling steaks came off the grill. Daniel and Victoria scrambled into their seats.

"How was everyone's day?" Anna began, hoping to put hers behind her.

"I've decided what I want for Christmas this year," Daniel announced. "Mom, this steak sauce that you make is my favorite. I want the Rosetta Stone."

"Oh, what languages?" asked his mother. Daniel was already studying Italian in school.

"I want both Spanish and Italian. I really want to speak both languages fluently. Italian is coming really easy to me, and Spanish is supposed to be similar. I'm doing so well in Italian that I can almost understand Nonna sometimes. Next time we go to Italy I want to be able to talk with Cousin Rocco without a dictionary."

His dad laughed as he said to his son in Spanish, "*Come tu comida.*"

"Mom, what's this steak called again?"

"Steak au poivre." Anna smiled. "It's a French dish."

"Hmmm. French? No, Uncle Pierre can teach me some maybe. I want the Rosetta Stone for Spanish and Italian."

"Oh, and guys…" Daniel continued. "I want to buy a book on Amazon. Can you give me the credit card number?

"Sure," replied his mother. "What do you want to buy?"

"I want to buy *1001 Comebacks and Insults*."

Anna and Danny looked at each other across the dinner table.

"Sounds like a strange book," commented his dad.

"Dad, I need to learn how to come up with quick comebacks. When people talk crap to me, I never have anything to say back, so I just have to sit there and take it. I need some comebacks." He then continued. "Oh, and I don't know that this cognitive behavior thing is all it's cracked up to be."

"Anything in particular you want to share?" asked his mother.

"No. Just that I don't know that the doctor gets me. That's all."

Danny and Anna recalled the doctor's lack of concern regarding Daniel's troubling e-mail, and they as well secretly agreed. Anna began researching new doctors who she believed might be better equipped to help her son. At least they could get yet another professional opinion.

———◆———

They chose a young doctor who was of Mexican origin and practiced family-based therapy. He explained that his approach considered the family unit as the nexus of all issues relating to the children, and so weekly sessions with the parents were critical. The approach sounded like a welcome relief to Danny and Anna after feeling so left out of the loop with the other two doctors.

The attentive parents sat in the new doctor's office. It was scattered with case files and papers. He seemed somewhat disorganized but was part of a major, well-respected network of doctors.

"People come to me thinking they can just drop their kid off and I can just fix them. Well, it doesn't work that way. I use the approach that the parents need to meet with me regularly, as well," Dr. T began. He seemed polite, young and sharp.

"Great," said Danny. "Let's get started." The doctor began with his list of questions.

"What kind of relationship do you both have? How long have you been married? Are there any previous marriages or previous children among the two of you? Is there any history of drug or alcohol abuse? Do you ever engage in activities as a family? Do you ever go on family vacations? Do you both ever take time for yourselves, like having a date night?"

Finally, at the end of the session with the parents and after being unable to find any issues within the family unit to hang his hat on, Doctor T threw up his arms. "Well, I just don't get it then. What's the problem?"

Anna explained that Daniel had been mercilessly bullied in middle school and high school. She told him about the *1001 Comebacks* book he had recently ordered and his renewed interest in martial arts. She told the doctor her son had expressed feelings of ending his life at one time but a full psychiatric workup had been done, and the doctors said he was fine. She told the doctor about the troubling e-mail Daniel had sent to his last doctor but how the doctor had felt there was no need for concern.

The doctor scratched his head. "Yes, I will need all of his previous medical records transferred to me for continuity before I can treat him," said the doctor. "That's just standard protocol. But is there anything in particular about him that you think might bring on the bullying?"

Anna shrugged her shoulders. There it was again. A search for the high risk factor that would logically make him a target.

"He's shy and shows low self esteem sometimes. I think that may be bringing on the bullying."

"I think this could all be just normal teenage stuff. Let me ask you, do you notice if he's particularly depressed at home?"

Anna shook her head.

"No. In general, he's great. He's usually in a very good mood. Laughing and talking. Then we'll notice he has a period of moodiness, but it doesn't last long, maybe a few hours, and then he's fine. He's never withdrawn for entire days at a time—nothing like that."

The doctor went to his door and motioned for Daniel to join him. Anna and Danny exited and waited outside as the doctor spoke to their son.

On the way home, Daniel was energized.

"I think he's going to be really good, Mom. He's a really cool guy."

As women often do, Anna compared notes with her friends about her child's behavior. The responses were sympathetic and encouraging.

"Don't worry."

"It's so normal."

"That's how teens are."

"My daughter is on meds for depression, and I'm not so sure they're helping. I think the meds have made things even worse."

"I wish a doctor would at least suggest that. They just keep telling us he's fine," Anna scratched her head. "They keep telling me all of his thoughts and feelings are perfectly normal. Maybe they're right. Maybe I'm overreacting. I know I'm a worrier anyway."

"I can tell you that my son went through a very dark period in his life several years ago," chimed in one of Anna's friends. "We would find strange poems he would write, visualizing his death and darkness. He talked about hating us. It was a little frightening at the time, but he grew out of it. He's fine now. It's like we finally have our child back after years of hell."

Anna liked the *grew-out-of-it* part. "I suppose I don't want to overreact."

"You definitely don't want to do that. That's like the kiss of death. Kids can tell, and doctors will tell you that," advised another friend.

"If the doctors are telling you he's fine, then he's fine. They're the experts. Sometimes it's hard for us parents to accept that."

CHAPTER
EIGHTEEN

There can be no keener revelation of a society's soul than the way in which it treats its children.

—Nelson Mandela

Two big birthdays were approaching, Victoria's twelfth and Daniel's big sixteenth. He had just gotten his learner's driving permit, and, unbeknownst to him, his parents had been shopping for his first car as a birthday surprise.

"Love, I don't think his first car should be anything really nice. He'll be banging it up anyway." Danny began his planned debate with his wife. Anna just smiled, amused at where she knew this was going. She knew her husband well enough to know it would be he who would insist on getting Daniel the best they could afford. But he'd always start out at least trying to be practical.

"Dad, do you have any spray paint? Aiden says we're not allowed to buy any because the stores think we're gonna spray crap on walls." The parents stopped the discussion as their son entered the room.

"What do you want it for?" Danny was curious what the boys were up to now.

"I wanna change the design on my skateboard."

"Sure, Son." Daniel followed his dad out to the garage.

"Be careful with it, Daniel. Don't make a mess."

"Don't worry, Dad! I'll be careful!"

His mother had just started dinner when Daniel came bursting in from the garage.

"Guys, my skateboard is awesome. Come look." They followed him out to find a shiny, freshly painted skateboard. Danny groaned and rubbed his forehead.

"Daniel, I told you to be careful and not make a mess."

"I didn't make a mess, Dad. It looks awesome. Just look at it."

"Look at my garage floor." His dad pointed in dismay. Spray painted onto the garage floor was a neat outline of a skateboard.

"Oh that. Don't worry, Dad. It's just a garage floor. You're the only one in the world who cares about a garage floor. It's no big deal!"

The day of his party was perfect. Lots of friends, cake, and a shiny black Lexus 300si parked in the driveway with a big red ribbon on it. Daniel stared at his new car in disbelief.

"Wait. So you got me a car?" he could only repeat over and over.

"Dude, you have a car." Aiden sounded incredulous. He slapped Daniel's back as he stared at the shiny black sports car sitting in front of them. "You have a caaaar!"

That night, the family celebrated at Daniel's favorite sushi restaurant.

"Thanks, guys. You're awesome. Now I'll have a car for college."

"Have you been thinking about where you might want to go?" asked Anna.

"Yeah," replied Daniel with an even bigger grin on his face. "I wanna go to the university in San Diego, and I'm gonna eat lunch every day at Junior Seau's."

Junior Seau's was a local sports grill that had been opened by a former NFL star. No matter how many times they went, Daniel was blown away by the place. There were giant big screen TVs playing every football game you could want to watch, cheerleaders serving cheeseburgers, and loads of football memorabilia plastered all over the walls. It was every football fan's dream.

It was late that evening when Danny and Anna settled down to unwind in front of the TV with Victoria and Nonna. Daniel's door suddenly flew open, and he came bounding down the stairs.

"Mom, you gotta come see this. Frank Caliendo's impersonating Robert DeNiro."

He grabbed his mom's arm and led her into his room to watch his favorite comedian. They laughed as the actor impersonated George Bush. They laughed harder when they watched him impersonating Robert DeNiro playing the Frankenstein monster. Daniel had all the episodes recorded.

"That's all I have on this video." Daniel turned off the DVD player as his mom got up to leave. "By the way, Mom, there's a really awesome kid I met in karate class, and I think it would be cool if we started hanging out."

"Great!" replied Anna. "Who is he?"

"He's a Greek kid. I'm teaching him Italian, and he's teaching me Greek. He's really chill. He doesn't have an attitude like some of the kids do. He's just a really laid back kid. I think he might wanna hang out one day."

Anna was happy to hear about her son's new friend. "Wonderful. It's always good to have friends outside of your every day circle. Invite him over for dinner one day."

"Yeah, maybe I will. I wonder if he likes Frank Caliendo."

———◆·◆·◆———

Danny and Anna sat in the doctor's office, listening attentively. They were in their twenty minute session with the doctor, but they were running way over the allotted time.

"Your young man has so much potential, and he's very smart. He just doesn't realize it yet at his young age. He's hard on himself. He reminds me a lot of me when I was his age. Talk therapy usually helps a lot and we're making good progress. We can also consider medication as an option at some point, if you're interested." Anna's heart sank.

"Why?" she asked. "You said he's doing really well."

"Oh, don't get me wrong. He's doing very well. Better than most of my patients. Sometimes he just gets into these moods where he's down on himself and can't see all of his values and attributes."

"But who among us doesn't do that? What does he say?" Anna wanted to know more.

"Yes, you're right. We all do," continued the doctor. "The other day he told me he wished he had been raised in a ghetto so he would know how to street fight. I responded by asking him why he didn't appreciate the fact that he had two professional parents who had been able to raise him in a privileged environment, that not many people have it as good as he did. I know I didn't. I just think he needs to get comfortable in his own skin. He seems to envy the kids from a different culture—either white kids or Mexican kids. I think he's having cultural-identity issues. I'm not saying he *needs* medication. It's just an option if you ever want it."

"Why is he having cultural identity issues?" Anna broke in. "He seems to be very proud of both of his heritages. He has a Mexican flag and an Italian flag up in his room. He's studying both languages. Last summer when he went to his leadership summer program in New York, he looked up his ancestors on Ellis Island. There must be more going on with this than we know."

The doctor shook his head. "Don't make this more than it is. He's a great kid, very level headed. These issues are very common in kids his age."

The creaking of the doctor's door stopped the conversation and the three looked back to see Daniel standing in the doorway.

"Look, guys, I don't mean to be rude, but I really need to talk to you, Dr. T. I've told you before that my problems have nothing to do with my home life. My problems are all at school. So you talking to my parents doesn't really help me at all. And I really do need to talk to you today, but it seems like we're running out of time."

"We'll wrap this up, then. Just give us a couple of more minutes," Dr. T assured the determined teenager.

Daniel shut the door again, sitting back down in the reception area. He waited patiently for the doctor to call him. He really needed to talk to the doctor today. But it never happened. A couple of minutes ended up eating away the rest of the appointment time. The door opened, and the doctor apologized to Daniel for having no time left to talk with him.

"I promise you'll get the whole hour next week," he said as he waved good-bye. Daniel nodded and walked with his parents to their car.

"Daniel, I'm sorry the doctor took so much time with us. What is it?" Anna was concerned.

"Mom, you know how some kids have a really bad home life, and they go to school to escape? Well, my problem is the opposite. I have a really good home life, and it's school that's the real problem."

"But what do you mean school's a problem? You're a straight A student. You have good friends that you enjoy hanging out with. What's the problem?"

"Nothing, Mom. No big deal." Daniel stared vacantly out the window at the suburban landscape that passed before him.

"Are kids bothering you?"

"Mom! No! I'll talk to the doctor next time." Daniel had shut down the conversation. *Now I'll have to wait a whole other week*, he thought.

As per the doctor's suggestion, Anna began researching medication. The more she researched, the less she liked the idea. With every new article or website she read, she felt more uneasy about the idea of putting her child on meds.

"Danny, what do you think? There seem to be so many risks tied to medication," she asked her husband as they both began to prepare for their early morning routine that evening.

"I agree, but Love, the doctor didn't recommend medication. He just asked us what we think about it. Let's see what he tells us at the next visit."

Their bedroom door opened and Daniel walked in.

"Hey, guys, can I ask you a question? Would you be mad at me if I got suspended?" Danny looked up from his hanging shirt waiting for the steamer to heat up and made eye contact with his son.

"Daniel, what's going on?"

"Well, you can get suspended for fighting at school. So if I got into a fight and got suspended, would you be mad at me?" Anna was right on it.

"Daniel, is somebody bothering you?" She was alarmed.

"No, Mom. No one's bothering me. I have it handled."

"Daniel, if some kids are bothering you, you choose the biggest one and hit him right in the nose." There was anger behind her words.

"No! What are you telling him?" Danny interrupted firmly. "Violence is not the answer."

Daniel looked slowly from his mom to his dad and then back to his mom again.

"No, guys, everything's fine. I have it handled." With that, he walked out of the room.

CHAPTER
NINETEEN

Be such a man, my son, and live such a life, that if every man were such as you, this earth would be God's paradise.

—Anonymous

The Chargers were playing the Kansas City Chiefs, and Daniel had convinced his dad to take him and his friends to the big game in San Diego. The boys met up at the Mendez house that morning. They were wide eyed and ready to go, which was a pretty big deal since getting out of bed before ten on a Saturday was not usually something any of them were excited about. As the guys arrived, Daniel came bounding down the stairs wearing his Phillip Rivers jersey with three other jerseys in his hand.

"Here." He tossed the pile toward his friends. "These are my extras. Choose one."

Aiden and Jeff pulled their jerseys over their heads.

"Thanks, man. This is awesome." Aiden looked down at his chest to see how the jersey looked. "Fits perfect!"

Jeff grabbed a Ladanian Tomlinson jersey and threw it on. Michael squeezed the only one left over his head and pulled it down over his abdomen. He didn't have as good of luck as the other guys with his jersey. It fit like a second skin, squeezing his midsection snuggly and barely hitting the top of his jeans.

"Sorry, Michael." Daniel stifled a laugh, looking at Michael, who was shrink-wrapped in a Chargers jersey. "That's one I had when I was younger."

"I don't care. I'm totally wearing it." Michael grinned as his friends laughed, knowing full well he'd be tearing it off in the car.

Daniel had a solution. "I know! You can use it like a 'terrible towel' and wave it around at the game." The 'terrible towel' was a rally towel for the Pittsburg Steelers, another one of Daniel's favorite football teams.

The game was more exciting than they even thought it would be. The Chargers scored a touchdown in the last quarter to win the game 20-19.

Aiden didn't know much about the game, but that didn't affect his enthusiasm as they watched the Chargers eek by with a "W." Whenever Daniel screamed out in elation, disappointment or anger, Aiden followed suit. He matched every emotion-filled "Come on!", "Throw the flag!", and "Touchdown!" that Daniel yelled out, only just a few seconds behind. He may have not had a clue what was going on, but that wasn't going to stop him from participating in the action.

"Yeaaahh!" Daniel jumped up and screamed at the top of his lungs as the final seconds ran off the clock.

"Yeaaahh!" Aiden jumped up and shouted toward the field right on the heels of Daniel's same war cry. "What just happened? Was it good or bad?"

Daniel looked over at his best friend and laughed. You had to admire the guy's enthusiasm.

———◆•◆•◆———

The calendar on the wall was marked with a big red circle. The day of Daniel's Confirmation in Christ had finally arrived. Anna's sisters, Dena and Lilly, and their families had traveled hours to be there for the occasion.

Lilly was helping Nonna in the kitchen with the food preparations as Dena tried to get her new baby Girard into his church clothes, but her attempts were met with Girard's many protests. He wasn't going to go easily into that tiny, uncomfortable suit. The little guy kept wriggling around on the bed with his mother on one side and Anna on the other, both women trying hard to make sure he didn't fall off. It was two against one, so the odds were stacked against him, but somehow Girard was winning by a landslide.

Daniel heard the commotion and came in to find his mom and aunt standing on either side of the bed, both armed with tiny little dress clothes and trying their darndest to get Girard into them. He stood in the doorway a minute and watched the comedy act that was taking place in front of him before coming to Girard's rescue.

"Mom, he doesn't want to wear that." Daniel looked disapprovingly at the miniature suit that the two had in their hands. "He's just a baby, Aunt Dena. Nobody will care if he's wearing a vest."

Girard stopped wriggling and looked up at the sound of Daniel's voice with a sweet, toothless grin on his chubby face.

"See, Mom? He understood me!" Daniel lifted Girard off the bed and walked away with him.

The sisters looked at each other in surprise and Dena called out hurriedly, "Be careful with him, my love! He's the only one I'll ever have."

"Don't worry, Aunt Dena. I've got him." Daniel and Girard disappeared into Daniel's room.

Both sisters tiptoed to Daniel's room and stopped to watch through the open door. Daniel had Girard sitting in his lap as both boys watched the computer screen showing NFL clips of Chargers' games. Girard was cooing happily, his eyes fixed on the screen as though understanding everything Daniel was showing him. There was some definite guy bonding taking place.

"I'm going to make you a Chargers fan, Girard. Your dad's gonna be so ticked at me!" Daniel said with a mischievous chuckle.

"I'm grateful that Daniel and Victoria finally have a cousin," Anna told her sister. "Even though they're so far apart in age, at least they'll have each other when they grow up." Dena had had only one child late in life, and Lilly had not had any children.

"And what sixteen-year-old loves a baby so much?" Dena marveled.

If it had been possible, they would have stood in that hallway and watched the cousins forever, but it was time to get to church.

The old mission was a national shrine. Although they attended mass regularly there, it was always breathtaking to experience the beauty of the hand-carved bench seats, the massive altar backing covered in cedar and gold leaf, and the decorative, sacred art that adorned the old walls. They made their way up the aisle, took their seats, and waited for Daniel to take his giant step forward in his faith.

Anna choked back tears as she watched her handsome boy walking down the aisle, hands clasped in prayer. Daniel looked so very proper and grown up in his dark suit and tie. The bishop bestowed the sacrament onto him, tracing the sign of the cross on his forehead. Daniel accepted the blessing and turned back, scanning the faces of the church goers to lock eyes with his mother, and flashed her his trademark smile. Anna could see how proud he was of himself. She felt gratified that she had been able to raise her son in God's presence and that he had affirmed it for himself when the time came. She knew that it was his faith in God that filled him with light and understanding and enabled him to endure his struggles. She loved him more than she thought it was possible to love, and she broke out into full sobs. Victoria looked up at her sobbing mother.

"Mom, why are you crying?" Victoria whispered forcefully.

"I'm just really happy, sweetie. This is what parents do when they're happy."

"Well, stop being so happy. Everyone's staring at us."

That evening, the family and friends returned to the Mendez home to continue the celebration. Daniel's parents, aunts, and uncles each presented him with gifts to mark this step he had taken in life with the Lord.

"I get gifts?" Daniel was pleasantly surprised as he was handed cards, wrapped boxes, and gift bags. Anna handed her son a small box. He opened it to find a gold chain with a beautiful, hand-etched crucifix.

"Grandpa wanted you to have this, son."

Daniel hugged his mom and proudly hung his grandfather's chain around his neck.

Wrapping paper was scattered everywhere as they gathered in to take pictures. Victoria had been standing next to her mother when she suddenly switched and squeezed in tightly beside her brother before the flash went off. She looked up at her big brother and smiled wide. Anna wasn't the only one who was proud of the young man in Christ Daniel had become.

CHAPTER

TWENTY

For by thy words thou shalt be justified, and by thy words
thou shalt be condemned.

Matthew 12:37 (KJV)

Monday morning. The start of another week of school and
another world. Another week of Sal and his goons, of verbal
assaults, and of being slammed into lockers. Daniel entered his
Italian class the way he always did lately, full of trepidation and
dread. As he walked over to his desk to sit down, Sal Gutierrez
was poised and ready for some quick cut downs he had thought
up especially for Daniel.

"Hey, dirty Dan. You make me sick. You walk like a n———.
Maybe you're not half Mexican. Maybe you're half black."

Some of the kids chuckled at Sal's racist comments, but there
were other kids whose expressions hardened. They had heard
enough of Sal's unwarranted attacks on Daniel. A select few had
begun to realize that neither Sal nor his stupid remarks were
funny anymore.

Daniel said nothing in response. He sat down. There wasn't a
doubt in his mind that Mrs. Conti had heard what Sal just said,
but instead of telling Sal to cut it out or sending Sal to the principal's office, she told everyone to turn their books to page 181.
It was par for the course. He would've been shocked had it gone
any other way. He had learned long ago that he was on his own
as long as he was on school property.

Daniel's confusion about his teacher's lack of involvement was compounded when the kids had to break up into teams to work on a group project. Mrs. Conti pointed to Daniel.

"You need a group. Why don't you join these two?" She pointed over at Sal and Allen. Did she think that putting them together to work on a project would somehow make the harassment stop? Or was she just clueless? It didn't matter. A guy couldn't help but think the universe was working against him.

Oh, this is going to be just great, thought Daniel. Sal and Allen wasted no time in letting him know that this little group project was going to be as bad as he imagined.

"Listen, faggot. You do the work for us and we get good grades too, or you and that trash can over there are gonna become real good friends," Sal spit his words at Daniel. "So far I've been pretty easy on you, wetback."

Day after day, Daniel had worked away with Sal and Allen breathing down his neck. They moved from insults to threats and back again. The last week the project was due, Daniel had had enough. He refused to show up for the group meeting and produce the project. He wasn't going to walk in front of the firing squad another day. That meant that Sal and Allen had to fend for themselves and put together a lackluster presentation. Needless to say, Sal was furious.

"Hey a—hole. What are we supposed to do now? You screwed us, loser. Guess what happens to losers like you!" Sal got in Daniel's face.

Even Mrs. Conti could no longer ignore what was going on in her classroom. She called Sal over to her desk and asked him to go to the principal's office for threatening a student. Sal left the classroom but not before shooting a death stare at Daniel. *Okay, that's over.* Daniel was a little relieved. Some action had finally been taken. He knew that school policy stated that this kind of offense should get Sal suspended for at least two days.

But Daniel didn't get even a 48 hour reprieve. The very next school day, there Sal was, walking the halls and as venomous as ever.

"Hey, faggot! You're a dead man! Everyone hates you, spic!"

Thank God I see Dr. T in a few days, thought Daniel. *Maybe Mom will move up my appointment.*

———◆———

Anna sat in the waiting room, texting her office on her blackberry. The doctor was making up the time Daniel lost the previous week by allowing him the full hour this time. As Daniel came walking out of the office with the doctor, Anna stood up.

"How's he doing today, Doctor?"

"He's great. He's very excited about his summer plans. He's fine. Sorry I didn't leave time to speak with you as well this week. See you next week." Dr. T and Daniel high-fived each other, and the doctor was off to his next appointment.

Anna was happy. *He must have changed his mind about the medication suggestion. Daniel must be doing really well.* She had no way of knowing that this would be her son's last session. She was unaware that one of the final comments reflected in the doctor's notes was how much Daniel hated violence and how Daniel thought that was one of his biggest problems. No one asked what kind of violence was occurring in his life. No one asked why hating violence should be a problem for a kid. No one got it. Not yet anyway.

CHAPTER
TWENTY-ONE

Could a greater miracle take place than for us to look
through each other's eyes for an instant?

—Henry David Thoreau

Candles burned bright against a night sky on the ground in the
very spot where Daniel had seen the last of the world. In their
midst, a photocopied picture of Daniel's smiling face with the
words *Always Courteous*, *Always Kind*, *Beautiful Smile* had been
placed in a plastic sleeve and stood between the candles in the little memorial. Bunches of floral arrangements, a miniature plastic
Chargers Jersey, and handwritten notes had been lovingly placed
at the site. Kids had gathered, some consoling each other, others
staring alone at the flickering flames. Danny parked his car and
quietly joined the small crowd of mourners. He walked to the
very spot where his life had changed forever. As he stood, trying
to comprehend that this memorial was for his son, his own flesh
and blood, he felt a hand on his shoulder.

"I'm Robert Harrison, Michael and Sean's dad. I light the candles for him every night."

Danny choked back tears as the two dads embraced.

The memories of their son would both comfort and torment
the parents after his tragic death. Amidst the condolences and
well wishes, the family began hearing more and more details
about their child's last few days on earth. Several bullies had been
targeting Daniel all year long, and things had escalated in the
weeks leading up to his death.

"I need to share something with you," a caller began. It was Sandra White, a mother of one of the boys at SV High. Anna didn't know her well, but both of their boys had attended some of the same classes together since middle school and had both been in the Italian class.

"My son, Steven and his friend Jeremy have told me that Daniel had been taking a lot of heat from several of the kids in that class. One troublemaker in particular, a senior kid named Sal Guttierez, had made it public knowledge that his senior class project was to harass Daniel to death." The mother paused as she considered the effect her words must be having.

"Steven said Sal was always trying to impress some girl in that class, and when he'd mess with Daniel, the freshman girl would laugh. She thought it was funny and that just egged Sal on even more."

Anna's heart broke with every word she heard, broke at the thought of how much her son must have hurt.

There was anger in Sandra's voice. "The environment in that Italian class is so toxic that, after being denied a transfer, even before Daniel's death, my son asked us if he could see a therapist just to be able to survive the school year there. Can you believe it? Even before Daniel died."

"I know this call must have been hard for you to make. Thank you." Anna was grateful. More pieces of the puzzle were filling in.

"You had to know. My son says the Italian teacher, Mrs. Conti, is completely out of control. Even other teachers at that school complain about her. Many of them have filed complaints to the principal about her incompetence. She often yells things at her students that a teacher should never say. Things like, 'I hate you kids,' and, 'You're my worst class ever.' She perpetuates the chaos and negativity. Her classroom is a breeding ground for bullies.

"And by the way"—the mother on the other end of the phone hesitated for a moment—"you need to know that students are being solicited by the school administration for statements about the bullying they saw related to Daniel. You have every right to a copy of those letters. Did anyone from the school notify you that this was going on?"

Anna's silence told Sandra what she needed to know.

"Yeah, I didn't think so. Let me know if there's anything I can do for you." She hung up.

That became the first of other similar messages. In their daily mail, the family received letters from other concerned parents. Some anonymous, some not. Copies of the school rules with sections highlighted, sections that had obviously been failed to be enforced by the school officials—the "zero tolerance policy," the suspension requirements and punishments for two or more kids fighting one kid. They were often sent in unmarked envelopes with no return addresses. Some people wanted to help. They were just afraid of getting involved. The political ramifications of angering the powers that be were too great. They might need them one day. Two moms, who didn't care who knew their names or the position they were taking, personally hand delivered a copy of the letter their kids had been asked to provide the administration during the bully investigation. Steven's mom handed her son's letter to Anna. She sat by her as they both read the handwritten document.

"Daniel was a great kid, but if you didn't know him well, he came off as shy. Daniel often showed no emotion and did not respond to the bullying. I believe that was one of the reasons why Daniel was targeted so often, many times by kids who were more popular or social than he was. The Friday a week before he died, Mrs. Conti sent one of the bullies to the principal's office. School policy says that he should have been suspended. But Sal was right back in class the following Monday, and his abuse toward Daniel didn't stop."

Another letter written by a freshman girl in the class read, "I told Sal to back off of Daniel, or else Daniel was going to snap one day, but he didn't listen."

It hadn't taken a degreed professional to understand what was bound to happen. A sixteen-year-old kid could see where this whole thing was headed.

———•◆•———

The kids at SV High felt an overwhelming desire to be heard. They began writing blogs in the local newspapers about the bullying. A few bloggers, whom Daniel's friends suspected were school administrators, tried to discredit the bullying accounts.

"There is no bullying at this high school. That kid had problems. Why can't the kids just toughen up on their coping skills?"

Other blogs were heart wrenching. All of the pain and confusion the bloggers felt revealed itself in every word they wrote. "Why are the bullies still in class?" "Why has no action been taken?" "Why are the bullies not being held accountable? We have to see them every day, pass them in the halls every day, while Daniel's desk remains empty."

One blogger wrote, "No one has impacted my life as much as Daniel did. He was a great kid. We were in karate together. I was teaching him Greek, and he was teaching me Italian. I will never be the same after his death, although I try to not show the outside world how much I have been affected."

Anna remembered her son's recent conversation about his new friend and cried when she read that entry. Because of the bullies, her son would never learn Greek, and a boy out there would never have a friend to teach him Italian.

Accounts of students turning on one of the suspected bullies began to surface. The bullying against Daniel was such common knowledge on the campus that one kid in particular, Phil Jensen, was feeling the backlash of having spewed hatred for so long. The kids who had watched for years as Phil tore people apart had all had enough. They began trashing his car and calling him names. Right or wrong, it seemed Phil was getting a taste of his own medicine. Three weeks before the school year ended, Phil Jensen requested a transfer to a different school.

"I need to transfer," he told the principal. "I'm being bullied."

"Why have we heard nothing from the school?"

Anna looked at her husband and wiped her tears. Her face was more wet than dry these days. The parents placed a call to the principal.

"Students are telling us that there's a bullying investigation going on at the school and that kids are being called out of classrooms to give their statements," Danny said into the phone.

"Absolutely not," replied the principal. "That's an absolute falsehood. No one is being called out of their classrooms for statements. There is absolutely no bullying investigation taking place here."

"Well, we heard that there was an altercation that occurred only hours before our son's death between him and two other students. Our son's autopsy shows cuts and bruising on his face and body," Danny continued.

"Well, yes," replied the principal, "we're hearing that something happened on the afternoon of May 1 between Daniel's lunch and Italian class, but we're still not sure what that was. And you have to understand that the other kid involved has an excellent record just like Daniel. And we also understand that your son was the one to throw the first punch. So you understand our dilemma."

Lunch and Italian…lunch and Italian. Anna's mind flashed back to Daniel's words the last morning of his life. *"Mom, can I skip lunch and Italian class today?"* Danny saw rage flash in his wife's eyes.

"Really? The other boy involved has an excellent record?" Anna was angry. "The kids are telling us that the primary boy involved in the altercation with our son is named Sal Gutierrez, that he has a history of bullying, and, according to the kids, had made it known to everyone that his senior class project was to harass our son to death. He succeeded, didn't he? This boy is two years older than our son."

"Well, we're still investigating," stuttered the principal, surprised that the family had so much information. "We're hearing from Sal Gutierrez that Daniel attacked him and that Allen Carter was just trying to restrain Daniel from hitting Sal more."

Danny tried hard to restrain himself. "My son was not a violent person. There is not a single record that shows he ever got into any sort of fight. He hated violence. Yet the records on the boys involved in the final altercation show a history of bullying. And you're trying to convince us that Daniel was the instigator and the other boys were just restraining him for his own good?"

"Like I said, we're still investigating, and I don't know what it'll turn up, but if it's determined that there was bullying involved, what are your intentions legally?"

Wait. Didn't he just deny there was an investigation going on? Now he's saying there is an investigation pending? I'm confused. And legally? Anna thought. That threw her for a loop. *What is this man talking about? Our son is dead and he's asking about our legal intentions? I'm being haunted by the vision of my son lying lifeless in a morgue. We need the truth. We need to know what happened to our child. Can't they understand that's the extent of our intentions?* Anna struggled to keep her composure and replied in a strained voice.

"Our son is gone. We just need to know the truth. We need to know what happened. As a fellow human being, can you understand that?"

"That's it? Okay. The Mendezes only want the truth to be known." The principal sounded relieved.

"And I want the bullies expelled," Danny demanded through clenched teeth. The principal promised to follow up with the parents as soon as more information became available.

"Why did *we* have to call him? Why didn't he call us? If kids weren't telling us what's going on and if we hadn't called him, I don't think the principal would have called to let us know."

Danny knew his wife was right. Their phone rang, and it was the detective in charge of the investigation. Danny had a few investigative questions of his own.

"Have you questioned the boys who were involved in an altercation with my son an hour before he died?"

"No," replied the detective. "What are you talking about?"

"Our son was being bullied."

"I didn't know," insisted the detective, "I spoke to the principal just an hour ago. I asked him questions, and he didn't mention that there was any bullying investigation going on or that an altercation of any sort had occurred."

"He denied that there was an altercation between Daniel and another student right before Daniel's death?" Anna asked, incredulous.

"Well, you better call him again," Danny insisted. "Because we just had a conversation with him, and he admitted that some students have been questioned, and he has documentation of an altercation that occurred within an hour of our son's death. After he died, there were cuts and bruises on his face and body."

The detective was silent. It was obvious that he knew nothing about what he had just been told.

"And will the principal be held accountable for obstruction of justice since he didn't reveal this to you when you first called him?" Anna wanted to know.

"Well, anything that didn't happen at the immediate scene of the incident is really outside of our scope of investigation." The detective was apologetic. "The death has been ruled as a suicide, and that's really where our investigation ends."

It was a sad day at SV high school. News of Daniel's death had spread like wildfire across the campus. Aiden walked slowly, purposelessly through the campus. His limbs felt heavy, disconnected from his mind. He shuffled on toward nowhere when he noticed Sal Gutierrez sitting on the curb outside the gym. There he was. The kid who had made his friend's life intolerable. The kid who had pushed his best friend over the edge. Aiden stopped, stared a minute, and then slowly began walking over to him. By now, other kids had noticed Aiden making his way toward Sal. They knew Daniel's death stood between the two, and like vultures, they began to gather in a circle around the two boys. Aiden stopped in front of Sal, arms to his side, looking down at him. Neither moved. Sal finally looked up from his crouched position to face Aiden, eyes squinting, not to protect them from the sun but from Aiden's stare that demanded accountability.

"You need to come to the funeral." Aiden's voice was low and strained. "You need to come see the damage you've caused."

There was silence as Sal stared back. The kids in the crowd shifted uncomfortably, expecting something to erupt. Aiden kept his eyes on Sal, not moving an inch. Sal finally spoke.

"I'll try to make it." Sal shifted his stare back down to the ground.

Aiden turned and slowly walked away.

CHAPTER
TWENTY-TWO

Good men must die but death cannot kill their names.

—Anonymous

The funeral took place at the same beautiful mission where just a few short weeks earlier Daniel had celebrated his confirmation in Christ. This time, instead of triumphantly walking down the aisle in a formal suit and tie, flashing his proud smile at his mother, he was being carried in a glossy oak casket.

Over a thousand people crowded the historic Roman Catholic Mission San Juan Basilica. Many of the priests and parishioners in attendance had known Daniel personally. The pall bearers were Daniel's best friends; two of them wore their Boy Scout uniforms.

They were all precious children themselves, and today their innocent faces were gaunt and pale. The boys, young and typically so full of hope and life, seemed lost and confused as they tried to muster up any fragment of courage they could find to make it through this day. Rather than laughing and jostling, planning a day at the beach or the movies, they were standing by their friend's casket, each wearing a white glove on one hand. A tearful mourner whispered, "Boy Scouts should never be pall bearers. There is something very wrong with a world that causes this to happen."

Surprisingly for such a traditional church, the priest began his sermon with some booming statements. "When everyone first heard that Daniel Mendez died, the reaction was the same. What? Who? *Why*?? And they say there's an investigation going on, but we have no answers, and *nothing makes sense!*" The priest's loud, angry voice reverberated through the old mission and shook the people sitting in the pews to their very core.

The raw emotion in the priest's voice comforted Anna. In her excruciating grief, she was comforted to know that she was not the only one who was angry and knew that the world did not make sense at that moment.

The principal of SV High School had come to the services. He sat in the pews, listening to the words, and felt them as daggers aimed directly at him. *I thought this was to be a service*, he thought. *Not a hearing.*

The priest finished speaking, and the heartbreaking eulogies began. Aiden was first. He began his eulogy by telling the story of how he and Daniel first met.

"We were in sixth grade, and I was the new kid. I was sitting by myself at the lunch tables when Daniel sat down next to me and started eating his lunch. He said, 'Hi,' but I was shocked at first since no one had yet talked to me. I literally stared at the side of his head wondering what this kid was doing and finally asked, 'Why are you talking to me?' Daniel was just that way, just kind to everyone. After getting past the awkward start, we realized we both loved basketball and started playing during lunches and even on weekends."

Aiden talked about their happy days, football games, movies, skateboarding, and hanging out at Michael's. "Daniel made us laugh, he made us think, and he was always there whenever we needed him. He was the most positive guy I knew, and it was his positivity that always let us know we would make it through the difficult stuff. He helped us all. I can't thank him enough for all the good memories I have. We had so many plans for the future. We were supposed to be hanging out at the beach all summer long in two weeks.

"Daniel was an amazing friend and a beloved member of our close knit group. He always seemed happy in front of his friends, and that's what we'll think of to keep his memory alive. Daniel, you'll be greatly missed. Cherish everyone in your life, and make sure they know you love them. I know he cherished his family and friends above all else."

Finally, he choked out, "I never got a chance to tell you this, but I'll tell you now. I love you, man." Aiden stepped off the podium and embraced the Mendezes with damp, red eyes.

Now, it was Victoria's turn. Victoria had told her parents that she wanted to read a passage at her brother's services. Her parents had agreed to let their daughter speak but told her if she felt like it was too much when the time came, she didn't have to do it. Now, her mother looked at her to see what she would do.

"You don't have to do this if you don't want." In her grief-stricken haze, Anna's sole concern was to protect her only remaining child from any additional pain.

"No, I want to." Victoria looked small as she purposefully made her way up the altar steps of the grand mission basilica and took her place at the podium. She was short for her age and barely reached the microphone. She pulled the mic down toward her, held her head high, and began her passage with conviction.

"Blessed are the poor in spirit, for theirs is the kingdom of heaven. Blessed are those who mourn, for they shall be comforted. Blessed are the meek, for they shall inherit the earth. Blessed are those who hunger and thirst for righteousness, for they shall be satisfied. Blessed are the merciful, for they shall obtain mercy. Blessed are the pure in heart, for they shall see God. Blessed are the peacemakers, for they shall be called sons of God. Blessed are those who are persecuted for righteousness' sake, for theirs is the kingdom of heaven."

She took a deep breath, bowed, made the sign of the cross, and returned bravely to her seat. Danny hugged his daughter.

Anna looked at her son's lifeless face in the casket. It seemed lit from within, a face of merciful serenity, with no more fear or pain. No more joy or laughter. She looked at the curve of his eyebrows, his dark lashes, the corners of his mouth, his full lips, the beauty mark on his right cheek. She placed her shaky hand over his heart and let out a cry of anguish that hardly seemed human. It was the sound of a mother's heart breaking forever, the sound of a good-bye that should never be spoken, the sound of a world that isn't understandable and never will be. The strange sound left the mother and marked in the universe a time when lives would be changed forever. The words her son had once spoken reverberated in her mind. "*Remember, Mom, if I die, I love you.*"

I remember, my love. She felt his strong arms around her, holding her up so she wouldn't collapse. Holding her up for the excruciating work that still lay ahead of her.

She watched as the casket was lifted into the waiting hearse. *My child is in there. I can't leave him alone. He needs me.* She began walking toward it as though to get in with him when her husband's hand pulled her away. The family had been asked to join friends in the recreation center. The large center was packed with mourners. A projection screen was broadcasting a powerpoint set to music with hundreds of family pictures flashing, and Daniel's beautiful smile filled the room. Their family pictures. The parents watched in disbelief. Nothing seemed real. Was this really their lives being flashed before their eyes on a big screen in a large recreation center while they wore black? How had it come to this?

Danny and Anna greeted mourners who were forming a long line as they waited to pass on their words of comfort and love. Kids that the parents had never met before greeted them.

"It's awful what they did to him."

"We are so sorry."

"We are going to take measures to fight bullying."

"This cannot be tolerated any longer."

One pretty, teary-eyed girl hugged Anna. "He was the first boy who ever told me I was pretty. We were in first grade together, and we knew each other ever since. I will never forget him."

Another boy timidly approached them. "I don't know if you remember me. I was Daniel's friend in fifth grade. We moved to

San Francisco, but I told my mom I had to fly down here to say good-bye to my good friend. I will miss him so much." He began to sob.

A reception was held at the Mendez household for very close friends and family. The backyard, as well as the house, was over-flowing with people showing their love, sharing their sadness, and offering their support.

Several of the mourners had gathered around the fire pit where Daniel had so often roasted marshmallows with his sister, laughed, and sang songs with friends.

"Aiden just told me Daniel talked about two boys named Sal Guttierez and Alan Carter that were making his life hell and that he didn't know how much more of it he could take." Daniel's Uncle Pierre spoke solemnly to his wife.

Lilly nodded. Dena's friend Gigi listened attentively.

"It's so horrible." Gigi's face was dark with sadness. "Why couldn't anyone do anything?" Daniel and her son had played together when they were younger, spent holidays together. No one could understand how any of this was possible.

Marla Schaeffer stood by, watching Anna solemnly. Her son Jeff had been one of the pallbearers. The two mothers didn't know each other well, but the evening would change that. Marla watched quietly. At a moment when Anna was not surrounded by well-wishers, she approached the grieving mother and took both her hands in hers. "I want you to know that many parents are very upset about what happened. We are not going to let this rest, and I promise you many good things will happen in memory of your son."

Aiden, Michael, Jeff, and Jeremy slipped upstairs to Daniel's bedroom. They now stood and looked at their good friend's post-ers, read the quotes Daniel had taped up on his wall, touched his homework books, his backpack, his pencils, his football, and finally allowed themselves to break down. From outside, seated with guests, Anna and Danny looked up at their son's lighted bedroom window and were at first taken aback to see any activity. Were their minds playing tricks on them? But instead of Daniel's profile walking back and forth across his room, they saw the silhouettes of four boys sobbing and holding on to each other for dear life. Clearly their son was loved. And clearly these boys were going to need love and support as well as answers.

CHAPTER
TWENTY-THREE

A sad soul can kill you quicker, much quicker, than any germ.

—Henry David Thoreau

The following days were mind numbing. It was as though they had stepped into someone else's lives. News media were calling, hoping for a statement of any kind from the family. Producers from Anderson Cooper 360 and Dr. Drew called, asking for an interview for bullying segments they were airing. Relatives came down to help keep the household running. One of them was an aunt on Anna's side from Italy. The death of her great-nephew was a shock to her, but it wasn't just the untimely death of a young loved one that the aunt couldn't wrap her mind around. She was shocked that schools in America didn't take bullying more seriously. In Italy, she told the family, upon the mere mention of the word "bully," parents would band together, march down to the school, and pull their children out if the bully was not immediately expelled. Schools had no choice but to take harsh measures against bullies. She couldn't understand why the issue was treated so differently in America. Neither did anyone else suffering Daniel's loss.

Anna's sister Lilly came down from Canada to be with her sister. She had made contact with an acquaintance who was a psychiatrist in Canada. She told her about the circumstances surrounding her nephew's passing.

"In Canada, the psychiatric community looks at bullying as an issue as serious as any traumatic incident in a person's life," the Canadian doctor had explained.

"Bullying is insidious and is typically not a singular event. If it continues to occur, it can reshape a person's self-image, no matter how strong or well grounded the person may be."

"That makes sense," Lilly had replied.

"In Canada, when a therapist even hears the word mentioned as part of the patient's past, we are required to take a completely different course of treatment because of the long lasting and serious effects that bullying can have on patients."

So why were Daniel's issues so easily glossed over? Anna was angry. *How different might our lives be if only the United States was as educated about the problem as other countries. Three separate doctors had been told by us about the bullying,* she thought. They had read about it in the intake notes, had been told by Daniel both directly and indirectly, yet all continued to shake their heads and wonder why he was depressed.

Why was American psychology so detached from such a major issue that many other countries realized was so damaging? Perhaps American society didn't want to admit that bullying was the root cause of so many problems. We will look to everything else for an explanation—sexual orientation, a divorce, family finance problems, the kid's personality, medication, a disability— anything else but seldom admit to the glaring fact that stands before us. It isn't that a kid is different, shy, or that he doesn't wear the right clothes. It is society beating him down at every opportunity that makes him finally hate himself.

———— ◦•◦ ————

Anna sat at the computer screen, trying to get into her son's personal Facebook account but realized she couldn't remember his password. He had just begun his Facebook account only weeks before he died. Aiden had helped him set it up.

"Victoria, do you know Daniel's Facebook password?" Anna asked her daughter.

"No, Mom. Maybe Aiden does."

Victoria sent a text to Aiden. Within seconds, Victoria called down to her mother.

"Mom, Aiden says it's Italianmexican55."

"I wonder what the fifty-five means," Anna said back as she keyed in the password to login to the site.

"Mom, that's Junior Seau's old football number," Victoria said. They both smiled. Daniel had taught Victoria a lot about the game.

Anna logged on to her son's Facebook page and was overwhelmed by what she saw. There, awaiting someone to hit "accept", were many friend requests from kids who knew that Daniel had died. They knew but wanted some way to hold on to him, even if it was only through the web. Regardless of who accepted the request and who read their posts, the kids needed a way to connect with Daniel now, so they reached out the only way they knew how.

"It's interesting," Anna commented to her husband after going through several Facebook friend requests. "This generation even uses social media to work through their grief. Good for them. Whatever they need."

———◆━◆━◆———

Tragedies reveal a lot about humanity. Some acts, like the overflow of kids and parents pouring their hearts out on Daniel's Facebook page and newspaper blogs, moved the family immensely and demonstrated how much compassion, love, and support was out there. But it wasn't all good.

The family was getting questioned in the court of public opinion, by bloggers, most of whom remained anonymous. People unfamiliar with the bullying dynamics or those that were bullies themselves were questioning what the family had done wrong that their child would take his life. Everyone gets bullied. It's just a fact of life. So why couldn't this kid handle it? What kind of a life had he led? Where did they live? What kind of food did they eat? Something else must have been wrong.

They found it necessary to view the tragedy through a veil of detachment. For their own emotional health, they needed to justify how they were different from this traumatized family and why this could never happen to them. Maybe the parents weren't fit. Maybe depression ran in the family. Maybe the kid was gay. Had Daniel been gay, the straight community would have blamed his suicide on his sexual orientation, that it was his sexuality that was the real cause of his issues. But Anna had many gay friends who were popular, content, well adjusted, successful, and the life of the party. So perhaps being gay is not the issue that causes some gay teens to take their lives, she thought. Perhaps it is the abuse, the torment, the bullying that some gay kids are subjected to as a result of being gay. Perhaps, just perhaps, it is the moral majority that is the root cause of the problem.

With the whirlwind of attention, they sat and wondered how their once peaceful lives had been torn open in such a violent way. Then a blog caught her attention.

"He was a great kid. Often spent time at my house with my two boys. He was polite, happy, had a beautiful smile. I'll always remember his beautiful smile. Just the kind of kid I wanted my own kids to hang out with. The kind I wished more were like. I don't know his parents well, but I'm here for them. Unless you knew Daniel, don't comment. Don't speculate. I knew him." This blogger didn't need to remain anonymous. He signed it simply, signed it proudly, "Mr. Harrison."

It was these diehard supporters that continued to give them strength. Strength to go on, even if for one more day. Marla Schaeffer began spending time regularly with Anna. She swore she would not rest until changes were made within the system.

After Daniel's death, media stories of children ending their lives as a result of bullying became more common. Anna didn't know if she just hadn't paid much attention to them earlier, or was it that society was finally getting at the root cause of what was causing the child suicides and finding a commonality—bullying?

They were finishing up dinner, as Marla and Anna were about to take their seats in the living room to watch an Anderson Cooper special on the suddenly hot topic of bullying and suicide. Anna stared at the images on the television screen.

"My child's picture could so easily be among those children," she observed sadly. Suddenly, she pointed to the screen. "Oh my God."

There was her handsome son's picture confidently smiling at them on the screen amidst many other beautiful teens who had also lost their lives to bullying. The reality of the situation hit her hard.

"I always knew I would see him on tv one day. I just never imagined it would be like this." Her words were slow and deliberate. She listened as the news anchor stumbled through the sensationalism of the bullied children who had lost their lives. For the sake of garnering the maximum number of viewers, the program focused upon the various manners in which the children had died and the wake of devastation that had been left behind, rather than exploring the root causes of the bullying and any potential solutions.

———◆•◆———

With so many people clamoring for change, an initiative began within the district to educate students about the dangers of bullying. But while the administration's intentions were good, their execution failed miserably. Hokey presentations were made by the school counselor in the middle-school classrooms that turned a serious problem into a silly cartoon, which made the issue even less significant for kids. The educational material was outdated and used a turtle, a shark, and an eagle to make the point that bullying was wrong.

Victoria wondered who had come up with the ridiculous program. She knew that portraying a victim of bullying as a shy turtle with no respect for itself would not encourage kids to come forward and admit they were being bullied. If you've been thrown in a trash can and called a snitch, the last thing you want is to be compared to a cartoon turtle with self-esteem issues. Having a great white shark play the role of bully seemed a little less than beneficial as well. The entire presentation only seemed to add more fuel to the fire, and, most importantly, it perpetuated some of the very damaging stereotypes that allowed Daniel to slip under the radar in the first place. Sometimes, victims didn't look like slow, nerdy turtles. Sometimes, they looked like her brother. As she sat and watched the meek little turtle and the powerful shark, she knew she had to speak up. The well-intended presentation was missing the mark to the point of being offensive. When the presenter proposed that the simple solution would be for the victim to report the bullying, Victoria couldn't stand it any longer and her hand shot up.

"Excuse me, but that doesn't work. My brother did just that, and it definitely didn't work for him."

"Oh." The school counselor was surprised.

The kids' eyes were all on him. Now the presentation was getting interesting. The counselor looked irritated. How was he supposed to answer this one? Why was this little girl putting him on the spot like this? He hadn't any experience with this sort of feedback.

"Oh, I'm sure he just didn't go through the appropriate channels. Or maybe his type of bullying just wasn't that serious. Does he go to this school?" The counselor leaned his head to one side with a placating look on his face.

"Umm, well, he *used* to." *Yeah*, she thought. *They're clueless.*

Anna and Danny sat at the memorial park office to begin the incomprehensible task of choosing a burial plot for their beloved child. Neither could focus. *How do I choose where to place my child for eternity?* Anna thought. No parent is ever prepared for this. I know how to choose his shirt, his vitamins, his car, his college. I don't know how to choose a burial plot for my child. *I don't want to do this*, she thought. *I want him with me. Nowhere else. Am I really having to go through this? Why can't we rewind back to a few days ago? Maybe this is a nightmare, and I'll just wake up from it. Maybe I haven't prayed hard enough.* Her cell phone rang, bringing her back to the polite, sympathetic woman with tears in her eyes as she gently explained the difference between a mausoleum and a columbarium. She pulled herself together and picked it up.

"Hello," said the voice on the other line, "I am with the SV middle school, and we're very concerned about an incident that occurred today involving your daughter. During a bullying presentation being conducted by the district, your daughter Victoria raised her hand and announced that the tactics being recommended were not useful. We didn't think it was an appropriate comment for a student to make. We are quite concerned that she doesn't believe in the effectiveness of the program and wanted to share our concerns with you."

"You're right," Anna replied dryly. "She does not believe in the tactics being suggested. Her only brother followed them and died as a result."

"Oh. I'm sorry. When did he die?" The woman on the other end of the phone asked passively. She asked the question, not as though she really wanted to know, but as though she just imagined it might be the expected thing to do.

Anna had to work hard to control herself. Her forced, monotone words came out slowly and emphatically, almost like a prayer. "My husband and I are at the cemetery right now choosing our only son's final resting place. You're interrupting us with a concern that the tactic you suggested to counter bullying was

179

questioned by his sister. Do you see an irony in that? Do you people know what is occurring on your school grounds? Do you know who your students are? Do you know who you're placing calls to? Do you care?"

She cried and made no apology for her tears. She was astonished at the apathy of the people in the system. Perhaps understanding was too much to ask.

———◆———

Daniel's friends had organized a tree planting ceremony in memory of their beloved friend and were now standing in the Harrison front lawn just steps from where Daniel had died, where he had gone to seek solace in the last moments of his life. Each friend took turns with the shovel, digging the hole and then filling it in with dirt. While the kids were posing in front of the tree for pictures, Aiden ran across the street to his house. He soon returned with a little wooden cross and a rosary strung on it. Sean had saved the miniature rubber Chargers jersey from the memorial and now planted it firmly at the base of the tree next to Aiden's cross.

The Mendezes had been invited, and as their car pulled up to the house, Anna's stomach was in knots. *This is where my son died*, she thought. *This very spot is where he took his last breath.* Although Daniel had spent a lot of time with Michael, the parents had never met. Daniel often spoke highly of Michael's parents, and Anna knew they had loved her son. She slowly got out of the car, and her eyes fell on a woman standing in the driveway who she concluded must be Michael's mother. The woman was standing proudly, solemnly but welcoming, greeting her guests for this special occasion that she and her husband had arranged. Anna was nervous to meet this woman who she had heard so much about through her son. Would she be judgmental of her family? Would she secretly wonder what they had done wrong? Why had they never taken the time to know each other while Daniel had been alive? The woman turned and saw Anna approaching. The two mothers' eyes locked. Without speaking a word, they walked toward each other and embraced. Both wept tears but did not speak. They were now connected by a bond that few could ever understand.

Days went by. Danny and Anna wondered when the nightmare would end. They always hated being away from their son, and this time they didn't have the comfort of knowing when he'd be returning home. If prayers could change reality, he would walk through the door and throw his arms around them like he had the last time he went on his trip to New York. But all the prayers in the world wouldn't bring their son back to them now.

Victoria was fighting her own battles, and in their grief, the parents were doing all they could to support her. She just couldn't comprehend how a few moments could have stolen something so important to her. He was her only sibling. Her big brother. He was always happy, and he loved her. He taught her all about NFL football, multiplying fractions, and the elements table. He taught her how to respect people, how to fight for the underdog and how to say no to peer pressure. He was proud of her, one of her biggest fans. Maybe if she had reminded him that she loved him before he left to go to school that morning…maybe if they hadn't quibbled over the bathroom sink…maybe, just maybe something she could have done would have made a difference. Maybe she could have said something that would have made Daniel think about her instead of the bullies. Why had the bullies been more important to him than she had? Why hadn't he remembered her? How could he have left her?

Anna watched as Victoria walked down the hall toward her bedroom. Her mother noticed the little girl cautiously steal a glance toward her brother's room as she passed by and then quickly look away. At that moment, Anna understood what they had to do. Although it would be one of the most painful acts of their lives, she knew that they had to clear out their son's room as soon as possible.

"His room mocks us." Anna could barely whisper the words to her husband. "It makes us believe it's waiting for him and he'll come home soon. We need to do it for Victoria if not for anything else." She didn't know if she had the strength to go through with what she was suggesting, but she had to try, for her daughter's sake.

So the broken parents began the heart-wrenching task of taking down their only son's room. Their firstborn. Their pride and joy. They began by taking down the posters on his walls. He had covered almost every square inch of available space and had even started on the ceiling. Most were football posters, NFL teams, some girls in bikinis, and some rock bands. There was the Led Zeppelin poster he had brought all the way to Italy and back, and quotes he had printed out and hung up. Anna had read the quotes a hundred times before, but they now had a completely different meaning. She looked around the room and read.

> We gotta make a change. It's time for us as a people to start makin' some changes. Let's change the way we eat, let's change the way we live, and let's change the way we treat each other. You see, the old way wasn't working, so it's on us to do what we gotta do to survive.
>
> —Tupac

And there was,

> Skateboarding in life is pretty much a fork in the road. You can go this way, you can go that way. Me, I went straight. I created my own path.
>
> —Stevie Williams

And,

> People have been messing with me my whole life. I learned
> a long time ago there's no sense getting all riled up every
> time a bunch of idiots give you a hard time. In the end, the
> universe tends to unfold as it should.

—Harold and Kumar

Anna had tears in her eyes as she and Danny began carefully peeling the posters and pieces of papers covered with Daniel's favorite quotes off the walls. Why hadn't she paid more attention to their meaning while he was still with them. Between his bed and the wall she found a *Playboy* magazine he had been hiding there. She felt a momentary pang of guilt that she was invading his privacy. As they worked, her sobs grew louder and her movements angrier. In the end, she was tearing violently at the paper as she screamed until she felt she had nothing left inside of her.

Completely exhausted, she came to a drawer she hadn't opened in years. At the top of the drawer was a poem Daniel had written for her years earlier.

> Mom,
> Funny, sweet, wonderful,
> Wishes to be with her family,
> Dreams of a happy family forever,
> Who wonders if I will stay healthy,
> Who fears bugs,
> Who is afraid of spiders,
> Who loves my dad,
> Who believes in God,
> Who loves me a lot,
> Who plans to love me even more,
> Who I love so much,
> And always will,
> No matter what,

Love, Daniel

"He knew he was loved." She sobbed as her husband held her. "No matter what, I know he knew he was loved."

———◆·◆·◆———

Dena and Lilly took time off work to come down and help their sister and her family continue functioning. In the midst of their own grief, they somehow had to find the will to stay strong. They would have their time to crash too, but it couldn't be now. They had to push everything deep down inside for now. They could fall apart later, but at that moment, their sister needed them.

Anna looked at Dena with sadness in her eyes. "Do you understand now why I wanted to make the most of every family holiday? I wasn't being unkind. I just wanted to appreciate precious family moments. I didn't even know how truly precious they would become. I just felt deep down that I had to cherish each one."

Dena began to cry. "I'm so sorry. I didn't realize. I just didn't realize."

"I know. It's okay." Anna comforted her sister. The two held each other and cried for lost family moments, for the past as well as the future. Lilly began remembering happy, crazy times, and they started laughing through their tears. There was no time for regrets. They had to remember the good. It was all they had left of Daniel.

———◆·◆·◆———

Victoria couldn't sleep. She tossed and turned as nightmares haunted her. She heard her parents crying in their room and knew they were still awake. She quietly walked into their room and saw her dad holding her mom. She put her arms around them both, and sobbed as she never had before in her young life.

"I love you both very much," Danny whispered. "We will survive this."

As Anna tucked Victoria back into her own bed, the little girl looked up at her mother.

"Mom, why did God take Daniel?" She wiped the tears from her eyes with the back of her delicate, little hand.

"What do you mean?" Anna's heart throbbed at the question.

"Well, Daniel was good, and God took Daniel. Why?" Anna knew her daughter was trying hard to find answers.

"No, sweetheart. God didn't take Daniel. God is crying, too, right now. Daniel was being bullied for years, and we had had real concerns about it."

"But no one told *me*," Victoria sobbed, turning her head on the pillow, as though to turn away from the searing pain of the new reality. "Everyone forgot to tell me."

She was struggling not only with her brother's loss but the extreme unexpectedness of it. Anna remembered her daughter's first words upon hearing the news that her big brother was gone forever. *Why did he do it, Mom? His life was perfect.* That's all Victoria had seen. A perfect life. She looked down at her daughter who was now drowning in questions and never felt so helpless as a parent.

"We didn't understand it ourselves. We didn't even know how bad the bullying had gotten. We thought it had stopped. I'm so sorry, sweetheart." All she could do was apologize to her child. There was nothing more she could offer.

She sat on the bed and held her daughter until she fell asleep. Once she was sure Victoria was asleep, Anna joined her husband in the kitchen.

"How did we miss it, Danny? As much as we tried to figure out what was wrong and as much as we tried to help him, how did we miss it?"

"No, you can't blame yourself. We did everything we could."

"But we knew. We knew he had been bullied. And we knew he had self-esteem issues. Why didn't we connect the dots? Why weren't we more forceful about it?"

Danny rubbed his tired eyes. "We tried to tell them. You kept telling them all the time. The doctors didn't even connect the dots. They kept saying it was normal teenage stuff. None of the professionals were concerned about the bullying, about anything. How could we have known?"

"Because we're his parents. It's so clear now. Why is it so clear now and we were in such a fog then?"

"I don't think we completely understood the seriousness of bullying. We just didn't know. He seemed to be handling it well. Don't do this to yourself."

"I had it all backwards." Anna spoke and her voice had the tone of someone who had been enlightened for the first time. "I thought his social shyness and self-esteem issues were causing the bullying. But instead, it was the bullying that was causing the anxiety and the self-esteem issues. We were treating the symptoms instead of the cause. That's why he was always fine around us. He didn't feel abused around us, only at school. I understand now what he tried to tell us, sometimes so clearly, when he said his problems weren't at home, they were at school, when he was so worried about defending himself. I could have helped him. I was almost there. I was really close. I can help him now. Why can't God give me just a few more days?"

The worst part was that there was no one to appeal to for a few more days.

———◆———

She was reading condolence cards. There were hundreds, too emotional to get through all at once. She put the last one aside when her phone rang. It was the pastor of the local community church where Daniel and his buddies had attended youth group.

"I just want to say how terribly sorry I am for your loss," he began. "Daniel was a great kid. One of my favorites."

"Thank you," replied Anna. "Your call means a lot to us."

He went on, choosing his words cautiously. "I just want you to know that I think what happened to Daniel was horrible. I know the family of Phil Jensen. I've known them for years. I've known Phil since he was born."

Anna tensed up. There was that name again. Phil Jensen was one of the bullies that other kids had reported as one of her son's main tormentors.

"I thought you should know that Phil's parents had a very ugly divorce." He paused. Anna waited, not speaking a word. "No, I mean really ugly." The pastor continued with trepidation. "And Phil has been scarred by that. He's had a lot to deal with. I know it doesn't excuse what he did to Daniel, but his parents are very sorry for the part that their son played in the bullying. His father has been in my office every night for the past week distraught and in tears. He wants to know if you would be open to an apology."

"Thank you," she could barely choke out the words. "Maybe one day. I hope you understand. It's just too soon for us right now." She hung up the phone. Later, she would come to regret that response.

CHAPTER
TWENTY-FOUR

The real war will never get in the books.

—Walt Whitman

"I didn't know!" The Italian teacher was waving her arms. She had asked Austin and Jeremy to stay after class so she could talk to them. "I didn't know he was being bullied! Why didn't anyone tell me?"

She has to be joking, thought Austin as he and Jeremy exchanged glances.

"Mrs. Conti, you saw it. It happened all the time. You sent Sal to the principal's office just the week before."

"But I just didn't realize! I didn't know that a child's life depended on my efforts. You kids should have done something. It wasn't my fault!" Her voice was shrill. The two boys shifted uncomfortably.

"Was it? Do you think it was my fault? What could I have done? Oh, why didn't you boys tell me?" The friends looked at each other. This was getting kinda bizarre now.

"Mrs. Conti, was there anything else you wanted to say to us?"

"Just that I didn't know! I should have been given a chance to help him! No one told me! No one gave me a chance!"

Austin and Jeremy quickly turned and left the classroom, leaving the Italian teacher still bemoaning the unfairness of her ignorance.

They passed a group of twelve parents led by Marla Schaeffer and Jillian Harrison. The team had marched down to the high school and demanded a meeting with the principal. They were sitting in the principal's office now, and their questions were numerous. They had no intentions of leaving without some answers. Italy would no longer be the only country where parents banded together to oppose bullying.

"What happened?"

"Why was the main bully removed from the classroom the week before Daniel's death and sent to your office for discipline but was allowed to go right back in the next day? This is clearly against your zero-tolerance policy, which calls for expulsion."

"Why were the bully's parents notified of the incident the week before but the victim's parents were never told? Do you think it might have been helpful if Daniel's parents had known he had been bullied?"

"Why have Daniel's bullies still not been expelled?"

"What disciplinary measures have been taken, if any, against the bullies?"

The principal put up his hands in a defensive motion. "I can't answer your questions. It will violate the bullies' privacy. I have to protect them. They're minors."

The questions continued.

"Why wasn't Daniel protected? He was a minor too."

"What is going to be done about this?"

"We want a school-wide anti-bullying assembly."

The principal looked pale. "I'm concerned that assemblies aren't always effective. Many kids don't pay attention," he replied weakly.

"We want a school-wide survey on bullying undertaken immediately."

"I'm afraid budget constraints won't allow that." The principal rubbed his forehead.

"The kids want to begin an anti-bullying club at the school. Will the administration support this?"

"I'm not sure," he shrugged his shoulders.

The team of parents wanted change. They wanted to know that what happened to Daniel would not happen to another child. They all agreed that bullying and the school's policies to prevent it needed to be addressed quickly. They were prepared with recommendations. They suggested training for teachers to recognize bullying and requirements for teachers to take measures when it was discovered; parental notification to both bully's parents as well as the target's parents whenever altercations were observed; and severe consequences for students who participated in bullying as well as teachers who turned a blind eye. The parents had done their homework.

The principal was overwhelmed. He promised to consider the recommendations and follow up.

The determined group of parents walked to their cars with their notebooks in hand, when Jillian and Marla spotted a teacher they were particularly fond of standing nearby. They both waved to Mrs. Campbell, a conscientious, hard-working woman. As they approached, the teacher nervously signaled for them to follow her and ducked behind a wall.

"We aren't allowed to talk to you." Her eyes darted in all directions. "They're threatening us with our jobs if we do. But we're all *very* concerned about what happened. Bullying is a problem that isn't being addressed." There was emotion in her voice as she whispered forcefully. "We've heard there was another attempted suicide just yesterday but they won't tell us anything. I want you to know that many of the teachers are supporting you. God bless your efforts." Mrs. Campbell looked nervously from side to side as she hurried away.

The principal sat alone after the parents had left his office. He had always felt so much in control. Always knew what to do. Up until this point in his career, his job had seemed so predictable, easy to perform. He felt a sudden jolt of anger. He was just a principal, for christ's sakes. He spoke at assemblies, signed off on performance reviews, and attended football games.

How was he to know that children's lives hung in the balance of his responsibilities?

Janet Dorsey, a local author who had been among the group of concerned parents, doubled back to the office and had quietly re-entered.

"Do you need to talk?" she asked softly. The principal looked up, but he was looking past her, as if in a trance.

"All the parents are asking for is that the district make needed changes," continued Janet. "That's all. The best thing you can do right now is become proactive in the measures against bullying. Legally, proactive measures you take after the death can't be held against you. You'll be protected. Convince the school board. You don't have to admit fault. All the parents want is change. It will be the best route you can take for the school and for the kids."

The principal stared blankly. "A child died under my care," he broke into tears. "A child died." The tragedy was sparing no one.

The following week, an article appeared in the local newspapers. The principal was quoted, "This death reveals that bullying does occur on this campus, and we can be more proactive about it."

Within hours of the story's release, school board officials were contacting the principal, and their warning was explicit. No more statements of that nature or his job was on the line. No more meetings with parents. No more discussion about bullying of any kind. The lawyers were moving in, and things were about to go from bad to worse.

Parents were incensed by what they saw happening. The school officials had shut down. Several parents contacted the Mendezes and pleaded with them to file a civil suit against the school district. Because of the district's refusal to address the problem, parents were convinced that there was no other way for positive change of any kind to take place.

"Schools are a business venture," explained one of Anna and Danny's friends who was the superintendent of an out-of-state

THE DANIEL MENDEZ STORY

school district. "Our decisions are measured by risk and return. Typically, the bullies' parents threaten legal action when any remedial action is suggested against their kids. However, because of the difficulty of the burden of proof and their fragile state of mind, the victims' families historically almost never sue. So the schools are more concerned with the rights of the bullies than they are the victim's rights. That's just the way the dollars work out."

The dollars. What about our kids? thought Anna. Although she desperately wanted to do all she could to change the broken system, she was hesitant about filing any kind of lawsuit.

"The last thing I want is to enter into a complex legal battle. I just don't have the strength. Why can't the school just do the right thing and begin implementing change?" She sat on her bed, rubbing the back of her neck.

There is something very wrong with this system, thought Danny. *But the kids need to be protected.* He knew Daniel would have wanted it that way.

———— •◦• ————

On top of the excruciating grief of losing her only son, Anna realized she was coming down with a bad cold and that she had most likely caught it from Daniel. Odd, but the cold was a welcome connection to her son—something still alive, albeit a virus. At this point, she would take anything. She remembered a few nights before her son died, they had just finished dinner when Daniel said, "Mom, I think I still have my cough from Park City."

Aiden and Victoria's friend, Cathy had joined Daniel and Victoria on that trip. It had been Aiden's first time snowboarding. The thought of riding a board on snow and ice was a little intimidating to him, but Daniel was a patient and determined teacher, and at the end of the trip, Aiden was able to come down the double blues with his friend.

Aiden and Daniel had spent countless sun-filled hours on the powdery, white slopes of Park City. They had fallen, rolled down hills, thrown snowballs at each other, kept count of who had the most bruises, and had barbeque rib-eating contests until they thought they would burst. On the last day of the trip, Aiden got a call from home that his new baby sister had been born. Aiden's parents had texted a picture of the beautiful newborn baby. Daniel had smiled and patted Aiden on the back.

"Welcome to my world, dude." Daniel had mischievously pointed his thumb at Victoria.

With all the snowball fighting and snowboarding, Daniel had ended up with a cold by the end of the trip.

"Do you think my lungs are congested?" Daniel had asked his mother.

"Let me listen." Anna had put her arm around her son's back and noticed that he seemed taller to her. *He's growing so fast*, she thought. Daniel's next sneeze took them both by surprise, and he accidently sneezed all over his mom.

"Oh sorry, Mom! Sorry!" He had muffled his laughter, trying not to be rude that he found it funny as he wiped his nose.

She had put her ear to her son's chest. She could hear his heart beat, and with her arm around him, she was taken by how perfect the moment was. *Let me enjoy this moment*, she thought to herself. She wished she could stay there forever with her arms around him just listening to his heart beat. Mozart couldn't have composed anything more beautiful than the rhythm she was listening to, the beating of her only son's heart.

"Uh, Mom, do you hear anything?" Daniel had asked impatiently.

"No, I think you're fine." Anna had reluctantly let go of her son.

"Okay. But if I still have my cough when you get back from Palm Springs, will you take me to the doctor?"

Anna snapped back to the present. There was a strange, sad comfort she felt as she remembered her son's words.

She wondered how everything had come to this. Only a few weeks before he had been worried about a cough, and now he was gone. She recalled how he had sobbed when he told them about the frightening thoughts of ending his life, how those thoughts had terrified him, how relieved he was that the doctor said it wouldn't happen again. She wondered how it was that people could claim someone makes the *choice* to end their life. She knew that her son had not *made* that decision. If he had decided to no longer live, he wouldn't have been concerned with congested lungs. He wouldn't have had his alarm set the morning after he died so he would be on time for his PSAT practice exam. He wouldn't have been excited for the check for his summer trip to Washington, DC. She started to think that perhaps people didn't fully grasp the dynamics of suicide just yet. She certainly didn't.

⸻

She opened her eyes to the sound of her cell phone ringing. She must have dozed off. She couldn't sleep at night anymore. Her body was exhausted, but her mind and her heart would not allow her to rest. She noticed it was her office calling and answered.

"Anna, it's Jeannie. How are you doing? We're all thinking of you."

Anna was glad to be talking with their VP of Human Resources. She had some questions for her.

"Jeannie, I don't think I can come back to work. I don't think I can function. At least not like I used to. I'm wondering about filing for disability. I know executives have a separate disability policy that the company provides for us in our benefits package. Can you give me some information about it?"

"I can. But why don't you think about it before you take that path. It's only been a few weeks, and you may feel differently later."

"I don't think so, Jeannie. I can't eat. I can't sleep. I can barely pull myself out of bed to take care of my daughter. And she needs me desperately right now. She's my highest priority."

"Of course she is, and that's the way it should be. But in a few weeks, you may want to busy yourself with work again. It may be a useful distraction for you. We know you won't be able to hit the ground running again and operate at the same level. We don't expect that. So much is happening here in your absence that we really need you to be a part of. We miss your participation greatly. All of us do, Dean, Harold, and you know your direct reports are lost without you. We all would love to see you back. Can you promise me you'll think about it?"

Anna agreed to give the disability claim more thought and hung up. But how could she function? Her son was gone. He was forever gone, and there was no one in the world she could appeal to, no one that could possibly change it, no matter how convincing or persuasive she made her case. This was permanent. Irreversible. A fact she would have to live with for the rest of her life. How was a mother expected to survive each day without her son, let alone function in a stressful corporate environment under those circumstances?

She looked up to find her husband's concerned eyes on her.

"I overheard the conversation," Danny began. "It's nice of them to be so supportive of you at a tragic time like this. It sounds like they really want you back."

"But, Danny, I'm just not sure. If I claim on the company's long-term disability policy, it'll keep us going financially until I can think clearly again, and I don't know how long that'll be. I know Jeannie said they understand that I can't go back to the same level of performance right away and that they don't care, but that's a really difficult environment to function in for anyone, let alone someone in my emotional state. I'm really worried."

"You'll make the right decision."

"I'm concerned that if I file a claim on the long-term disability policy, it'll reflect poorly on me at the office. I'm basically telling my bosses, and the rest of the world, that I can't function. And the company will hate it because it'll be expensive for them.

No, they don't want me to file on the company disability policy. I know they don't. It'll definitely be frowned upon. That's one reason why Jeannie's trying so hard to convince me to go back."

Danny rubbed his wife's shoulders. "You need to think about yourself right now, not what they want. Still, Jeannie sounded sincere, like they'll work with you if you decide to go back. It may be something to consider."

CHAPTER
TWENTY-FIVE

Peace if possible. Truth at all costs.

— Dr. Martin Luther King Jr.

It was weeks after Daniel's death, and the student body at the high school was traumatized. They wanted answers, and the administration was providing none. They organized a unified outcry of protest. Kids began rallying in front of the administration office, demanding to know what actions would be taken as a result of Daniel's death. They weren't going to let the bullying death be swept under the rug.

The principal had no choice but to finally agree to meet with a group of the students. Among them were Aiden Kai and Jeff Schaeffer. Jeff was a smart, sensitive kid who had known Daniel since elementary school. They had been in scouts together and spent many hours camping, talking, and just having fun. Since his friend's passing, Jeff had been agonizing over thoughts of life and death. He had been at home that day, finishing up homework, when he had received the phone call from Aiden. The phone had fallen from his hands as his entire body had frozen up in blinding torment and confusion. Why? He didn't get why his friend had to die. Daniel was kind and shy, just like he was. They shared a lot of the same qualities actually. It could so easily have been him to have been targeted by the bullies. Try as he may, Jeff couldn't figure out why Daniel died but he was still alive. What did it all mean?

"I know you're mourning your friend's loss, and I understand that you're upset with Sal Gutierrez. But Sal's not a bad kid. He

199

once saved his uncle's life. He deserves a break," the principal said to the kids from behind his large oak desk littered with papers and planners.

"What does saving your uncle's life have to do with bullying another kid?" asked Aiden from his seat opposite the principal's.

"I'm just saying that there may have been teasing going on, but…"

"Excuse me, sir," interrupted Jeff. It was out of character for him but he couldn't help but challenge this authority figure. "But with all due respect, Daniel and our group teased each other all the time, and all of us laughed, including Daniel. Just the day before, we had all been having a food fight at the lunch tables and laughing and joking. But when someone is not laughing back, that can't be called teasing. And that's what happened to Daniel."

And there it was. Jeff Schaeffer had unknowingly come up with a definition of bullying that had eluded politicians, legislators, school officials, and scholars for years. That still eluded them. While the adult world continued to debate how to define bullying, how often the incidents should occur, should intent of the perpetrator be considered, should it include only physical acts, etc. etc., this unassuming teenager had succinctly defined it for them in a matter of moments. When someone is not laughing back.

These kids are sharp, thought the principal. *And they're not letting this die. Maybe they'll lose interest and the whole thing will eventually go away. Yes, that's my plan*, he thought.

———◆•◆———

Aiden was sitting alone at the lunch table where he and Daniel had sat talking and laughing a thousand times before. A counselor had been going from classroom to classroom addressing the recent suicide. He had appeared at two of Aiden's classes that day. He had started his speech out the same both times.

"We cannot confirm that bullying was a factor in Daniel's death." Each time, the classroom of kids had rolled their eyes. The kids knew. There was no denying what they had seen. A counselor telling them to ignore what they had witnessed for years was just making matters worse. Austin had caught up with Aiden earlier in the day.

"Dude, do they think we're idiots? They think they can just state that 'they cannot confirm' and we'll buy it? Who gives a crap if they can't confirm it? They never handled it to begin with."

Aiden had just nodded to his friend.

He was remembering all the good times he and Daniel had had over the years. His mind went back to the day he had climbed up the slope of Daniel's backyard and how Daniel helped him up that terrible last part, physically and mentally. "Don't give up. Just trust me. Hang on a little longer. I'll help you."

I listened to your advice, Aiden thought as he blinked back tears that he'd been holding back for too long. *I grabbed your hand and made it to the top. Why couldn't you listen to me? Why couldn't you grab my hand—hang on just a little longer?*

He sat with his head bowed so no one would see the tears, the searing pain of his memories immobilizing him until something caught his attention out of the corner of his eye. It was Sal Gutierrez, and he was slapping a girl. They were in the bleachers. Aiden watched the bully lift his hand up and then send it right into the girl's left cheek. He shook his head in disbelief, got up, and sprinted over to the principal's office. He wasn't in.

"I have to report an incident," Aiden panted, out of breath from running the entire way. The sympathetic office assistant pushed a piece of paper toward him, and Aiden's hand shook from anger as he quickly wrote out what he had seen. Nothing was changing. Not only had the bully not been expelled, but he was out playing Ike Turner without a single person blinking an eye. Aiden left the written complaint, and just as he turned to leave, he saw the principal coming in. Aiden asked to speak to him.

"Sorry, Son. Really busy." The principal kept walking, but Aiden wouldn't let him off so easily. He followed along, his words keeping pace with his footsteps.

"Why is Sal still on campus? What's being done to enforce the no-bullying rules? Why is Daniel's chair in the classroom empty while the bullies are out slapping people around and doing the exact same stuff to other kids that caused my best friend to kill himself?"

The principal finally stopped and turned to make direct eye contact with the boy. "Aiden, I said I'm really busy. I have no time for this right now. If you want to make an appointment with me, you'll have to come back later."

"I just saw Sal Gutierrez slapping a girl. What are you going to do about it?"

"Did anyone else see it? Are you sure they're not just joking around? I need to run, Son. I have an important call to take." The principal ducked into his office and shut the door.

Aiden was becoming more and more impatient. He looked at the clock. It was time for his science class. He figured that he had better just keep going through the motions. He turned and left the office, making his way to science, Daniel's favorite subject, but they had never been lucky enough to be in the same science class together.

Aiden entered the class and took his seat. *I just want to get this day over with*, he thought. *I can't handle any more crap today.* Aiden sat down and forced his mind to focus when the teacher's words began to sink in. He had to be hearing things. This could not be real. The teacher had begun to give her own editorial on what her opinion was of the tragedy that had affected their campus.

Mrs. Johnson was a science teacher but also the coach of the high school rugby team and a rumored romantic interest of the principal's. The high school rugby team had several winning seasons, and she felt a particular sense of pride for that. She also believed it made her untouchable, and it was obvious in the way she conducted herself on and off school grounds. Some parents had complained that she would conduct herself inappropriately when out with the rugby kids at tournaments, getting intoxicated and driving the kids back to the hotels in an unfit condition.

"That kid wasn't being bullied," she announced in her usual cavalier manner. "Don't believe it. That kid had problems. They're just after money if they think they're going to sue."

Aiden's pulse skyrocketed, and his face burned hot. Enough was enough. He stood up, heart pounding in his throat. "That's not true. He was bullied to death! I lived through it with him. You take that back!"

But Mrs. Johnson didn't take it back. "I guess you didn't know your best friend very well then." She was goading Aiden now.

"I knew him better than you. You never even had him as a student. How can you say those things about someone you never knew? He was bullied to death! I lived it!" Aiden was shouting now. He was outraged. *How dare this moron sit and talk about Daniel that way? She didn't even know him.*

"We took care of the bullies. Why doesn't everyone just leave us alone?"

"The bullies have not been dealt with." Aiden was shaking. "I sit and watch them do the same thing they've always done every day while my friend's seat is empty! My friend's *only* issue was the bullying, bullying that you people ignored, and the fact that you would now talk crap about him after he's dead in a class full of people is just plain wrong!"

Other kids in the class who had known Daniel shook their heads in amazement. They looked at Aiden to see what he would do next. Aiden walked out of the classroom and directly back to the principal's office where he had left just minutes before. The principal was no longer in his office, so Aiden filed yet another written complaint. He was going to try as hard as he could to work within the system. He handed the complaint to the office assistant who looked at him with pity in her eyes.

———◦•◦———

Several days had passed with no word for him so Aiden decided he'd had enough waiting. He noticed the principal walking down the hall and cornered him.

"What are you going to do about Mrs. Johnson? She shouldn't be making irresponsible statements like that. It's not right."

"Sorry, Son. I'm really busy." The principal dodged into a back room. He was getting good at that.

More parents began to hear about the statements Mrs. Johnson had made about Daniel in her class, and calls began pouring in to the parents from people offering their support.

"There's nothing you can do," Danny and Anna were told by the parents, some of whom they had never met before.

"She has a lot of pull at the school. She has a very close relationship with the principal. And because the rugby team is doing so well, she'll be protected to the end. She's in very tight with the principal. He's smitten by her. She does what she wants and gets away with it every time. She denigrates her student athletes, belittling them at the games and in public. Many people say she's a bully herself. That's why she has no empathy for your family. You should get an attorney to file a restraining order against her."

Aiden wasn't the only one having a rough time with the administration. Daniel's good friend Sean Harrison was also finding the status quo to be unacceptable. Sean had been the first one to find his friend lying in the street that day. At first, he hadn't recognized him. He had run back into his house and told his older brother he thought they were being punked. When the two boys came back out, they saw a neighbor kneeling over someone and the man had yelled out that he had just called 911. Michael grabbed Sean and pulled him back into the house. They had been worried sick for what seemed like forever. They still didn't know who the boy was, hoping against hope that it wasn't someone they knew, wasn't one of their friends. They had stood motionless, faces pressed against the window of their game room, looking out at the horror that was unfolding in front of their house, the police cars, the ambulances, the covered body, while their mother had rushed home from work to be with them. When Sean had heard his mother utter the words, his friend's name and the word 'dead' in the same phrase, he felt in that single shock of a moment like something inside him had exploded and died. He had collapsed to the floor while Michael had slumped back in a chair, hands over his face, both boys struggling hard against the tidal wave of pain and confusion that had just engulfed them.

Sean always wondered if he could have made a difference that day, if only he had come outside just a few minutes earlier. If Daniel had seen him and would have remembered how much he was cared about, how much fun they would have later. Daniel had been coming to be with them at that moment. Had he been hoping that their company would comfort him? Snap him out of the darkness that had consumed him? He was only steps away from their home before he died. He had almost made it. Maybe, just maybe things could have been different but for a few seconds.

Sean was still attempting to deal with his own personal pain as he tried to make sense of this system that the adults seemed to be making such a mess of. He sat in science class now and noticed a guy named Jordan, an unassuming kid who never said a lot, being harassed by several rowdy boys. The unruly little group had a history of being aggressive and had chosen their new-est victim. Jordan got up out of his seat and walked up to Mrs. Johnson's desk.

"Can I move to another desk? These guys are really bothering me, and I can't focus on my work."

Good for you, thought Sean. Maybe things will start to change. But he was stunned by Johnson's reply.

"You don't need to move. You're fine where you are." The teacher casually dismissed the quiet kid and went back to her books. Sean, who was a quiet kid himself but also someone who wasn't afraid to take a stand against injustice, wasn't about to let this one go. He was going to make sure his friend's death hadn't been in vain, even if the administrators were refusing to learn anything from it. He got up out of his seat and approached Mrs. Johnson's desk. He stood quietly, not speaking a word, until the teacher looked up slowly.

"With all due respect, Mrs. Johnson, Jordan said he needs to move. If he said he needs to move, then he needs to move. Move him. Now."

Mrs. Johnson was taken aback. This kid had obviously lost his mind talking to her that way. Didn't he know who she was? Her record with the rugby team? The pull she had at this school? Sean stood determined. He knew he was right. The whole class was watching now. The teacher didn't budge. Finally, Sean turned to Jordan and motioned to him, "Dude, switch seats with me." He walked quietly back to Jordan's seat while Jordan took his. Sean sat down between the rowdy bullies, as they continued on with their antics. *Man,* he thought, *they just don't get it.*

The bell rang, and Sean was on his way out the door when Mrs. Johnson called him back. "Sean, can I have a word with you?"

Sean approached her desk with reluctant resignation, like someone having to take out a trash can that had remained unemptied far too long. The teacher leaned forward with one hand planted firmly on her desk.

"Don't ever pull that crap with me again. Do we understand each other?" Johnson's eyes narrowed beneath her wrinkled brow.

"He needed help and—"

"Do we understand each other?"

He did not take his eyes off of hers. His face showed no surprise, no anger, no astonishment at her words. He would not grant her the satisfaction of a reaction. He looked as though he had given up hope of any reason or understanding from certain school administrators long ago. After a period of silence, he spoke.

"No. I don't understand you," Sean said with an innocent sincerity. "But whatever." And he walked out of the room.

———— ••◦•• ————

Marla and Jillian sat with the Mendezes in their dining room with a pile of letters on the dining room table. Daniel's English teacher had accumulated letters written by Daniel's classmates in his memory and had sent them to the family. Anna had been reading the heartfelt letters written by kids still racked with pain.

"He was a great kid. Always so helpful and kind. I will never forget him."

"I remember most his kind smile. He never had a bad word to say about anyone. I will always be affected by his death."

The letters had become a source of comfort for the mother during her darkest moments of grief.

"It was kind of his English teacher to do this," Anna began. "I remember she told me how Daniel was one of her favorites. I hope one day I can let her know how comforting her thoughtfulness has been to us."

The pasta and salmon were growing cold. No one had an appetite. Marla kept her eyes down and spoke quietly as she carefully chose her words. "The way the district is handling this is an atrocity. Nothing is changing. We're embarrassed for our community and so very concerned. We're all hoping you'll consider filing a lawsuit against the district and the bullies."

Anna lifted her face and her eyes met her friends' eyes.

"Marla, believe me, we know how unjust it all is. But the very last thing our son would have wanted is to be remembered as a bullied victim, a weakling. That's why he didn't speak up about it more than he did when he was alive. He was ashamed of it. If we go public with this, I feel like we're dishonoring his last wishes. His legacy will be that of a bullied victim. That's all anyone will remember of him. How can I possibly do that to him?"

Marla listened sympathetically as Anna continued.

"And we don't know that we're strong enough for a lawsuit right now. We've spoken to other parents who lost children to bullying, and those who filed lawsuits against the schools all said that it was the most difficult process of their lives. They said the district will viciously attack our family and friends in their attempt to fend off any responsibility."

"And you'll have an army of parents right behind you," Marla assured Anna. She gripped her friend's hands tightly as she continued.

"We understand your fears about the stress, the accusations, the ugliness that a lawsuit may bring with no promise that justice will prevail. But we know that there is more healing in building up rather than tearing down. We know Daniel bore a cross that he did not deserve. We also know that he bore a cross that will help save lives. And because Daniel was so loved, so kind, so beautiful in his soul, God will be able to use his life in a mighty way. Please just think about it."

The tired parents promised to sleep on it. The next morning, when their mail was delivered, they were surprised to find a letter from the school. Anna opened it. The letter began, "We wish to express our condolences for the loss of your son. We know José had a lot of friends…"

She couldn't finish reading. She cast the letter down and turned to her husband, choking back tears. "They couldn't even get his name right. He's gone forever, and they couldn't take the time to get his name right. He was a human being. He laughed. He loved. He had dreams. They didn't care. He was that insignificant to them, in life and in death. They stole his soul, and they still don't know who he is."

With the administration's unwillingness to meet the issue head on and pleas from their friends and concerned parents in the community, Danny and Anna finally realized they had no choice but to begin the arduous process of finding legal representation.

CHAPTER
TWENTY-SIX

You are a human being. You have rights inherent in that
reality. You have dignity and worth that exists prior to law.

—Lyn Beth Neylon

Several law firms shied away from a bullying lawsuit of any
nature. One attorney explained it would be too difficult to
prove causation.

"Psychiatric injury, unlike physical injury, is very difficult to
prove after a death. Even prior to a child's death, it's difficult to
prove that years of verbal and physical bullying resulted in psychiatric injury to him. But now that he's gone, it's too late. All the
coroner has is a body with cuts and bruises."

Another attorney agreed with the futility of the action.

"The school district will dig for any dirt they can possibly find
within the family to blame you for the suicide. At best, even if
there is proof of bullying and proof that the school failed to do
anything about it, negative issues of any kind within the family
will be enough to convince a jury that the bullying was only a
contributing factor to your son's death. They'll turn the issue on
its head, point to the emotional weaknesses your son developed
as a result of the bullying, and blame those very weaknesses for
his death. They'll claim that the weaknesses were a result of a
mental illness, not the consequences of psychiatric injury that
results after long-term bullying. They'll drag your family through
the mud to make their point because they know that you'll still
be fresh in your grieving process and that in the long run it will
just be too much for you to bear."

Some attorneys suggested they would be more interested in the case if they sued the therapists.

"Suing the therapists will be an easier case to win. All you have to prove is that they were incompetent and missed the signs of suicide—only one benchmark to meet. And the therapists will have professional liability insurance to attach. But to sue the school, you'll have three benchmarks to meet. You have to prove that your son was bullied, that the school knew about the bullying, and that the school did not do enough to prevent the bullying. So the bullies may be found liable, but the school could still get off. And the underage bullies won't have much in terms of attachable assets."

"No," Anna was firm. "While there's much that the therapists missed and the psychiatric community needs to change, his doctors cared about him and wanted to help. Whatever they did, they did with the best of intentions. That isn't the case with the bullies and the school system. It doesn't matter that suing the therapists will be an easier case to win. This isn't about money. It's about changing paradigms. And the biggest area of change needed is within the school system. That's who I entrusted the care of my child to every day. Let them try to find mud. They won't find any."

One attorney, after hearing the specific facts of the case, did not agree with the others. His name was Tom Dunn, and he had children of his own, so he had a personal interest in seeing justice done. He felt that due to the specific actions by the school along with the actions of the bullies beginning years before and then just hours before Daniel's death, there was enough there to link the school's actions, or lack thereof, to the death.

Danny and Anna were instructed to ask for copies of Daniel's therapists' notes. Anna contacted each of the three medical offices. The first two said it would take at least two to three weeks before they could get the notes sent out. When the third doctor gave Anna the same response, she had to ask, "Why on earth does it take so long? I just need someone to go in to the file and make a copy. We can come pick up the notes ourselves, if that's easier."

"Oh, it doesn't work that way," the last doctor explained. "The notes have to be reviewed by our risk management department before they can be released."

"What does that mean?" Anna turned to her husband, perplexed. "What if their 'risk management department' determines there's too much *risk* in releasing the notes as they're written? Are they going to change the notes to protect themselves from liability? How can they legally do that?"

Danny shook his head.

Upon receiving a call from the cognitive behavior doctor that his notes were ready to be released, the parents scheduled a visit.

Anna sat in the doctor's cluttered office, looking around. She sat in the very chair her son had sat in when he so desperately wanted to save himself. She scanned the notes she had been handed and noticed something missing.

"Doctor, do you recall when I spoke to you about his merciless bullying experiences in middle school? It's even written here in my handwriting at the initial intake notes you asked us to complete at our first meeting."

"Yes, I do remember," replied the doctor. "And I remember that Daniel himself told me that he had been bullied."

"Thank you. It's not written in any of your notes that you took documenting your sessions with him." She was relieved that the doctor was admitting to the recollection of the bullying conversations, both with the parents and with their son.

"Can you give us something in writing that states what you just expressed?"

"Yes, I'll send you notes of this meeting with my statements in it," replied the doctor.

Anna's eyes were still fixed on the doctor's notes. She noticed a message that Daniel had written to his doctor.

I know you don't like rap music, but I feel a need to express myself through music. I feel like it's me speaking in those songs and that it's me expressing how I feel. Like Tupac said, I need changes, but I don't see any, though I've been working at it. Here are some of the biggest songs I listen to. You don't need to listen to the entire ones, but if you could just listen to some parts I think it would help you understand more. Listening to the entire part of "Changes" might help.

Thanks. Dan.

She scanned further and her eyes landed on another message,

I am trying to remember what you told me. It just seems so hard right now. I'm trying to get better, but things haven't changed that much. There are still the everyday struggles I go through like saying the wrong things to people, etc. High school is a war zone—kill or be killed. Make fun of someone or get made fun of. I'm still trying to cope with not allowing other people to get to me. People talk crap to me because they know they can and they know I won't do anything about it. I would if I could but I can't. I look forward to coming in on Saturday. Thanks. Dan.

Anna and Danny shut the file folder and got up to leave.

"I'm so sorry," the doctor continued. "He showed no signs of suicidal risk."

He hugged the parents on their way out.

———◆———

Tom Dunn reviewed the therapist records.

"You realize these will all be subpoenaed," he said calmly to the parents.

"Tom, I feel like I'm invading my son's final right to privacy." Anna was torn. "Hasn't the world violated him enough? He made those statements to his private doctor firmly believing that

THE DANIEL MENDEZ STORY

they would be kept confidential. Now we'll be releasing them to the courts. To the bullies and their hostile attorneys. It's just not right."

"What's really good here is that the medical records don't show any kind of serious problem within the family or any other area of his life," Dunn continued. "Usually, significant family issues can be uncovered, like alcoholism, drug abuse, marital or financial problems, sexual identity issues, anything that the kids tell their doctors about that the defense can grab onto and point fingers at. There's nothing like that in here at all. For the most part, you can tell he's just tortured by the low self-esteem, and he mentions several times that he's being harassed and that he hates school. This is good."

"Tom, they'll have a field day with Daniel's e-mail to his therapist."

"Oh, you can bet they will," Tom agreed. "But it doesn't take a Ph.D. to see that it was his low self-esteem that was talking. Self-esteem that was torn away by the harassment and abuse he was suffering. He says it in numerous places."

Tom Dunn began his due diligence by questioning some of the other boys that had been in Daniel's circle. Several had witnessed the bullying and wanted to help. Others had witnessed the bullying but were concerned about the repercussions if they spoke up. One boy that had been one of the last to see Daniel alive had initially offered information and support to the Mendezes. The entrance essay he had written for the university he was hoping to attend had been about Daniel's death, how it had changed his life forever, and how the bullying and his lack of action would haunt him always. But he had become legitimately concerned that his teachers would refuse, or be forced to refuse, to give him the recommendations he needed if he agreed to speak up for the prosecution. He spoke to the parents with sorrow in his voice.

"My mom says we just can't afford being involved. I'm really sorry."

"We understand." Anna was saddened that it had come to this.

But other kids did speak up. They had a need to be heard, to get the real story out, and to see justice done, regardless of the political ramifications.

"I know exactly how Daniel felt. I was also targeted by Phil Jensen in middle school. And I also thought about taking my own life. Several times. Thank God the kid finally left me alone. I wish he could have just laid off Daniel," one boy told Tom Dunn.

The lawsuit was filed against the school district as well as four individual students.

"Tom, we need copies of any prior bullying complaints the school has received about the kids who harassed our son. In fact, we need copies of all bullying complaints they received and documentation showing how they've handled the complaints to date."

"We won't get that." Tom shrugged. "The bullies are protected. They're minors, and they have an even stronger right to privacy than adults do. That's just the way our system works."

———————

Anna sat in the formal conference room. Her face was expressionless. Being back at work after her son's death was surreal. Life had now taken on a whole new meaning. Why didn't these people understand that there was more to life than business plans and corporate profits? Did it take a child's death to teach us that? She looked around at the anxious faces of the participants. Dean Hathaway had called the unscheduled meeting and no one knew why. The executives, all armed with their binders of information, were eager to impress, dodge bullets, or avoid getting hit by shrapnel, whatever was required, and the situation could change quickly at a moment's notice. They had to be prepared. Anna's mind was numb. Her heart was heavy. Her entire being felt weighed down, as though she was wearing a coat of armor that weighed a ton. Daniel was gone. Her sweet child was no longer on this earth. She was not focusing on the conversation around her.

"It seems to me…"

"What happened…"

"Whose responsibility was it…"

"What was represented…"

As she forced her mind to focus, she realized they were speaking about a contract within her scope of authority that had been executed while she was on bereavement leave. A contract executed with a government agency that was turning out not to be in the best interest of the organization. In fact, it was costing them money on a regular basis. Dean was angry.

"Anna, can we fulfill the terms of the contract?" Dean was asking.

"We can but very inefficiently. And it applies to all of the loans in our portfolio." Anna's response was matter of fact.

Dean rubbed his eyes and leaned his face up toward the ceiling. The senior managers nervously watched. That was what he did when he was really angry.

"Anna, can you please tell me why we would ever consider signing such a contract?" Dean pressed on.

Anna realized that Dean thought she had signed it. While she had been on leave, Christy, her subordinate, had recommended the contract be signed and their new boss, Harold, had complied. According to a new corporate policy, only senior vice presidents could execute contracts. Anyone else only had authority to recommend or co-sign.

"I'm not sure. I wouldn't have signed it." Anna didn't want to hang her new boss, especially not in a public forum, but Dean was being very direct.

"Who signed it?" Dean looked directly at Anna. The executives in the room held their breath. Most were grateful it was not they that were involved in the drama unfolding. Harold shifted in his seat uncomfortably. He remembered he had signed it. It had seemed harmless enough. Christy had recommended it, so he had signed it alongside her recommendation. He hadn't really been able to follow her rationale with all of the particulars because this business was very new to him but it had seemed reasonable enough.

Harold remained silent, waiting for Anna's response.

"Christy signed it." Anna's reply was almost inaudible.

"Ha! Someone who's not even authorized by the organization to sign contracts! The contract is meaningless! Tell the agency we do not intend to uphold it!"

Harold looked at Anna. Was she going to drop him in the grease, in front of everyone to boot? She remained silent. Once the meeting had ended and the managers had all scurried back to their individual offices, Anna followed Dean into his.

"Dean, I can't debate the validity of the contract with the agency. It was also signed by one of our senior vice presidents. Harold signed it."

Dean pounded his hand on the table.

"Thanks," he muttered. His voice was low with anger. Anna turned and left. Finally, she could get home to her family.

CHAPTER
TWENTY-SEVEN

Peace has its victories but it takes brave men and women
to win them.

—Ralph Waldo Emerson

The SV high school students decided change was needed at their
school. They could not allow what had happened to their friend
to get swept under the rug. Aiden, Michael, and Jeff were huddled together talking. With them was Lisa Hydes, a beautiful,
petite blonde who had known Daniel from elementary school.

"We need to do something." Aiden was adamant. "This can't
just end here like this. It's not right. We need to take action.
Do something."

"Look, if the school doesn't have an anti-bullying program in
place, we can create one ourselves. We can start an anti-bullying
club in Daniel's honor," Lisa suggested.

"Yeah, just what I was thinking. We can do it. We can't just let
them act like nothing happened," Jeff added. "For something like
this to happen to someone as good as Daniel has to shock us all
into action."

"We can call it 'Cool To Be Kind.'" Lisa liked where the conversation was taking them. "The point of the whole thing will
be that it isn't cool to be a bully. Our message will be that being
decent is what makes you cool. It'll be perfect because it would
be like peer pressure, but in a good way, like peer influence. It can
be a place not just to start promoting kindness but also a place for
kids being bullied to come and talk and get support from other
kids. We'll give other kids something Daniel didn't have, a safe

place to talk to other people about what's going on and to get support when they really need it."

Their words became quick and excited. Ideas were pouring out. For the first time since Daniel's death, there was something to feel good about. After they figured out a general plan of what they were going to do, they petitioned the school administration to begin an anti-bullying club in Daniel's memory. They were kids with a cause now, and nothing was going to stop them.

At first, they were met with bureaucratic resistance and red tape. The principal couldn't support them. There was too much to lose. He couldn't put his career on the line. To stand behind a club that was in memory of a student who had been pushed to suicide by bullying was basically admitting that the school had failed somewhere, he thought to himself. He had worked too hard to get where he was, for his retirement fund, to risk everything so that these kids could start a club. Besides, they didn't need another kindness club. They already had Character Counts and Hug A Tree. So what did they need an anti-bullying club for? He reluctantly told them it was a no go. But the kids refused to be dissuaded.

They began searching out adults outside the school to help them get the ball rolling, anyone who would help. They petitioned their parents and the parents of their friends. People in the community came together to help the kids structure the club. Janet Dorsey became the club's adviser. She worked tirelessly with the kids, serving as their subject matter expert. Within a month of Daniel's death, the Cool To Be Kind club began planning its first event to raise awareness of bullying—a school dance.

Lisa came up with the idea to make T-shirts. "My mom is a graphic designer. She can help us. We can design them with the phrase 'I've got your back' written on the back of the shirts." The kids were officially getting the word out in a big way.

The administration would not hear of allowing a dance for the new club, but the kids wouldn't accept that answer either. Aiden decided he had to meet with the principal.

"This isn't a suggestion, sir." Aiden spoke authoritatively as he stood, leaning over the principal's desk, his hands planted firmly on its surface. "Consider it a bona-fide offer. If you don't allow us to have the dance on the school premises, we'll simply have it off the premises. And seeing as how the press has become very interested in the case, I might not be able to speak so kindly about the school in future press articles when I'm interviewed."

Aiden looked innocently at the principal and shrugged his shoulders. He was young, but he was already learning the power of negotiations. This boy, who just a few short weeks ago didn't have a care in the world, was definitely stepping up to the task.

With Aiden, Lisa, and the rest of the kids' persistence, the administration acquiesced, and the Cool To Be Kind leaders received permission to go forward with the dance. There were conditions, however. Nothing could be mentioned relative to the bullying that Daniel had experienced. But the kids had their own ideas.

It was the largest dance in the history of the school aside from the annual prom. The line to buy tickets wrapped around several buildings. Hundreds of students showed up to show their love and support, many wearing T-shirts with the new Cool To Be Kind logo on the front and "I've got your back" plastered across the back. The music blasted as kids filled the auditorium. This was definitely no small event, and it had been sparked by kids who refused to let a tragedy be hushed by politics and bureaucracy.

Without notice, the music stopped, and a video of Daniel's life that the kids had put together started playing while the lyrics of Daniel's favorite songs bounced off the walls. The very last slide read, "Daniel was a wonderful son and grandson, an accomplished athlete and scholar, a fun brother, and a trusted friend. He died as a result of bullying. Do not let his life be one lived in vain. Do something. Cool To Be Kind."

As the very last slide faded, the auditorium roared with cheers and applause. The lights came up again, and Lisa walked onto the stage with a quiet and determined grace. The audience hushed as they stared forward at the tiny girl with serious, blue eyes who stood before them.

"Thank you for joining us tonight in support of this very important cause. Daniel thanks you as well. He is smiling down on all of us from up above."

Again the crowd erupted in applause. The entire building seemed to shake with the thunderous reaction of the student body. Lisa waved graciously and exited the stage. The principal almost passed out. The music started again, and the dance was back in full swing. That night, the kids didn't dance to impress a crush or to mark the end of a school year. They danced to remember a kind boy who just wanted to live his life in peace; they danced for all the kids who were losing their lives because they were too kind; they danced to show they were bigger than bullying; and they danced to make a difference. The Cool To Be Kind kids knew they officially had people's attention.

Realizing that for every action there is generally an equal and opposite reaction, there had been some security concerns about the dance. There was a possibility that bullies might show up and start problems. Parents were concerned that there might not be enough security present. So the Hydes, the Schaeffers, the Harrisons, those who had been involved in the initial meeting with the principal as well as the parents of the Cool To Be Kind kids, pitched in their own time and money to be sure the dance was going to happen. They were also there in presence that night, working and monitoring the situation to make sure everything ran smoothly. They were taking back their community and helping their kids to heal.

In the end there was no trouble at all. It could not have gone smoother. If bullies had been present, they had hopefully been converted. The Cool To Be Kind kids had experienced their first success.

———◆•◆———

They say that time heals all wounds, but they unfortunately don't say how much time. Weeks turned into months and Daniel's friends continued to struggle emotionally. Their personal pain over the loss of such a good friend, a good person, was overwhelming, and even months after he was gone, they still couldn't make sense of everything that had happened. They had seen him only hours before he died. It happened so suddenly, so out of the blue. Just the day before Daniel's death, they had had a food fight during lunch. Daniel didn't do drugs, he didn't drink, he didn't do anything that the press said most kids do who take their own lives. They weren't the kind of kids who had friends who died young, not like Daniel did.

Nothing made sense. But as devastated as they were, they fought on. Instead of giving into the grief, they used it to create awareness. They turned their anger and confusion into fuel for Cool To Be Kind. It was their way of taking back their lives, of reasserting themselves, of refusing to remain victims.

The students were gathering in the classroom ready to begin another Cool To Be Kind meeting. The membership was growing, and they were excited. Aiden was about to call the meeting to order when he noticed Allen Carter was in the group. Aiden and Jeff spotted the bully at the same time and shot looks at one another from across the room. Neither had any idea what the troublemaker was doing there. He was one of the ringleaders of the bullying circus, one that Daniel had often complained about to his friends, and there he was sitting in a meeting that spoke out against bullying. Both boys were thrown off by his presence, and, although anger kicked up inside them at the sight of this kid, they hoped for the best and thought maybe he was remorseful and trying to make amends. After the meeting had ended, Allen walked up to the boys.

"Hey, guys. What's up? Wanna hang out after class?"

"What do you want, Allen?" Austin answered for the group. "Why are you here?"

"Hey, man, I just want you guys to know that I didn't do anything to that kid. I know that there's stuff going around about a lawsuit, and I just want you guys to know that I had nothing to do with the bullying. I mean, I was just in the wrong place at the wrong time, ya know? I mean, like, I threw him one of his touchdown passes. Daniel and me, we sorta had a bond because of that."

Yeah, a bond that bonded your hands to his arms as Sal unloaded on him the last day of his life, thought Jeff. This kid obviously wanted something. Was he scared that the boys would implicate him in the bullying charge? Did he think if he befriended them, they wouldn't flap their jaws to the Mendez attorneys?

For the next several months, Allen made it a point to stay very close to the Cool To Be Kind kids. Even though he was never a participating member of the club, never really contributed anything to the cause, he was always loitering around. The kid who used to help throw Daniel into trash cans was now high-fiving the Cool To Be Kind kids and asking them to hang out after school. Maybe he was changing, but the sudden change of heart seemed a little too coincidental to Daniel's friends. They couldn't help but be suspect.

Anna was carefully going through the boxes they had accumulated when they cleared out their son's room. *What do I do with it all,* she wondered. She picked up his wallet and looked inside. She pulled out a picture of the four of them, standing in the Medici Gardens from their trip to Florence. Nonna wasn't in the picture so she must have been the photographer. The picture was off center. His father was waving his arms with a frustrated look on his face, obviously instructing Nonna who knew nothing about cameras, and Daniel and Victoria were laughing hard. This was the picture he had chosen to carry with him. He always did love a good laugh. Her cell phone rang and brought her back to her new reality of life without her son. She picked it up to hear Austin's mother, Cindy Gomez, on the line.

"Austin told me that Allen Carter is trying to befriend them. I've heard he's afraid of what the boys might say now that a lawsuit is filed that might incriminate him. I think it's disgusting. I told Austin to stay as far away from him as possible. That kid turns my stomach."

So there it was. No one had really believed that Allen had had some epiphany that made him realize what he did was wrong or decided to turn over a new leaf. He was just afraid of getting into trouble. He was scared that he was going to be held responsible for the role he played in Daniel's death. So his strategy was simple. Turn up the charm and start brown nosing the kids who could implicate him.

Cool To Be Kind was going better than the kids could have hoped. It was getting real attention, not just within the school but throughout the community. Kids and parents were excited about the awareness they were raising. But the powers that be were not particularly pleased with the attention the club was getting. They just didn't know quite how to stop them. The harder the school tried to squash things and throw obstacles in their path, the more the kids relentlessly worked.

The club created a charter, a mission statement, and began talking to students about the dangers of bullying. Other schools began to take notice and started their own Cool To Be Kind chapters. The SV High School administrators began to receive kudos and recognition from community leaders for putting together such an effective anti-bullying program. The kids even got the mayor to attend an anti-bullying rally they held at the school. They organized and executed a school-wide petition, which required constituents to vow never to harass others and to stand up for friends. The mayor's office issued a public commendation for their efforts to raise awareness of bullying across school districts. As the Cool To Be Kind kids lined up on the stage to accept their award, they felt overwhelming pride at how much they had accomplished. But their success had come at a price. Many of Daniel's friends and Cool To Be Kind organizers were getting attacked in the blogs and in person.

"If you were his friend, why didn't you stop the bullying?"

"How come you let it happen?

"What kind of a friend are you?"

"Why did you start this club now? Maybe you're just doing it for the attention."

"Maybe you're just doing it because it'll look good on your college application."

The Cool To Be Kind kids heard it all, but nothing the critics could say would stop them. They had learned that when someone is a beacon of light, there will always be someone else trying to steal that light. When someone confronts evil, there will often be a malicious attack in return. The attacks were coming in the form of mounting denials from school administrators, lack of support from uneducated adults or sensational attacks from the press. But they knew that anything worth fighting for comes at a price, and they were ready to pay it.

CHAPTER
TWENTY-EIGHT

Everyone knows how my brother died. I want you to know
how he lived.

—Mary Nell Verrett

She was only thirteen, but Victoria as well had begun feeling the
political effects of the lawsuit. Her middle school was planning
to conduct an anti-bullying assembly in response to an initiative by her Peer Assistance Leadership class. The Peer Assistance
Leadership (PAL) class was to conduct a presentation during the
assembly on the topic of bullying. Victoria had been enrolled in
PAL class for the past two years, even before the death of her big
brother. Some of her closest friends were also in the program.
Lisa Hydes's younger brother Collin, a socially conscientious girl
named Cathy and a quiet girl named Serena were among them.
As his older sister was the president of the Cool To Be Kind
Club at SV High, Collin had a particular interest in the anti-
bullying movement.

Victoria and her three friends sat in their vice principal's office
with their request to present. The stout man with thinning, dyed
hair read their request and peered over his spectacles at them.
He was reluctant but agreed to give them a few minutes at the
assembly. But there would be caveats.

"We have to be very careful what we say about suicide. We
probably shouldn't mention it at all. Too traumatic for kids, I
think. And we have to be careful what we say about bystanders being able to make a difference. We don't want bystanders to
think that victims will just go home and kill themselves."

The kids couldn't believe what they were hearing.

"We need people to take this seriously," Victoria said, rubbing her forehead. "Suicide is real, and people should know that." She tried to keep her voice steady as she spoke. Had they learned nothing from her brother's death?

The vice principal didn't want to argue with her. What did this little girl know about how the adult world worked, how adults could get into hot water with their superiors about these things? How could he explain the world of corporate games and the politics of covering yourself at all costs?

"I need to see a draft of your presentation and approve it in its entirety before you'll be allowed to present it at the assembly." He continued in a monotone voice. "Remember, I can't stress enough that you will only be given ten minutes and not a second more to speak because a local police officer is going to be giving a very important presentation that he needs adequate time for. I suggest that you each take a letter of our school acronym and have each letter stand for a topic related to bullying." *That should be harmless enough*, he thought to himself.

The students agreed. Ten minutes was better than nothing. Each child had a letter to present, and Victoria's letter was *S*. She chose "serious consequences" as her topic. She prepared her speech to share information about bullying and how it had affected her brother. She wrote about who her brother was, what his life was like, and what his interests and dreams had been. She included how and why he had been targeted by the bullies and the ultimate consequences of lowered self-esteem and suicide. Victoria was proud of what she had written and was ready to share it with her school for the anti-bullying assembly.

The PAL teacher read her speech, and tears filled her eyes. She was a compassionate woman with kids of her own, and she loved Victoria as she loved all of her students. She asked Victoria if she could speak to her after class.

"I really enjoyed your speech," she began, "but the vice principal wants to read the final version before you present it."

The kids waited. It was several days later that they received their reply.

"Due to the pending lawsuit, the vice principal is asking you to further edit it. I hope you understand."

She didn't understand. Victoria, accompanied by Cathy, Collin, and Serena, tracked down the vice principal after class to find out what kind of "editing" she was expected to do.

"What parts do you want me to take out?" Victoria asked with her speech in her small hands.

After a slight pause, he answered. "We want you to take out that bullying occurred in this school to your brother, and we want you to take out his name altogether. No mention of him at all. See, we don't want to personalize this."

Victoria was astounded. Her three friends stood by her side, just as shocked as she was. *My brother died from bullying*, Victoria thought. *And you don't want me to personalize it?* It was a little late for that now. Bullying had already become very personal to her without her permission. She would have loved not to be so personal about it, but that wasn't possible. Why should she have to silence herself now? Silence was what created the hell her family had to live through in the first place.

Without another word, the young friends walked out of the vice principal's office, all of them trying to get a hold of what had just gone down. Collin couldn't think of anything to say to his friend, anything to lessen the blow. But he had to think of something. Finally he spoke.

"Don't worry, Victoria," Collin assured her, putting a caring arm around her shoulder. "I'll record any more conversations we have with the school people on my iPhone so we can prove to everyone how much they just don't get it." He may have not been able to stand up to the vice principal that day, but he could prove to the world what they were fighting against, if he had to in the future, with some help from his new smart phone.

——•◦•——

The day of the anti-bullying assembly was upon them, and the PAL kids were excited. The assembly began, and the police officer started with his very important presentation that the kids had been ordered to work around. He spoke on the importance of doing your homework on time, picking up trash, walking around the planters instead of jumping over them and putting the plants in harm's way, and how the kids shouldn't use sharpies to write on school property. Students yawned and shifted in their seats. Some were annoyed. None of what the officer was rambling about had anything to do with violence or bullying. Some of the student body was left wondering if the administration assumed they were stupid—or maybe they just didn't get it.

One speaker after another droned on about keeping the campus free of litter and respecting the foliage, until it was finally the PAL kids' turn. The students stood up on the stage to conduct their presentations. Cathy, Collin, and Serena talked about the realities of bullying. They explained how to recognize and prevent it and the importance of bystanders speaking up. Victoria was the last to speak. Her speech may have been edited by the administration, but Victoria knew that she had the stage and no one could edit her voice now.

"S stands for serious consequences," she began and continued on with the way that bullying can affect self-esteem, cause self-hatred and lead to depression and suicide. "Many of you have heard about what happened to my brother. The bullying he suffered started right here in this school. He was a great kid and none of it had to happen. The story speaks for itself."

Her words were powerful. Some kids in the audience cried as she spoke. One boy who was infamous around the school campus for his bullying antics stayed after the assembly and approached

Victoria. As Collin saw the bully walking toward Victoria, he protectively moved toward his friend. He wasn't sure what the kid wanted with her, but he was going to be sure he was there if she needed him.

"You're really brave," the boy began. "I enjoyed your speech." With that, he put his arms around Victoria and gave her a bear hug. He wasn't there to hassle her; he was there to commend her for what she was doing. Her speech had helped him understand how ugly actions can affect lives. He wanted to have no more part of it. Out of the corner of her eye, Victoria caught a glimpse of her PAL teacher's face beaming with pride. It wasn't necessarily all of the school administrators who needed to change. It was just the system itself.

As shattered as their protected world had become, the family was determined not to become a house of mourning. Their home was regularly filled with friends and relatives. Victoria's friends, each of whom seemed wise beyond their years, were a constant bright spot in her life, giving tirelessly of their love and support. Although some of the family's old friends no longer knew what to say and were afraid that the mere mention of Daniel's name might break open old wounds, there were plenty of friends who knew exactly what to say, and thankfully they did. The family also made a number of new friends through the tragedy. After their son's death, the parents of many of Daniel's friends became their closest allies, always present with their support and counsel. *The friendships are his parting gift to us*, thought his mother.

The family had to relearn how to live life without their boy, their loving son, and the protective big brother. Victoria began struggling with class choices she needed to make for her next year's school schedule. She was a smart kid just like her brother and was in advanced placement classes at school, but she was afraid of stretching herself too thin by adding yet another intensive class—World History—to an already challenging schedule. Yeah, she wanted to be studious and get ahead, but life wasn't all about books and tests. She thought that World History might be a bit too much with everything else she had going on, and her parents were supportive of anything she decided.

Dinner had ended, and Victoria was helping her mom and Nonna clear the dishes. "Mom, did Daniel take World History his freshman year?"

"I'm not sure, love. Is it important for you to know?" asked Anna. "If so, I'll find his schedule for you."

"I'd like to know, if you don't mind doing that."

The two of them walked upstairs and dug through Daniel's records. *Such wonderful accomplishments*, thought his mom as she leafed through reports and certificates. They eventually found his freshman class schedule. Indeed, he had taken World History.

"I think I'm gonna take World History." Victoria looked up at her mom.

Anna realized that, in her own way, she was still seeking her brother's guidance and still following his direction. Even after his death, he was still influencing her choices. But in a few more years, Victoria would be older than Daniel had been, and his path could no longer provide guidance for her. Somehow Anna knew that, even then, Victoria would still find a way to be guided by her big brother.

Before Anna turned in that night, she checked Daniel's personal Facebook page. Victoria had posted three short words on it: *I love you.*

CHAPTER
TWENTY-NINE

No poet ever interpreted nature as freely as a lawyer inter-
prets the truth.

—Jean Giraudoux

Legal proceedings began. The first one to be deposed was Anna.
A team of eight opposing counsel sat at the large conference table.

The lead opposing counsel was a man named Mr. Renfrew. He
was an older man with ink blotted skin, yellowed teeth, and hair
that did whatever it wanted, but he wore an expensive Italian suit
that looked as though it was trying hard to make up for his physical appearance. As the proceedings began, he flashed an arrogant,
nicotine stained smile at her.

"I must give you some very specific instructions before we
begin," the unkempt attorney started. "If at any point you get tired,
you can ask for a break, but you will be required to answer any
outstanding question on the table before taking that break. Do
you understand? It's very important that you follow this process."

Tom Dunn had already explained this process to them. The
questioning attorney had to be sure that the witness's attorney
wasn't coaching them on how to answer the specific question that
had been asked and still unanswered. Anna acknowledged that
she understood, and the attorney began the questioning.

The questions covered every part of Anna's life.

"Where was your mother born?"

"Where was your father born?"

"What kind of home life did you have?"

"What are the names of all of your aunts and uncles?"

"What kind of marriage did each of your aunts and uncles have?"

"Did either of your parents drink?"

"Did either of your parents take antidepressants?"

"What prescription meds did your parents take?"

"Were either of them depressed?"

"What are the names of your siblings?"

"Have any of them been diagnosed with depression?"

"How many previous marriages have you had?"

"What medications have you ever taken in your lifetime?"

"Have you ever been diagnosed as being depressed?"

"How do you discipline your children?"

"Do you work outside the home?"

"How many hours a day do you work outside the home?"

"Was Daniel gay?"

"Was Daniel on medication?"

"Did Daniel drink or take drugs?"

"What did Daniel do for entertainment?"

"Had Daniel been abused by priests?"

"Had Daniel been abused by scout masters?"

Their plan was clear. The goal was to prove that there were problems of any kind in the household and blame the suicide on whatever they could uncover. They were reaching for anything that could take the heat off the bullying and the school. They wanted to show that perhaps Daniel's depression didn't result from the bullying but that it ran in the family; that maybe there were marital problems; maybe Anna and Danny were bad parents. Anna had a full-time job—maybe they were latchkey kids and weren't paid attention to enough. Or maybe it was Daniel's sexual orientation that caused it or some medication he was on. Then there was always his religion. Daniel was Catholic, so maybe a priest abused him. There was the fact he was a boy scout. Maybe it was a scout leader that abused him and sent him to his untimely death.

If only they could uncover one of those things or even the slight possibility that it existed, they could argue it could have been something else that caused the depression and suicide and they'd be home free. They were determined to find that something else. All families had something to latch on to. Put any family under a microscope and you can prove even the tiniest bit of dysfunction. They just needed to find out what the Mendezes' "something" was. If they could come up with anything at all, it would be enough to file a motion for dismissal. So they threw as much mud on the wall as possible to see what would stick. Something always did. And they began to turn up the heat.

"Did you ever stop to think that perhaps you pushed him over the edge because you were overprotective of him?" The attorney smirked at Anna as he flashed her an arrogant, dingy grin.

Anna stared back. "No, I was not overprotective."

"On the day that Daniel died, he knew you were both leaving to celebrate your anniversary, isn't that correct?"

"Yes."

Mr. Renfrew leaned forward real Perry Mason like as though he was about to blow the lid off this one.

"Did you ever stop to consider that perhaps he chose that particular day to kill himself to send you a very clear message that he hated you?" He finished his sentence and flashed another exaggerated, wide-eyed smirk. *Surely she'll crack now*, he thought to himself. *If my questions don't kill her, my facial expressions will.*

He's got to be kidding, Anna thought. "No. He loved us."

"Did your son ever take illegal drugs?"

"No."

"How do you know?"

"My son talked to us a lot. His friends did not do drugs. The toxicology report from the coroner's office came back showing nothing in his system. Kids at school will testify that he did not do drugs. My son once wanted to stop taking protein drinks because he thought they contained steroids. We had to convince him they didn't. He was very health conscious—"

"Did your son ever drink alcohol?"

"Yes."

At this, Renfrew perked up. Finally he was getting somewhere.

"Please tell us when he drank alcohol." He sat back comfortably, ready to finally start getting to the good stuff.

"Once when we were vacationing in Italy eating dinner, I encouraged him to taste wine," recalled Anna. "He took a sip, and we took a picture of it with our camera. I'm so glad he was able to do that once before he died."

Renfrew glared at the mother. He was losing his cool with her now. He had built a business on his reputation of being able to break people. He wasn't about to let this case end any differently.

"Other than tasting wine in Italy, did your son ever drink alcohol?" His voice was sarcastic and his words exaggerated.

"No. Oh yes, he sometimes drank wine at Mass. You know, the blood of Christ?" The mother looked the angry attorney directly in the eyes. His piercing stare finally shifted.

"We have an e-mail here that you sent to the principal stating that Daniel was not enjoying his high school experience and telling him you had thought about enrolling Daniel in a different high school. Do you recall this e-mail?" He handed a paper to Anna as he spoke. She looked over the document.

"Yes, I sent that."

"Did you discuss with your son the possibility of him attending a different high school?"

"Yes, I suggested it to him before his freshman year after his bad experience at middle school."

Renfrew leaned forward to emphasize his next point; his eyes narrowed into slits and his voice was low with sarcasm. "Did you ever stop to think that perhaps you demonstrated to your son that you had no confidence in his ability to attend public school? Do you think perhaps that you yourself damaged his self-esteem by making that suggestion?" Again with the nicotine-stained, exaggerated grin and wide eyed stare.

"No," replied Anna. "I'm glad I made the suggestion and wish I'd been firmer about it."

The interrogation went on for hours. As Anna's parenting skills were scrutinized and the relationship she had with her son was put on trial, she wondered how these people slept at night. Was a dead child's reputation really worth the paycheck this disheveled lawyer with no scruples in an expensive suit was receiving? How was it that the most highly paid, seemingly most cultured members of our society would stoop so low on the moral compass? What value did society find in their methods that they were so highly compensated? By what code of ethics did they operate? Was there no limit to what some would do for money? She wondered how this man, who she assumed must have family of his own, lived with himself as he sat in front of her and threw out every malicious speculation he could think of, knowing well the facts surrounding the case and the bullying that had transpired. Did he, at the end of the day, despise his money, knowing full well the means he had used to attain it? Is this the system that professes to protect our children? What rights do our bullied children have today? Anna's mind raced as she sat and answered one biting question after the next that rolled off Renfrew's tongue.

Everyone struggles to define bullying on the school grounds, but harassment in the workplace has been clearly defined, Anna thought to herself. If an adult was walking down the street and was accosted, they could press charges. Or if an adult in the workplace was harassed, they could file for damages and the harassment was dealt with immediately. We wouldn't have had to come here today if Daniel had been an adult in a workplace. But when our children walk onto school grounds, they give up all their rights. They have no protection. If they fight back, they have a record, and things become even worse for them. Daniel was aware and fearful of that very dynamic. The school can claim both parties are at fault, and there is nothing the victim can do about it. Daniel never retaliated until the very last day of his life when he threw the punch after being pushed to his limit. He finally told the bullies he wouldn't take it anymore, and now his last attempt at self-defense had become the school's primary defense.

If the children become depressed and are given medication, then the medication is blamed for pushing them over the edge. If they aren't on medication, then the death is attributed to "untreated depression." As though medication is the only way to treat depression. Let's not consider stopping the cause of the depression, stopping the bullying and abuse. Let's just blame it on the fact that the kid wasn't on meds that would have put him in a fog so that he wouldn't have given a crap what names people called him or what violence was perpetrated against him.

"We have an e-mail here that Daniel wrote to his therapist." The district's attorney was on a new mission. "Please read it with caution. The words are very disturbing." He spoke with an ugly chuckle. *This should make her squirm*, he thought. *Her perfect son isn't so perfect after all.*

He's got to be kidding, thought Anna. *They drove him to this point of despair, and they're going to use against him what he said to his doctor in privacy about how the abuse made him feel?* She wanted to ask, "Have you not ever used that kind of language, Mr. Renfrew? I believe I heard you saying much worse in the hallway just this morning as you bemoaned your lack of progress with this case."

But instead, she replied, "I know exactly what it says. After that e-mail, his own doctor said he was fine. Check the written notes taken by the doctor right after that appointment with my son. And after each subsequent appointment. They all insisted he was fine."

Anna's deposition painfully dragged on, each preposterous question piercing her heart until she thought she could bear it no longer. After the third day, the Mendez attorney threatened to file a protective order with the judge due to the protracted period of time they were taking. Tom Dunn was frustrated.

"The drawn out deposition is part of their strategy to make the case so expensive with legal fees and so draining on you that you would be taking a huge risk by going to trial. It's all about discouraging you from continuing. And they're going to try to ruin your family's reputation in the process."

"Our reputation be damned," replied Danny. "My family stands before a jury of one – God. This isn't just about our only son. It's about all the children out there that still have a chance if changes are made." Danny assured Dunn that they couldn't be discouraged.

But they knew the obstacles in their way. The school district had more money at their disposal than the family, so they could afford the strategy, which was to win at all costs.

At the end of four exhausting days, Renfrew appeared tired and irritable. Things had not gone as he had hoped. The questioning was not producing the results the district's side needed.

"They're worried." Tom Dunn looked pleased. "After questioning the mother, they typically would have accumulated a lot of dirt on a family by now, but Renfew's coming up empty handed. They can't find anything on you guys."

All the other side had so far was a quiet, kind, conservative kid with no alcohol or drug problems, no tattoos or body piercings, no sexual identity issues—a kid who had not been on medication, was never in trouble, had no family problems, and had good grades and good friends. Nothing to point a finger at. The kid's clean past was going to be a real issue for them, but there was still the father to depose and then the grandmother. Surely Renfrew could break one of them. Hell, no one's perfect.

The day of Danny's deposition had arrived, and the parents were taking a few minutes to meet with their attorney before beginning.

"I've talked to Renfrew," Dunn began. "They're planning to make the argument that because Daniel ended his life on May 1, which was only a short time before school let out for the summer, the school could not possibly have been the source of his depression. They're going to argue that, if it had been school that was causing his problems, he wouldn't have taken his life when he did because he knew school was about to let out in a few months and he would have been looking forward to summer. They're saying that his date of death was too close to summer vacation to try to blame it on the school."

"That's the most ridiculous statement I've ever heard." Anna had to laugh at the absurdity. "They obviously know nothing about post-traumatic stress syndrome that results after abuse has been suffered."

"Or they're hoping a jury doesn't." Tom shrugged. "So they'll grab at anything. And who knows what a jury may buy."

Danny's deposition began and with it the same nature of questions. "What kind of discipline issues did you have with Daniel?"

"Our biggest issue with him was that he refused to eat a sit-down dinner with us every evening. Nonna would always cook a sit-down dinner for us, and we insisted on eating together as a family. Daniel wanted to be able to sometimes eat at a different time than us or eat with friends. We compromised and allowed him to eat at a different time three nights a week."

Renfrew glared straight through Danny's eyes. "Surely there must have been other issues than eating dinner together every night," he hissed.

"Not really. Oh, sometimes he wore his pants a little low, and we would ask him to hike them up."

Renfrew was growing more irritated with each response. This was getting him nowhere. There had to have been some real conflicts between these parents and their kid. There always was. This was a sixteen-year-old kid, for christ's sake. They were always screwed up. He just had to dig harder.

"Who did you specifically tell about the bullying of your son?"

"We told the middle school teacher as well as the middle school principal," Danny replied. "We also told the high school principal, guidance counselor, and the English teacher."

"In what form did those communications take place?"

"In person, and there were several e-mails to the high school principal, the guidance counselor, and the band teacher about the entire class harassing him that he was gay."

"Do you have copies of those e-mails?"

"Yes, we have some we wrote to the high school principal as well as Daniel's counselor, and we've already filed those as evidence. We didn't keep a copy of the band class incident emails. Unfortunately, back then we had a Cox e-mail account that we've since stopped using. Those e-mails have been deleted, but we're sure the school and the band teacher have copies." Danny pointed to Renfrew's pile of documents in front of him.

"Why do you presume to know what evidence I have?" Renfrew snapped angrily.

"I'm only saying that we know for a fact they exist, and we know the band teacher will tell you about them." *And,* thought Danny, *our attorney told us you're legally required to produce those records or you commit perjury.*

"Was your son gay?" Renfrew's question had an accusatory tone.

"No."

"In the therapist records, it states that Daniel was experiencing *identity issues.*" Renfrew made sure to stress the last two words.

"Yes, and if you read on, it states that his identity issues were regarding his ethnicity. As I'm Mexican and my wife is Italian, kids harassed him and often called him 'half-breed' and 'wetback' and 'spic.'"

"Did you refuse to put your son on medication?"

"No."

"Well, why wasn't he on it then?"

"His doctors hadn't recommended it to us. One specifically advised against it. We were researching the possible effects at the time of his death."

Finally, another day of depositions was about to wrap up. One of the bullies' attorneys stood. "We would like to amend our defense to include first amendment rights to free speech," he announced. "We need you to sign it."

"What does that mean?" Anna whispered to her attorney.

"That their clients had the right to call your son whatever derogatory names they wanted under their first amendment rights of free speech," Dunn growled under his breath.

The opposing side was now using the Constitution of the United States of America to proclaim their rights to deride, harass, and persecute—surely what James Madison most likely had in mind.

They sat in Dunn's office, waiting for him to finish speaking privately with the opposing counsel.

"Well," announced Dunn, walking in to his office. "He's trying to tell me we don't have a case because we have no 'temporal proximity.'" He could tell by the expressionless faces on the parents that they needed more explanation.

"It's a legal premise. They're positioning it that the only thing we have is a boy in a physical altercation with another boy an hour before he took his life. And the event was not significant enough to have caused someone to take his life."

"He was harassed for years," Danny began tiredly.

Dunn put up his hand. "I know that but they'll say the other bullying events weren't 'close enough in time' to his death. So they'll argue that the other events must be discounted and they're banking on the fact that they can minimize the final event to a jury."

That evening as they were turning in for the night, Anna turned to her husband.

"I know we said we wouldn't sue the therapists. I'm not angry with them, but if someone would have listened to him more carefully, if someone would have taken the bullying more seriously, they could have helped him. He needed to hear that it was not his fault. Just like any abuse victim. Abuse victims and children in particular have a way of blaming themselves. No one told him it wasn't his fault. He needed to hear that. I could tell him now. But I ran out of time."

CHAPTER
THIRTY

This is a court of law, young man, not a court of justice.

—Oliver Wendell Holmes, Jr.

It was Aiden's deposition day. Aiden's mother was Japanese. She had left Japan when Aiden was a baby and moved to America where she married Aiden's stepdad. The couple owned a lovely home in a neighborhood close to Michael and Sean's house and had just had a beautiful baby girl together. Opposing counsel had claimed that because Aiden was foreign they needed to videotape his deposition, as they claimed he was a "flight risk" and could possibly move back to Japan before trial began.

"That's ridiculous. It's part of their continuing strategy to run up the costs so you'll be forced to settle before getting to trial," Dunn explained, "as well as to intimidate the witness who they know is young and inexperienced in court proceedings."

Aiden sat in the large, cold board room with floor-to-ceiling windows and a giant, glossy conference table. Wearing his usual skate shorts and sneakers, he seemed calm and unaffected by the pomp and circumstance. He yawned wide.

"This is super early for me to be up." He stretched his arms, yawned again, rubbed his face, and ran his fingers through his hair. "I didn't even get a chance to comb my hair this morning."

The team of attorneys sat surrounding him in their well-pressed suits and two-hundred-dollar ties. He was sworn in, and the questioning began.

"How long did you know Daniel?"

"I met him in sixth grade. I was a new kid and really didn't know anyone. Daniel was my first friend. One day he sat down beside me and said hello. I was happy someone was finally talking to me. I think he saw I was alone a lot and wanted to reach out to me."

"Was he your best friend?"

"We were like brothers."

"Did you ever witness anybody picking on Daniel?"

"Yeah. And most of it, whenever Daniel would talk about it, would be in his classes and when there's a teacher there and stuff. And he said that kids were always picking on him and calling him racist names. But he wouldn't do anything—because he was just a really nice kid."

"Did you ever have a class with Daniel?"

"Physical education. And he took band, and I took orchestra. And we would often group up for performances, and that's the worst I saw of the bullying with all the kids picking on him and stuff. It was just sad."

"Have you ever heard the name Allen Carter?"

"The only thing I knew about Allen Carter was when Daniel mentioned his name. He just said this guy was picking on him… like this guy's being a total jerk."

"What else?"

"Well, sophomore year we'd just talk, and Daniel kept on saying, 'These two guys are harassing me all the time. One of them is Sal Gutierrez. I'm trying to tell my teacher, but nothing's happening.' And then Daniel's like, 'Allen Carter's being a jerk, too.'"

"Okay. During your friendship with Daniel, did he ever seem depressed to you?"

"He wasn't the happiest kid after a while, after all the kids would bully him. So not depressed but just not, like, eager."

"Who would bully him?"

"Like the football team, classmates. The thing that really got to me most was that Daniel was one of those kids who would never blame anyone for anything. And he would never tell me names because he knew if I knew who, I would step in. And then one day he told me who."

"Did you know Daniel was in therapy?"

"Yeah, I obviously knew why because kids were picking on him, and no one ever did anything about it. Daniel was always not feeling well from kids picking on him. And no one ever did anything. It was in classrooms, for God's sake, where there are teachers, and they did nothing. Kids would call him racist names and make fun of him for the way he walked, tell him he walked like a gangster, the way he talked, and then one incident in particular became violent, and the teacher didn't do anything. He would try to change the way he walked. He just kept on asking me, 'Does this walk look different?' but I always told him, 'There's nothing wrong with your walk. Kids are just mean.'

"So the last day of his life I heard from my friends that there was a fight between Sal Gutierrez and Daniel. And I heard that Allen Carter was holding Daniel back. And they threw punches at each other. And the teacher knew about it, and nothing happened. So I know that if either one of them throws a punch they would both be punished by the school because, no matter what, they're both supposed to get in trouble. And from what I know, nothing ever happened to Sal Gutierrez," Aiden continued.

"And then when my dad was driving me home that day he was acting a little weird, like, telling me he loved me over and over. And then when I got home that day, I saw all the police cars a couple of blocks away, and I tried to go over there, but nobody would let me. They wouldn't let me past the yellow lines or anything. I saw what looked like Daniel's car, but I kept saying, 'No way that's Daniel's car. No way in hell. That's not him.' I just remember spending hours calling him over and over again just hoping he'd pick up. And he never did."

"Who in sixth grade particularly made fun of him?"

"Phil Jensen. He was just the school jerk. Phil Jensen picked on every single kid he could find. And with Daniel, Phil Jensen went in for the kill."

"Why do you say he went in for the kill?"

"I mean he was mentally trying to hurt Daniel. Phil Jensen was the kid no one wanted to deal with. Phil Jensen was the kid you wanted to be friends with because you didn't want him to pick on you."

"But do you know for sure that Phil Jensen picked on Daniel?" asked the attorney.

"Yes, he always isolated Daniel out of everyone. He had the same classes with me. He talked about picking on Daniel. He took orchestra with me, and Daniel was in band. Orchestra and band would get together to practice. And he always picked on Daniel every chance he got.

"I asked him why he picked on Daniel, and he said he was just the kid to pick on. Daniel was actually defensive about it, and he thought it was funny, so he picked on him."

"Did you ever tell anyone at the school that Phil Jensen was picking on Daniel?"

"Yes. I told my band teacher, Mr. Cooper. I told him that Phil was picking on a lot of the kids, including me and Daniel. So from the sixth grade to the eighth grade, Phil Jensen picked on Daniel every chance he got."

"How often was that?" asked the attorney.

"I said every chance he got—whenever he saw us."

"So you told the band teacher about the bullying. Did you talk to any of the administration about it?"

"I was in sixth grade. I talked to my teachers. I didn't know the administration office in middle school."

"And when you told Mr. Cooper about the bullying, what did he say?"

"He was like, 'Oh, boys will be boys.'"

"So how many conversations did you have with Mr. Cooper?"

"At least once a week, and nothing ever happened."

"You specifically had a conversation with Mr. Cooper at least once a week about Phil Jensen picking on, bullying, or harassing Daniel Mendez?" The attorney was not happy with this statement. It proved that the school was made aware of the bullying and it would be very damaging to their case.

"Yes."

"At what point did you see Mr. Cooper having a conversation with Phil Jensen about it?"

"Never."

The attorney became more annoyed. He didn't like the answers he was getting and refused to accept them. Maybe if he just kept asking the same question, eventually something different would come of it. It was a common tactic used to confuse witnesses.

"You specifically told a teacher once a week about the harassment?" He asked yet again. By now, Aiden had had enough.

He had noticed that periodically an attorney would ask to go off the record, and the court reporter would stop typing. Aiden looked up at the reporter, "Can we go off the record?" The attorneys looked confused. Usually it was an attorney who made that motion. The court reporter stopped typing. Aiden turned back to the district's attorney and looked him square in the eye.

"Dude, with all due respect, what's up your ass?"

The attorney was taken aback by Aiden's question. His ass had never been mentioned in a deposition to date.

"Let me explain," he began, holding up his hands, palms facing Aiden in a defensive motion. "It's my job to make sure I'm getting clear answers. That's all."

"I have answered the same question for you twenty times. My answer is not going to change. Got it? Maaann!" Aiden shook his head in apparent exasperation, then nodded with authority to the court reporter.

"Okay. Back on the record."

The court reporter obeyed. What should have been a few hours turned into a full day. Aiden remained calm and periodically texted on his cell phone while the questioning attorney continued to hammer into him.

"You're really making me nervous with that texting. Can you please put it away?" the attorney finally barked as he wiped sweat from his forehead.

"Oh, sorry. Didn't mean to make you nervous," Aiden replied sincerely. "You guys could have just told me when we started. I'm hungry. Can someone get me a sandwich?"

This only irritated the attorney even more. This kid was supposed to be sweating, not the attorney. He was supposed to be near the breaking point by now, not asking for a sandwich. This was one of the prosecution's main witnesses, and the defense's attorneys were going to get what they wanted from the punk no matter what.

"Did you ever notice Phil Jensen picking on Daniel during PE?"

"Yes. He just made fun of him for everything—just how he would run funny or walk funny, how he talked, and his heritage. Called him hairy kid, dirty Mexican, you have greaser hair, you walk like a black kid, blah, blah, blah. I mean, he didn't say black kid, he used the *n* word, but I don't want to repeat it here. Just whatever he could find."

"Did you see other kids in PE picking on Daniel other than Phil Jensen?"

"Yes. There were other kids."

"Did you ever tell Mr. Cooper that kids other than Phil Jensen were picking on Daniel?"

"Yes, I would tell him that there were kids picking on Daniel more than not."

"So the bullying and harassment that Daniel underwent in middle school, it was more common than not for him to undergo that kind of treatment?"

"Yes, it got harder and harder for him because it just wouldn't stop. And so it was reinforced over and over every year. And he just took it to heart. Like, 'Where did I go wrong?' kind of a deal."

"Okay. You went to youth group together, and Phil Jensen was there as well. And it's your contention that Phil Jensen harassed Daniel at youth group. Is that correct?"

"Yeah. Phil Jensen and his little crew."

"How often did Daniel go to youth group?"

"We went every couple of weeks."

"Okay, so he had a choice not to go to youth group, correct?"

"Yes."

"But he went anyway."

"Yes."

"Did Daniel ever tell the pastor that he was being picked on?"

"Yes. I recommended that to Daniel, and I know he did. Nothing changed."

"Did that make you angry that Phil was doing this?"

"It pissed me off, but every time I would say something, nothing would happen anyway."

"Say something to whom?"

"To the pastor, to the school, the administrators—nothing ever happened."

Aiden's words were brutally honest, and the attorney had to dab at another pool of perspiration that had formed on his forehead. If they were going to move this case in the right direction, he needed to turn up the heat on this kid. He was not going to be defeated by some punk in skate shoes.

"Did you ever try to stop the kids from picking on Daniel?" The tone in his voice was accusing.

"Yes, I would tell them, 'You mess with him, you mess with me.' I would talk to them and ask them why they were doing it. They would laugh, walk away, or make fun of him even more. I would get angry, but Daniel didn't want us to fight them. Daniel just told me that would just make us as bad as them if we fought back, and he just didn't want any harm to come to anyone."

"I kept on telling Phil just to back off. He never did. He always acted like he never did anything wrong. I'll bet you right now he'll tell you he did nothing wrong."

"Did Daniel tell you he was seeing a therapist?"

"Yeah, he told me he needed to fix things. And I told him, 'No, people are just dumb.' He started feeling like he was wrong. Because after a while when he would complain to people about it, they wouldn't do anything. So he thought something had to be wrong with him. And I was like, 'No, it's not you. It's everyone else.'"

"Do you believe Daniel fit in?"

"I believe that Daniel was a good person, and nobody accepted him for that."

Lunch break. *Finally*, thought Aiden. *I'm starving.*

The Mendezes, Tom Dunn, and Aiden walked to a little Mexican restaurant nearby. Tom Dunn noted how big Aiden was. At sixteen, he was already over six feet tall. Aiden ordered three salmon burritos and began chowing down.

"Aiden, the district's attorneys were upset that you weren't answering your summons to appear at this deposition," Danny said.

"Oh, I was just busy. My dad told them I could, but it had to be after my exams." Aiden took another bite of burrito.

"They were threatening to get a court order to have you picked up by a sheriff's car and physically brought in," Anna thought she needed to inform him of how close he had come to that.

"Awww, man," Aiden stopped eating, looking dismayed. "That would have been so awesome if it had happened during school!"

"Man, I was hungry," he began again. "I know we haven't talked about any of this since Daniel died." He was apologetic to his best friend's parents between mouthfuls. "It's just kind of uncomfortable, I guess."

After lunch, Aiden took his seat again and the questioning resumed.

"We know you said you witnessed bullying in middle school. Did you actually witness any bullying or harassment of Daniel in high school?"

"Yes. The first incident was football kids just picking on him, making fun of him for his size and how he walks and stuff."

"Was Daniel smaller than average?"

"He was just average. He wasn't like the biggest, buffest guy, and so they would just pick on him about that."

"When did you see them picking on Daniel?"

"After school or after wrestling where the guys would be at the locker rooms."

"Did Daniel ever express an intention of quitting the football team?"

"At the end of the year, he was just fed up with all the kids picking on him. Something I remember a lot was that Daniel would talk to me about how everyone was so mean to each other and that the coaches would see it, and nothing was done about it. That bothered him a lot."

"So you play lacrosse, is that right? Don't you have that kind of behavior in lacrosse?"

"No. Our coach is very hands-on, and he gets involved right away if there's anything negative happening, and the team is more like a family."

"How did you choose lacrosse?"

"Well, I heard from Daniel crazy things about football, just like how much they'd pick on you and how no one got called on it, and whenever the coaches saw it they would just reinforce it. It's just ridiculous. There's no supervision there. And that's the biggest reason I didn't do football."

"Did Daniel ever join any other sports clubs?"

"He did track, but then he just didn't want to go anymore."
"Did he ever tell you why?"

"Sal Gutierrez kept trash canning him."

"When did Daniel tell you this?"

"About twice a week."

"Did anyone else tell you they saw Sal Gutierrez harassing Daniel?"

"Yeah, Eric, Jeremy, Thomas. Sal would just come up to the lunch tables and start calling Daniel 'dirty Mexican, dirty Dan' and going off on him. And kids in the Italian class, like Austin, saw it. They said Sal was picking on Daniel all the time. And Daniel would say, 'He's harassing me. I don't know why. I try to be friends with him, but he just keeps on harassing me.'"

"Did he say anything more?"

"Yeah, he complained about the teacher not doing anything about it even though she's right there."

"Since Daniel's death, did you ever hear of Sal Gutierrez hitting anyone?"

"Yeah, I was on the bleachers and saw him hitting a girl, and I'm like, 'Wow, this guy is friggin' crazy.' So I went to the administration office and reported it."

"But that was after Daniel died, correct? Not before?"

"Yeah, but I know he's done it before. I've heard of Sal incidents where he hits women. Sal just treated women like crap."

"How do you know that? You only saw him hit a girl one time."

"One time? Are you just saying, 'One time,' like one time is okay? One time? How many times do you need before it's not okay?" Aiden was getting angry.

"I'm just asking. Tell me who else told you that Sal was striking girls," the attorney pressed on. This kid was making him look pretty bad at this point.

"Jeremy, track kids."

"The last incident on the day of his death, were you aware that Daniel pulled the first punch?"

"Yeah, I heard that. And I heard it became a full-on fight."

"Did Daniel complain about anything else, like how difficult his classes were?"

"No."

"Did Daniel ever complain that his parents were putting too much pressure on him regarding his academics?"

"No."

"Daniel was in advanced classes. Did Daniel ever complain that he had too much homework?"

"No, he just did it before we hung out."

"Did he ever complain that he thought his parents were overprotective?"

"Yes, one time he did."

"Why was that?"

"His parents came down to talk to the school administrators. He was upset that after they spoke to the administrators the school didn't do anything about the bullying, and he just finally gave up because he was like, 'If my parents can't make the school do anything, who can?'" Aiden continued. "After Daniel's death, the school started trying to help because they thought they were in trouble."

"Okay. And when did you start the Cool To Be Kind club?"

"After Daniel died, a bunch of us kids got together and decided we had to do something. We all went to the principal's office, but they weren't letting us do anything for a while. Everything we were proposing, even little things like meeting at lunch where kids could all talk and share what was going on, the school was like, 'Oh, you can't do that.' Everything we suggested was like, 'Oh, due to this and that, you can't do that,' so finally we just started the club."

"Did Daniel ever express to you that he was having difficulty in Italian class?"

"No. He just told me about Sal Gutierrez. He was two years older than us, and he was just mean. He thinks he's better than everyone."

"Did you witness Sal picking on or bullying Daniel?"

"Yes, at lunch. He made fun of Daniel for his nationality and everything. And Daniel told me Sal would pick him up and throw him into the trash can. And Eric Peters also saw it and would tell me Daniel was getting thrown into the trash can by Sal. Eric would say that Daniel wouldn't fight back, and he just didn't understand why someone would treat someone else like that." Aiden continued. "And I remember Jeremy Harmon telling me about Italian class and that Sal wouldn't stop assaulting Daniel verbally. And Daniel was like, 'Yeah, Sal treats me like crap. He does it in front of the teacher, and the teacher doesn't do anything.'"

Aiden's deposition was the first time Anna had heard much of the detail surrounding what her son had lived through. She had suspected it, was afraid of it, but had never heard the gruesome details until that day. As Aiden described how her son was tortured on a daily basis and how it often happened in front of teachers who ignored it, Anna's heart ached, and she forced herself to blink back tears. She thought of her kind hearted son being shoved into trash cans and mocked at every turn, and it took every ounce of self-control she had not to break down right where she sat. How can so many adults, adults with their own children who were supposed to be protecting the kids from eight o'clock to three o'clock every day, have just ignored it? She struggled to keep her composure so she wouldn't affect Aiden's testimony.

"And what did Daniel do about it?" the attorney pressed on.

"Daniel would just say that he was going to try to be friends with him. But it never worked. Sal was the kid who made fun of everyone, but mostly he picked on Daniel a lot. Sal would just make fun of Daniel for everything, walking, talking, just breathing. Just Daniel being alive pissed Sal off. It was stupid. Sal would make fun of anyone, but Daniel most of all. I have no idea why, but he did it a lot more sophomore year." Aiden continued. "And after Daniel died, Austin told me the Italian teacher called

Austin in and was like, 'Did you guys see the bullying? I never saw it,' and Austin was appalled because it was in front of her the whole time, and she never did anything. But Sal just kept on."

"So how would Sal do that?"

"Daniel talked in a kind of deep voice for his age. I thought it was cool. He'd be made fun of for that. Kids would say he walked like a gangster, a black kid, and use the N word. I thought he walked like a normal kid. He was made fun of for the way he dressed. It was ridiculous. Daniel couldn't go for a full day without Sal or someone being on his butt." Aiden's voice was pensive.

"Daniel made a T-shirt once about his heritage. He put something on it like, 'Better to be half Mexican than none at all.' He loved making stuff, and he was proud of being part Mexican and part Italian. He would always say he was one hundred percent Mexican and one hundred percent Italian. So, like, he was always being made fun of for his nationality, so he just wanted to show off like, 'You know what? I'm proud of it.'"

"Did you ever communicate with Daniel in writing, like e-mails, notes, or texts?"

"Yeah."

"Do you have those today that you saved?" The opposing side was trying to assess how much exposure they had. If the kid still had the messages, they were really in hot water.

"No, I got a new e-mail address."

"Did he ever text you about the harassment or bullying at school?"

"Yes. He texted that he was being picked on by Sal. He didn't know what to do. He needed help, but he didn't know who to ask and all that kind of deal."

"Did Daniel ever make fun of Sal for being Cuban?"

"No."

"Did you ever see Daniel bully, harass, or intimidate other kids?"

"No. Daniel wasn't like that. Like, Daniel and I talked about joining the gay/straight alliance club at school. We just thought how so many people call each other faggot and make fun of gay people and stuff, and we were like, 'Wow, you guys are jerks,' and we wanted to get involved and do something positive. That's just how Daniel was."

"Did Daniel ever get made fun of for his sexuality?"

"No. Kids called him gay and faggot, but he wasn't gay."

"Did Daniel ever take a girl to the homecoming dance?"

"No. None of us did. We all went as a group."

"Who called him faggot?" asked the attorney.

"Sal Gutierrez, Phil Jensen, football team kids, even random kids that didn't even know him were like, 'You're a faggot.' Phil Jensen would call him dirty Mexican and say, 'Why do you walk like a black kid? You walk like 'the *N* word,' blah, blah, blah—all that kind of dumb stuff that shouldn't be said. You know…and they would say, 'You look like greaser hair…'"

"When did this incident happen?"

"It wasn't one incident. It happened over and over, way too many times. And other kids would join in."

"Did Daniel ever refer to anyone as a faggot or any other names?"

"No. Daniel would never talk back."

"Did Daniel have a temper?" *Surely there must be some dirt we can scrape up on this kid*, thought the attorney.

"He'd just get frustrated about himself more than anyone else, which was really weird because he'd get made fun of, and he'd be mad at himself. He would believe what they would call him because so many people told him these things. And we trust people. It's, like, one of our flaws as humans." Aiden calmly analyzed humanity in a way a lot of adults could not have.

"Did you ever see Daniel lose his temper?"

"I've never seen him lose it," Aiden stated matter-of-factly.

"Okay. And you both were friends with Michael Harrison?"

"Yeah, we'd talk and hang out. We'd always be at Michael's house. That was just like the house to be at. He had every single video game console. We'd just play a lot of video games and skateboard a lot."

"Were Daniel and Michael close?"

"Yeah, like, Daniel would talk to both of us about things that bothered him. He didn't understand why people made fun of him so much. How, like, he's just trying to be himself. And then whenever someone would harass him, and then he would ask for help from the teachers, nothing would happen. He was crying for help, and there was no one there who stood up for him who could actually do something. You know, not another kid but a teacher. Daniel would say that he didn't understand how school could be a prison to him. When you think of school, it's like you go to learn, have fun, get an education, and be with your friends. But he would say, 'I have friends there, but it feels like a prison with all the crap I have to deal with.' Daniel would talk about not feeling like he fit in. He would say, 'I don't fit in anywhere. What's the point of being here?'"

"Did you ever get tired of dealing with his phone calls?" The attorney looked hopeful.

"No, I just stuck with him. I actually thought things were getting better for him. Some of the guys were like, 'What's the big deal? Everyone gets bullied at some point.' But I would be like, 'Yeah, but not everyone gets bullied over and over again for the same stupid things from everyone nonstop for years.'"

"Did you ever feel that school was a prison?"

"I felt like none of the teachers or administration ever gave a crap. They made you feel like a nobody. Like, if you work at a school, it shouldn't just be a job, you know? Like, when you got sick and had to go to the nurse's office, no one gave a crap about you. After Daniel died, I just kept thinking, 'How can no one give a crap when one of their kids died?'"

"Why did you think they didn't give a crap?" the attorney asked in an irritated voice.

"It's just that they were treating the club like a business and trying to tell us why we couldn't do it," Aiden continued patiently. "We needed to do something, and they were like, 'No, you can't because of all these reasons, and it's the end of the school year.' I felt like I had to become an adult real quick, and it was hard."

"How did you have to become an adult?"

"To deal with everything. The school was trying to make it sound like they didn't do anything wrong. The media was trying to bend the story. And the advisor telling us we couldn't do anything. I was like, 'Um, a student died, and something needs to be done now, so no, I don't think we're going to wait a year.' The principal tried to get more hands on after the death. Once they felt like they were in trouble, they started helping."

"How did you come to the conclusion that the school thought they were in trouble?"

"Because we'd go to the office, a big group of kids—all the kids were rallying about it. I remember all the teachers would go out of class and talk about what happened to Daniel that last day in Italian class. It was weird. And the Italian teacher was freaking out, like, about what she could have done and all that."

"So you feel like the school should have done more for Daniel?"

"Definitely. First of all, they shouldn't have held off on that message to all students that was sent out a week or two after his death. They shouldn't have sent the parents a condolence letter with another boy's name on it. Imagine his parents. Their kid just died, and they get a letter from the school with someone else's name on it as their son. The principal heard about the letter at a group meeting, and he was like, 'That can't be right. No one can screw up that badly.' But it was. And they shouldn't have tried to make it hard for us to start the club."

"In terms of preventing Daniel's death, do you blame the school for not doing enough?"

"Yes."

"Did you ever have to attend any meetings of the students in which rules were discussed during your attendance at SV High?"

"Maybe my freshman year."

"Do you remember during that meeting with all the students if they went over rules regarding bullying, harassing, or picking on other kids?"

"No."

"Do you remember them discussing the fact that if you are bullied, harassed, or picked on you should go to the school?"

"No. But even if they did say that, what did it matter? Daniel had reported it to the school, even at the middle school, and nothing happened. Why would that change in high school?"

"Do you remember talking to Daniel on that day that he died?"

"Yeah, he asked me to hang out on the weekend, and we made plans."

"Did Daniel express any fears of being alone and not having his friends?"

"No, because his family was really close and loving. They were always doing stuff together and planning events that I was invited to also, like football games, Chargers games, which are really exciting."

"Did Daniel ever complain about his parents?"

"No."

"Did you ever feel like Daniel was a needy friend?"

"No."

"Had you ever heard of Daniel talking about suicide prior to his death?"

"Yes. He just asked why he couldn't fit in with anyone at school. Like, how when he met people they just didn't get along with him when he was just, like, the nicest kid. And he didn't understand how much he tried to do the best and right thing and tried to find the right answers and help people. And he tried to get people's help, but there was just no response. He once said that, because he couldn't fit in, maybe the world would be better without him.

And I talked to him, and I know he talked to his therapist. I think that's when his parents took him to the hospital."

"Did you ever get the feeling that Daniel didn't fit in?"

"No. I felt the kids would not let him fit in, and they did it on purpose. They just kept putting him down. And later Daniel would be like, 'What did I do wrong?' and I would say, 'You didn't do anything wrong. They're just jerks.' At one point I felt like he was getting better."

"Why did you think that?"

"Because he began brushing a lot of it off. But then at one point he realized it just didn't stop. He was like, 'Maybe if I fit in for a bit, maybe it will stop.' And he'd just go with it. But then when people reinforce something over and over again, don't you think you're going to start thinking that it's true?" Aiden sat up to give more emphasis to his next words. In his innocence, he believed that the attorneys were there to learn something, to seek to understand, and he wanted to educate.

"I mean, you guys all look around forty, right? Let's say you're forty without being too nice, and you think back to when you're in school. At anytime can you remember who picked on you? Do you remember the kids that picked on you? Can you remember their names and faces? Because I can remember the kids in school that picked on me—all the way back to elementary school. I believe I will for the rest of my life. And Phil Jensen was the kid who enforced all the negative things in Daniel's head from elementary school to middle school to high school. Daniel didn't even get to start living his life yet. High school's still going on."

"Did you ever tell Daniel's parents about the bullying?" the attorney avoided Aiden's comment and moved on.

"No. He didn't want me to," answered Aiden.

"Why not?"

"Because he was afraid they would get involved. Because they found out about the bullying in middle school and they reported it, and his life became a living hell."

"What do you mean?"

"Even more kids turned on him. His life became hell, and they called him snitch and loser."

"Did you enjoy taking part in the Cool To Be Kind club?"

"I felt it was my responsibility."

"Did you enjoy the notoriety of being the president the first year?"

"No."

"Do you feel at all responsible for Daniel's death?"

"I feel like I did the best I could."

"Do you feel like his parents are at all responsible for Daniel's death?"

"I feel like his parents did the best they could."

"Do you feel like Daniel's therapists are at all responsible for his death?"

"I feel like Daniel looked for things to help him, and some worked and some didn't."

"But do you feel like they have responsibility for his death?"

"I do not believe the therapists have responsibility for Daniel's death."

"Were you aware of any other issues with Daniel that bothered him other than being teased by other kids?"

"No."

"Was Daniel your best friend?"

"Yes."

"Were you his best friend?"

"I hope so."

After an entire day of questioning, Aiden's deposition was finally over. In the end, the sixteen-year-old had unknowingly put five attorneys through the ringer. The lawyers were exhausted as they huddled to assess the damages they had sustained from this one witness alone.

That evening as Danny and Anna prepared to turn in for the night, Anna turned to her husband.

"As difficult as it was to hear the details of the bullying, it was also very validating. After his death, I used to sometimes wish he could have been stronger. Now, after hearing everything, I'm amazed at the strength he had to hold up as long as he did. Throughout it all, he refused to let himself sink into a deep, dark depression. No matter what they did to him, he just kept pulling himself up by the bootstraps. He was funny, he was engaged, and he laughed. Right up until the very end. Until it was too late."

Her husband agreed. "That's why we never saw how bad it really got. He just refused to let himself buckle under the pressure, and then he crashed. What is it that they say? Even rocks will erode under the constant dripping of water. That's how it happened for our child."

CHAPTER
THIRTY-ONE

A reliable witness always tells the truth, but an unreliable one tells nothing but lies.

Proverbs 14:5 (GNT)

Danny and Anna were concerned about how Nonna would fare during her deposition. This had been the worst devastation she had ever had to face during her already difficult life. Although she was in fairly good health, she was in her early seventies and had not fully recovered from mourning her husband's death when her beloved grandson died.

She had been racked with guilt from the moment Daniel had died, feeling as though she should have been able to do something to prevent it. After all, he had been left in her care that day.

Both parents were painfully aware of the unfounded guilt she harbored, and they were very concerned about the loving grandmother having to sit in the hot seat with the attorneys who were on a mission to prove Daniel's death was tied to anything other than bullying. She was part of the family, though, someone they considered dangerous to their case, so she would have to withstand the barrage of questions that were cloaked in insinuation and accusation like the rest of them. Anna and Danny prayed for her as she sat in front of the attorneys and awaited the questioning.

The district's attorneys began with questions about her past, where was she born, what type of home life had she had, and what medications was she on.

"You were the last one in the family to see him alive, is that correct?"

"Yes," replied Nonna. She spoke in her thick Italian accent. "I just drop him off at home and hurry to pick up Victoria at school."

"Did he say anything to you before he left?"

"Yes." She choked back tears. "He say, 'Nonna, you always say hugs make you feel better,' and then he came and gave me hug. That was all. I was in hurry to pick up Victoria. And then I left."

"Did Daniel ever tell you he was being bullied?"

"He did not say that word. I went to pick him up from school one time, and when he got into back seat with Aiden, I heard him say to Aiden, 'Man, they really bother me today.'"

Nonna paused and took a deep breath. "One week before he die, I drive him to school, and I say, 'Daniel, I can tell something is bothering you. Whatever it is, you need to tell Mom and Dad. They help you,' and Daniel say, 'What can they do for me, Nonna? Hire bodyguard for me?'"

Anna's heart throbbed as she listened to her mother have to recount that to a room full of antagonistic strangers.

"Anything else?"

"One time he listen to phone message on speaker phone. I walk in and I hear someone with very angry voice say, 'Meet me at four o'clock.' Daniel was very upset and throw the phone down. I say, 'Daniel, what is going on? Is this joke?' and Daniel say, 'Yes, Nonna, it's joke. No big deal.'"

"Do you know why your grandson died?" asked the district's attorney.

"Yes. The bullies kill him," Nonna said with anger in her quiet voice.

"How did they do that?"

"They make big hole in his chest!" Nonna beat her chest with her fist for emphasis. The attorneys looked confused.

"They made a hole in his chest?"

"Yes."

"How do you know that?"

"I know. I'm his Nonna!" With that, Nonna's deposition was concluded.

———◆◆◆———

Now, it was the time for the other side's depositions. The first to be deposed was Mr. Sacker, the principal of SV High. As he walked into the room, he avoided all eye contact with Danny or Anna. He was shown to a seat directly across from Anna, but he turned his chair sideways so he wouldn't have to look the mother in the eyes and stared at the floor as he began answering questions. Anna felt a twinge of pity for the man. He looked frightened and uncomfortable.

Tom Dunn gave him the same instructions that the district's attorneys had given to Anna and Danny. "Prior to taking any break, the witness is to answer the question on the table so that the witness's counsel does not inappropriately coach the witness as to how to answer the question asked." Danny and Anna had abided by that rule, and the school administration would be expected to do the same. With the rules explained, Mr. Dunn began his questioning.

Tom Dunn started by asking background information regarding his education and credentials, which Mr. Sacker proudly provided. Then the real questioning began.

"Did you ever talk to a member of the press about the death of Daniel Mendez?"

The principal's eyes stayed fixed on the tiles beneath his feet. "I don't recall."

Tom Dunn continued. "Okay, so you don't have a strict prohibition against talking to reporters. You may have or you may not have, but you don't recall. Is that correct?"

The principal shifted in his seat. "I need to take a break."

"Yes, but we ask that you answer the question on the table first."

The principal glanced at his attorney for direction. His attorney shrugged.

"I need a break right now," the principal repeated. As the principal and his attorney walked past the Mendezes, Renfrew stole a quick glance at Anna and flashed the smirky, yellowed smile. *Unlike you, we aren't going to follow any rules,* it seemed to be mocking. As the two left the courtroom, the court reporter looked surprised. People didn't generally just walk away from the witness stand after a question had been asked without answering it.

After a short amount of time, the attorney and his client re-entered the room, and the Mendezes' counsel continued.

"After conferring with your counsel, are you now prepared to answer my question?" Dunn made sure a jury reading the deposition would understand that the district's attorney had taken ample opportunity to instruct his client how to answer, clearly indicating the answer would be less than honest.

The principal nodded.

"Yes, my answer is I don't recall."

Interesting, thought Anna. *His attorney told him not to recall.*

"Did you start a bullying investigation shortly after Daniel's death?"

"Yes."

"How did you conduct the investigation?"

"I called students into my office and asked them to write about the final altercation between Sal Gutierrez and Daniel Mendez."

So that had been the extent of the so-called bullying investigation. They had sought out only details about the final fight, nothing else. Danny and Anna looked at each other in disbelief.

"How many interviews did you conduct?"

"I don't recall."

"Was it more or less than ten?"

"I don't recall."

"Did you keep notes of the interviews?"

"I don't recall."

"Okay, so you called the students in. What was the longest interview you conducted with any one of the students?"

"That depended on how long it took them to write their statement." The principal finally recalled something.

"Oh. You called them in, and in front of you they wrote out statements?"

"Most."

"Did you contact any of the students' parents to get consent to get written statements from their minor kids?"

"Not that I recall."

"Did you have those kids sign those statements under penalty of perjury?"

"That's on the form, yes."

So the kids as minors had been called in and forced to write their recollections of only the final altercation, nothing else, under penalty of perjury with the principal watching them the entire time and with no approval or guidance from their parents. Coercion at its clearest.

"Other than getting written statements from some of the students in the Italian class in your presence, did you conduct any further investigation?"

"Not that I recall."

"Did you call the homicide detective who was investigating the death to determine if perhaps one of your students was involved in some type of foul play?"

"No."

"Did you call anyone during the time you were conducting this investigation pertaining to Daniel Mendez?"

"Not that I recall."

"So the totality of your investigation was to bring in certain kids from the Italian class and have them write out statements in front of you, is that correct?"

"Yes."

"Did you interview Mrs. Conti, the Italian teacher?"

"I don't recall."

"Did you get a written statement from her?"

"I don't recall."

"This was a fairly significant event. A child died on your watch. Did you do anything to memorialize your investigation to help you better understand what happened?"

"I don't recall."

"Is there a reason why you didn't better memorialize your investigation?"

"As I recall, the lawsuit was filed, and I was advised—"

Tom Dunn interrupted. "Okay, I need to stop you there. I don't want to know anything about what your lawyers told you in confidence because you can't tell me that, but prior to the lawyers getting involved, did you do anything to keep track of your investigation?"

"Yes."

"So I'll ask you again, sir. Did you talk to the Italian teacher about the incident?"

"Yes."

"Okay, when did you talk with her?"

"I don't recall."

"Okay. What did she tell you about the incident?"

"I don't recall."

"Did you get a written statement from her?"

"I don't believe I did."

"Is there a reason?"

"I don't recall."

"Did she tell you whether she noticed Mr. Gutierrez and Mr. Mendez having a conflict between them?"

"I don't recall."

"Is that something you asked her?"

"I don't recall."

"Did any kids ever complain to you that Mrs. Conti would often say to the class, 'I hate you kids'?"

"No."

"Had any other teachers at the school ever told you that they thought Mrs. Conti had no control over her Italian class?"

"No."

"How many classrooms do you have at SV High?"

"About 110."

"All right. Do you visit each of the 110 classrooms at least once per year?"

"Yes."

"How often do you visit each classroom?"

"I make it a goal to visit 10 classrooms per week."

"Do you know how long Mrs. Conti has been with the district?"

"I believe 12 years but I'm not 100 percent sure."

"In the 12 months preceding Daniel Mendez's death, how often were you in that classroom?"

"I don't recall."

"Did you talk to any of Daniel's other teachers about possible bullying that may have occurred in other classes he was taking?"

"I don't think so."

"Did you do anything to ascertain whether or not Daniel was involved in any sports?"

"Well, the Mendezes told me that Daniel had been on the football team when they called me after he died."

"Did you contact the football coach to see if there had been any hazing or inappropriate conduct by any of the other players or coaches?"

"Not that I recall."

"Did you make any efforts to contact any of Daniel's friends to find out if they knew about the bullying that had occurred on the campus?"

"Not that I recall."

"Did you ever talk to Aiden Kai?"

"Yes."

"Do you recall what he told you about bullying that was occurring?"

"I don't recall."

"Did you ask him if kids were bullying Daniel at school?"

"I don't recall."

"Did you get a written statement from Aiden?"

"I don't recall."

"Did you do anything to try to find out about any bullying, such as post something on a blog or put up flyers asking people to come forward with any information they might have about the bullying of Daniel Mendez?"

"I don't recall."

"Did you ever think about maybe sending out a survey to kids asking whether or not they had been bullied in the last school year?"

"No."

"Did you talk to friends of Daniel's during the investigation?"

"I'm sure I did."

"Did they identify any of the boys they suspected were bullying Daniel?"

"I believe they identified one student."

"Was it Sal Gutierrez?"

"Yes."

"Any other individuals?"

"I don't recall."

"Was it Phil Jensen?"

"Possibly."

"Did you discuss with Phil Jensen whether or not he was involved in any type of harassment of Daniel Mendez?"

"No. Phil had left the school."

"Do you know why Phil left the school?"

"He told me he was being harassed."

"Did he say by whom?"

"No."

"Did he tell you that he was being harassed as a result of Daniel Mendez taking his life?"

"He did not."

"Did he tell you he wanted to transfer before Daniel's death?"

"No, it was after Daniel's death."

"So after Daniel's death with only a few weeks left of school, Phil tells you he wants to transfer out because he's being harassed but not as a result of Daniel's death, is that correct?"

"Yes."

"Do you recall the quote you gave to the paper after Daniel's death?"

"I don't recall."

"Okay, let me read it to you. You stated, 'I don't know how much the weak levies had to do with the tragedy in New Orleans, or was it the hurricane? I'm not sure, but the levies were weak. This death revealed—not saying it was the cause—but it revealed that bullying takes place on this campus, and we can be more proactive.' Do you recall making that statement?"

"I don't recall."

"Okay, were Sal Gutierrez and Daniel Mendez involved in an altercation on April twenty-fourth that you were aware of?"

"I think so."

"What do you know about that altercation?"

"Well, Mrs. Conti wrote a referral saying that Sal had been insulting to Daniel."

"Did you ask her specifically what she meant by that?"

"Not that I recall."

"One week later, after Daniel's death, did you ever contact her and ask her for more specifics?"

"Not that I recall."

"Based upon your investigation, did you feel that bullying played any part in Daniel Mendez's death?"

"No."

"Why is that?"

"Because I believe that Aiden told me that Daniel had talked about suicide the summer prior."

"So based upon those comments by Aiden Kai, you formed the understanding that bullying played zero part in Daniel's death, is that correct?"

"The students' statements, as I recollect, also indicated that there had been a fight wherein Daniel had struck Sal."

"And how did that factor into your determination that bullying was not a factor in Daniel Mendez's death?"

"I'm not sure."

"Did you ever talk to the school psychologist about the possibility that bullying may have played a role in Daniel Mendez's death?"

"Not that I recall."

"Okay, did you ever find out if anything was done in response to receiving the referral that Sal Gutierrez was insulting Daniel Mendez?"

"Sal Gutierrez was counseled by the assistant principal."

"Did Sal Gutierrez receive any type of discipline other than counseling?"

"I don't recall."

"Was he placed in detention as a result of the altercation between himself and Daniel Mendez?"

"I don't recall."

"Was he suspended as a result?"

"I don't recall."

"A child died after being harassed by a student and you don't recall the disciplinary measures that were taken against the student?"

"No. I don't recall."

"Did you ever tell anyone that one of the reasons Sal Gutierrez was not more sternly disciplined was his involvement in saving his uncle's life?"

"I don't believe I ever said that."

"Do you recall a parent meeting of approximately twelve parents who met with you after Daniel's death?"

"I think so."

"Did those parents ever express concern to you that Daniel's parents should have been notified of the altercation between Gutierrez and their son?"

"I don't recall."

"Did the parents at the meeting ever voice criticisms for the way the April twenty-fourth altercation was handled by the school administration?"

"I don't recall."

"Do you recall talking to the homicide detective about Daniel's death?"

"I don't believe I did."

"Did you ever tell the coroner's office that there was no bullying that was occurring at the school?"

"I don't believe I did."

"Did you ever discuss Daniel's death with anybody from the Orange County sheriff's office?"

"I believe so."

"Did you mention to the lieutenant that Daniel had been involved in an altercation with Sal Gutierrez?"

"No."

"After May fifth when you found out that an altercation had occurred, did you contact the sheriff's office to let them know that an altercation had occurred?"

"I don't believe so."

"When you got written statements from the kids in the Italian class, did you ask those kids to describe any incidents outside the classroom where Daniel may have been a victim of some type of harassment or bullying?"

"I don't think I did."

"Why didn't your investigation encompass other possible bullies or other possible incidents of bullying?"

"I don't know."

"Is there any reason why you didn't talk to other students and other faculty about allegations that Daniel was being bullied outside of Mrs. Conti's class?"

"I don't know."

"Did you ever meet with a group of Daniel's friends that included Aiden Kai and Jeff Schaeffer after Daniel died?"

"I believe so."

"Did you make the statement that some teasing may have occurred but not bullying?"

"I don't recall."

"Do you recall Jeff Schaeffer ever saying, 'Excuse me, sir. But Daniel and our group teased each other all the time, and all of us laughed, including Daniel.' Do you remember that?"

"I don't recall."

"And then he went on and said, 'But when someone is not laughing back, that can't be called teasing, and that's what happened to Daniel.' Do you recall Schaeffer telling you that about Daniel being bullied?"

"I don't remember."

With every question asked and with every "I don't recall," the principal's face turned a deeper shade of red. Anna couldn't help but think that, if it had been up to him, there would have been more substance to his answers. She got the feeling from the frightened look on his face and his downcast eyes that he didn't have much of a choice in what he did and did not recall. He became more desperate with each response he gave.

"At some point in time, did you receive complaints from any of the students that Mrs. Johnson was making inappropriate comments about Daniel Mendez and his death?"

"I believe so."

"Who complained about it to you?"

"I think it was Aiden Kai."

"Did you ever have any discussions with Mrs. Johnson regarding those allegations."

"Yes."

"All right. Where did you talk to Mrs. Johnson at?"

"Say what?"

"Where was this conversation with Mrs. Johnson?"

The principal looked guiltily amused.

"At SV High School."

"Were you and Mrs. Johnson friends?"

The principal's face turned crimson. He smiled like a school boy caught with his hand in the cookie jar. His attorney shot him a disapproving glance.

"We're professional and I care about all my teachers."

"Okay. What did she tell you?"

"I don't recall."

"Was Mrs. Johnson ever formally reprimanded for the alleged comments that were attributed to her?"

"I recall Aiden reporting it, me speaking with Mrs. Johnson and me being satisfied."

"When the parents first called you after their son died—did you ask them if, when your investigation was over, if it was determined that bullying had occurred, what their intentions were legally? Do you recall speaking those words?"

"I don't remember that."

"During the conversation you had with the parents, did you confirm that, 'All the Mendezes want is for the truth to be known.' Were these the words out of your mouth during the conversation the first week after Daniel Mendez took his own life?"

"I don't remember."

The principal's deposition was over, and he barreled out of the meeting room so fast he knocked over a chair on his way out.

CHAPTER
THIRTY-TWO

If you tell lies in court, you will be punished—there will
be no escape.

Proverbs 19:5 (GNT)

The next witness for the district took his seat at the table. It was
the band teacher's turn. After Mr. Cooper received preliminary
instructions, the questions began.

"Do you remember Daniel Mendez as one of your
band students?"

"Yes."

"Do you remember what instrument he played?"

"Trumpet."

"Was he pretty good?"

"Yes."

"Good kid, polite, quiet?' asked Mr. Dunn.

"Yes."

"At some point in time, did you notice that Daniel was picked
on by the other kids?"

"No."

Anna's pulse raced. *How can he deny that?*

"Did the parents ever contact you to discuss the fact that they
felt their kid was getting picked on?"

"I don't have any recollection of that."

"Do you remember a kid named Aiden Kai, a big Japanese kid?"

"No."

"Did you receive any e-mails from anyone in the Mendez
family notifying you that they felt there was a problem?"

IF THESE HALLS COULD TALK

"I have no recollection of that."

Anna's heart sank. He was under oath. All of her life, she had believed that you had to tell the truth under oath. She could not comprehend that the teacher was sitting in front of them blatantly lying about what had happened. How could he deny their e-mails, and what had happened repeatedly in his class to Daniel? Especially knowing that Daniel was now dead? What brings a man to this level of moral bankruptcy?

"Do you remember Phil Jensen?"

"No."

"Was Daniel an incredibly skilled musician?"

"Based upon my knowledge at the time, I wouldn't have expected that he would be the next Miles Davis." The band instructor smiled nervously. He had made a joke.

"Is there a reason then why you remember Daniel Mendez but none of the other boys? You stated that he wasn't an incredibly skilled musician. So why did he stand out in your mind, or was there anything about him that caused you to remember him and not Aiden Kai or Phil Jensen or the other kids?" continued Mr. Dunn.

A flicker of fear entered the band teacher's eyes. "I don't know." He fidgeted in his chair.

"Why do you remember Daniel Mendez but not the other kids?" pressed Mr. Dunn. "Was there something in particular about him that stands out in your mind?"

"Nothing that I can put my finger on."

Perhaps it's all the bullying and the complaints from us that you recall, thought Anna.

"Did you ever become aware of the fact that Daniel had complained that kids in the band class would call him gay?"

"No."

"Did you ever become aware of the fact that some of the kids in the class, including Daniel, alleged that some of your students would refer to him as Mexican in a derogatory manner?"

"No."

"What training did you receive regarding bullying from the district?"

"I'm not sure I understand the question."

"Were you given any type of criteria to follow that dictated when you were required to refer a student to the administration for guidance and/or discipline?"

"I'd like to take a break and talk to my lawyer now."

"Of course. But you must answer the question on the table first."

"I need a break now."

The band instructor and his attorney got up and left the room. The court reporter looked up, baffled yet again by this obviously inappropriate bend in protocol. Anna and Danny leaned toward their attorney.

"What the heck is going on?" Danny whispered to Dunn. "How can he just take a break with a question on the table unanswered? He's making it obvious that his answers are coached by his attorney and not truthful."

Tom Dunn shook his head in amazement. "It's going to look really bad for them if this ever gets to trial."

The witness and his attorney came back into the room ready with their prepared answer.

"Now that you have had an opportunity to confer with your counsel, are you prepared to answer the pending question, sir?"

And the questioning continued.

"Based on your understanding of the criteria that you were required to follow within the school district, if a Caucasian student referred to a Hispanic student as Mexican in a derogatory manner, is that something that should have been referred to the administration if you became aware of it?"

"I think that depends on the details of the situation that aren't defined here," came the weak reply.

"What are the criteria that you are to use in determining whether or not a kid should be referred to the administration for discipline?"

"Well that depends on the context and the details of the situation."

"If one kid calls another kid a faggot, is that supposed to be referred over to the assistant principal?"

"That depends on the context and the situation and the details."

Anna could not believe her ears.

"During the initial training that you had at the beginning of your school years, did you discuss only disciplinary protocols, or did you discuss other things?"

"Can we take a short break?" Again, the teacher needed a break with his attorney before he could reply to a simple question about any training he may have been provided by the school district regarding disciplinary protocol. The witness and his lawyer left the room.

"This is a circus," Danny muttered to Tom Dunn.

When they had re-entered the room, Mr. Dunn continued.

"Now that you have had yet another opportunity to confer with your counsel before answering the question, do you have one for me now?

"Can you repeat the question?"

The court reporter reread the question from her records.

"That question is too specific for me to answer."

The question is too specific? This has become absurd, thought Anna.

"All right." Tom Dunn smiled to himself and kept on. "In 2006 was there a discussion in your preliminary workshop meetings of the teachers regarding zero tolerance for bullying?"

"I have no recollection of that 2006 meeting and the specific topics."

"Was bullying a hot topic at the 2009 to 2010 preliminary workshop meeting?"

"I don't understand the question. I don't understand 'hot topic.'"

"Okay, I will represent to you that Daniel Mendez died in May of 2009 toward the end of the school year. I assume—and correct me if I'm wrong—that by the time the 2009 to 2010 preliminary workshop meeting was held for the next academic year that was something seriously discussed, right?"

"I don't understand the question."

It's a simple enough question. What is he hiding? thought Anna.

"Was the Mendez suicide discussed at the August 2009 workshop?"

"I would say no."

"Daniel died in May of 2009. By August of 2009, it was totally forgotten, and no one is addressing it at the workshop. Is that an accurate statement?"

"I have no recollection of that."

"Thank you. Prior to the August 2009 preliminary workshop, had bullying ever been discussed that you recall at any of the prior workshops?"

"I have no recollection of the first time I heard the term *bullying* in a workshop."

"All right. In calendar year 2007 to 2008, how much time in the workshops did you spend discussing bullying?"

"I have no recollection of that meeting."

"Same for 2005 to 2006?"

"I have no recollection of that meeting."

Their workshops are certainly not very effective if he has absolutely no recollections of them, Danny thought. *Or perhaps he doesn't remember because bullying wasn't covered in their workshop trainings at all.*

"Can you give me your best estimate as to the amount of time that the school district or your school specifically has provided any type of training on bullying?"

"Bullying is covered under the discipline polices that are covered at the beginning of each school year and ongoing throughout the year."

"Can you give me your best estimate as to the amount of time that is spent on that topic?"

"No."

"Okay, for this year so far, how much time have you spent on bullying training specifically? Your best estimate."

"I need a break."

"We ask that you answer the question on the table first."

"I need a break now."

Yet again, the school district employee and his attorney left the room before the witness would answer the question asked. The court reporter, who typically would have remained very quiet to maintain an uninvolved, arms-length distance, finally had to speak. She looked at the parents with wide eyes.

"Never in my career have I ever seen anything like this before."

The witness and his counsel re-entered the room. Renfrew led him in with the sly smile Anna and Danny were getting to know so well.

"After another opportunity to confer with your counsel, do you have a response for me?" Tom Dunn continued.

"Yes. My response is I don't know."

Wow. He doesn't know how much time the teachers spent being trained on bullying. And he needed coaching from his attorney to come up with that as their best answer. Anna was incredulous.

"Okay, but you spent some time discussing bullying in at least one of your workshops in 2009 to 2010, right?"

"I don't recall."

"So it's possible you had no instruction in academic year 2009 to 2010 dealing with bullying, is that right?"

"I don't recall."

"Did you receive any bullying training from the school district in academic year 2008 to 2009?"

"I don't recall."

"What instruction did the school district provide to you to identify bullying?"

"I don't recall the specifics of what instruction the school district provided regarding identifying bullying."

"Has the district ever provided you with a specific definition for bullying?"

"I don't recall."

"All right. Is it your understanding that the district's definition of bullying includes sexual harassment?"

"I don't know the answer to that question."

"Under the district's definition of bullying, can a verbal comment, without any threat of physical force, constitute bullying?"

"I'm not sure."

"The district has never defined bullying for you in your nine years with the district, is that correct?"

"I'm not sure."

"As you sit here today, you don't recall if they gave you a definition of bullying at any of those workshops?"

"I'm not sure."

Tom Dunn was ready with his concluding questions.

"Okay. I'm going to cut you loose pretty quickly and wrap this up. Just a couple more questions. Mr. Cooper, in your nine years at the district, have you ever witnessed one act of bullying?"

"No."

Of course not, thought Anna. *You aren't trained to even recognize it. You can't even recall a definition of it.*

"Have you ever in your career noticed or observed one act of harassment?"

"No."

And we wonder why, thought Anna.

"In your nine years with the district, has any student or parent ever complained of conduct that you considered bullying?"

"No." The band teacher avoided eye contact with the parents.

"Thank you. I have no further questions."

Anna sat in the armchair in Dunn's office. Danny sat on its arm, rubbing her shoulders.

"I know that was really frustrating for you," began Dunn. "All of the denials and the, 'I don't recalls,' and continual breaks to ask for coaching from their attorney prior to answering the questions. They know what they just did made them look like liars to any jury. Quite frankly, I'm shocked at their performance. Obviously, they have something to hide. But they know that the only way this will hurt them is if these depositions are heard in trial. Their strategy is to squash anything that could surface in these depositions at all costs because then they won't have to pay you much in terms of settlements. They're banking on the fact that because they've driven the costs up so much, you won't even get to trial. So they're protecting their settlements at the sacrifice of a trial, and they believe this is a good gamble."

"I'm so confused." Anna rubbed her temples.

Dunn continued. "They believe your chances of getting to trial are almost zero because they've driven up the costs so much. The only thing they have to worry about is a settlement. So the more evidence that can be suppressed in these depositions, the less they'll have to pay you in a settlement."

The parents sat still, disillusioned by the whole process. They had come to court to get to the truth, and instead they found themselves playing poker with scheming attorneys.

Danny looked up. "Tom, these depositions make it clear that the district negligently breached its duty to protect Daniel and all students in general from harm by instructing its staff to ignore bullying and by not providing adequate training on bullying or harassment. I don't care what their strategy is. That's the bottom line."

"Unfortunately, there's nothing in the current education code that requires schools to act when they see bullying or when bullying is reported or imposes penalties when they do nothing," explained Tom Dunn. "I've reviewed the current code backward and forward. It only uses language such as, 'Schools are *encouraged* to establish policies…' It's all very loose. And the school policies are also very vague. It's a problem, but until laws change and new legislation is introduced, there's really nothing we as attorneys can enforce in a court of law."

Danny's eyes were tired as he sat behind the wheel trying to focus on the traffic ahead. "And they say we have enough legislation on the books." Anna shook her head. "Yet when the cases get to trial, the attorneys say the legislation is too vague. They have nothing to enforce in a court of law."

"You know," Danny began, "I've been so naïve. I just assumed that under oath, everybody tells the truth. We kept our oath. We told the truth, the whole truth, and nothing but. I really just believed that's how it worked."

"Yeah. Daniel did, too." Anna leaned her head back and closed her eyes.

CHAPTER
THIRTY-THREE

Evil can only proliferate if good men do nothing.

—Anonymous

On the eve of the anniversary of his death, Daniel's friends organized a vigil. Michael's parents, Jillian and Robert Harrison, whose house abutted the greenbelt, had worked hard to organize it. Friends, relatives, and people from the community, many of whom had never met Daniel but learned about him after his death, showed up to give their support. The vigil was held on the very greenbelt where the boys often gathered to play football. This was the greenbelt that his mother would watch him walk through as a shortcut whenever she dropped him off to go to Michael's house. But today Daniel was not walking on the grass, not heading toward a friend's house to skateboard and play video games. Today there would be an 8x10 of a smiling boy propped on a picnic table surrounded by flowers and candles.

Daniel's friends lined up to speak on their friend's behalf as kids held their flickering candles. Aiden began with words of encouragement, hope, and peace that he knew his friend would wish upon everyone there. Lisa was emotional as she stressed the significance of carrying on their mission to make sure that the damages that bullying causes were brought to the forefront. She read the lyrics that Daniel had kept up on his bedroom wall.

"We gotta make a change. It's time for us as a people to start makin' some changes. Let's change the way we eat, let's change the way we live, and let's change the way we treat each other."

Jeff reminded everyone of everything that they had accomplished in Daniel's name so far but also of the work that still needed to be done in order to save future lives. Joshua Bennett, a quiet, unpretentious boy with sad, brown eyes who had shared a locker with Daniel, walked up to the microphone as Jeff took his seat. He had not yet been able to speak publicly about his friend's death. Everyone watched as he took the microphone in his hand and hesitated. His friends silently rooted him on.

"He was a really great guy." He had to force every word out as he struggled to keep composure in front of the group. "He was a really great guy. You need to know that. He was just a really great guy." His words were few but for Joshua and his friends, they spoke volumes.

Jillian had organized a dinner for the friends after the vigil. As the dishes were being cleared from the table, Aiden put down his fork and pulled up his shirtsleeve. There on his left arm was a large tattoo, a cross with a ribbon intertwined and flowing down the center were the words "Daniel DiPronio Mendez" inscribed on it. Jillian's son, Sean, took his friend's cue and lifted his shirt to reveal a tattoo on his chest, directly over his heart. "Daniel Mendez. You may be gone, but you're never over." The boys needed to know that they would never forget. A part of their friend would be with them forever.

It had been an emotional evening, and the family was exhausted as they were finally back at home, getting ready for a new day.

"A new school year is around the corner," Anna said. "Victoria, have you thought about possible high schools for next year?"

She absolutely did not want to send her daughter to the same high school that Daniel had attended.

"Guys, I want to go to SV High. I want to play basketball there and take a leadership role in the Cool To Be Kind club for Daniel. It's important to me," she explained as her eyes shone with determination.

"I just think we've learned our lesson with public schools," Anna said, looking at her daughter with concern.

"Love," Danny began to his wife. "I don't think this is about public or private schools. I'm not sure that SV High School is any different than ninety percent of all the high schools. You heard parents talking to us about how their kids were bullied in private schools. I think that this high school is just like the overwhelming majority of all the high schools, public or private."

Victoria looked at her mother with calm resolution. "Mom, I don't want the bullies to affect my life more than they already have. They've affected us enough. I want to go there. That school is more than just bullies and bad administrators. There are good kids and good administrators at SV High too. The Cool To Be Kind kids already started the change, and I want to continue it. And besides, SV High has the best basketball team in the district, and I want to play basketball there."

"But you know a lot of the kids and teachers at the Catholic high school. The basketball coaches there love you. And you could start a Cool To Be Kind club there," Anna persisted.

"Mom, I talked to one of Daniel's friends, Carlson, at the vigil tonight. He's been Daniel's friend since kindergarten. He told me his sister just became the basketball coach at SV High and that she really supports kindness and respect and anti-bullying. No, guys. I'm going to SV High. That's where Daniel went, and that's where I belong."

———◆◆◆———

The following week, the judge ordered a mandatory settlement conference in an attempt to get all sides to settle prior to a costly trial. Anna and Danny made the long trek down to the courthouse. As they stood holding hands in the wide open hallways of justice, outside the courtroom, they noticed the school district representatives, the bullies, and all of their individual attorneys gathered together in small clusters.

Danny leaned towards his wife and whispered, "There's Sal Gutierrez." The words pierced Anna's heart as she looked over to find him.

There he was, the senior kid two years older than her son who had tortured him all year long. The bully who had the altercation with him on the last day of his life—one of the last human beings to see her son alive. His face was likely one of the last images in her son's mind the last few seconds of his life. Anna's eyes met his, and their stares locked. He then shifted his stare quickly down at the floor. Anna's eyes shot from Sal's face to his parents' eyes. She was looking for something, any spark of acknowledgement that they understood the pain their son had caused. But as far as she could tell, there was nothing.

"And there's Phil Jensen." Danny leaned over and whispered, breaking Anna's concentration. Her heart pounded harder.

Phil Jensen. The kid who had begun bullying Daniel in middle school and had made a career out of it—had stolen her son's self-worth, stolen his soul. As her eyes landed on his profile, she froze. That was the face she remembered at the band performance. The monster with the bright green eyes she wanted to grab by the shirt collar before her husband had pulled her back. She could never forget that face; it was burned into her memory. Anna knew now that the band concert was not the only time he had harassed and humiliated her son. He had continued his attacks until Daniel was buried. As she studied his face, she couldn't tell if she was seeing indifference or arrogance in his eyes, but she was sure it wasn't remorse or repentance.

Anna watched the expressions on the parents' faces. The families stood in small groups in the large hallway as they chatted and laughed with one another. Their demeanor was more indicative of people at a cocktail party.

Anna and Danny watched as Tom Dunn approached Phil Jensen's family and his attorneys. After a brief conversation, they saw Phil Jensen waving his arms.

"I didn't do anything! I never said anything to him. I barely knew the kid," Phil's words had the exaggerated emphasis of a daytime soap opera actor.

Anna flashed back to Aiden's words at his deposition. *Phil always acts like he never did anything wrong. I'll bet you right now he'll tell you he did nothing wrong.*

Tom Dunn looked the kid in the eye.

"You don't get it. The mother recalls seeing you harassing her son at a band concert. She personally witnessed it."

"We weren't even in the same band class," Phil snapped back. "He took trumpet, and I was on strings."

"Nice try, kid. You often practiced together. And you definitely got together for the concerts."

"My son has done nothing wrong," Phil's mother chimed in indignantly, hand on her hip. "He's being unfairly accused. We want an apology."

Tom Dunn then made his way over to the Gutierrez party.

Sal looked up at him. "Look, I may have joked around with the kid some, but it was all in fun. I didn't think he'd kill himself. Everyone thought it was funny. And he was the one that punched me first that last day. Actually, I kind of respected him for that. I never thought he had it in him, to tell you the truth."

"We have testimony that you were throwing him into a trash can on a regular basis. One of the students in the class told you that if you didn't stop, Daniel was going to snap," continued Dunn. "Why didn't you listen?"

"Hey, other people thought it was funny, too, not just me." Sal gave an apathetic shrug.

Danny and Anna were escorted by their attorneys into a small conference room. A short, wiry man with thinning, gray hair quickly entered the room.

"I'm the mediator," he announced in a booming voice. He spoke loudly, almost as though trying to make up for his lack of size. He looked around the room and then directly at Danny and Anna. "I'm a retired judge. I've made my millions, and now I'm doing this as a way to keep myself busy. Let me first tell you that I often deal with parents who have lost children, and when I look into their eyes, I see their blank stares expecting me to bring them justice as though I can somehow bring their child back to them. And I just want to clarify that we are not here today for justice. We're here to see what either side can make a jury believe. So if you expect me to bring you justice, you came to the wrong place." His words were punctuated with emphasis.

Anna's muscles tensed. She really wanted to say, "I'm sorry if other parents who have lost children have given you a God complex. I know my child is gone, and no one can bring him back. I live with that painful reality every day." *Why does losing your child seem to come with the assumption that you've also lost your senses?* Anna thought. *Who are these people who think they can interpret what you're feeling in the grieving process for your child? What qualifies them?* But Anna could tell that this man, who was to be the mediator, had an enormous ego, and it would be best not to offend him. Both she and Danny remained silent and allowed the dramatic little man to continue fervently attempting to assert his intelligence.

"I have heard the facts about your case, and I believe it's very weak. Yes, you have evidence of bullying, and, yes, there are kids willing to testify to that, but your e-mails to the principal and the teachers are not specific enough as to your concerns. They do not specifically mention the word *bullying*. Instead they say things like 'problems with peers' and 'peer issues.' So the school is denying that they knew about the bullying. In addition, the principal will deny that you ever called him on the telephone or had any meetings with him, and the vice principal and teachers will deny you ever met with them. And your e-mails to the band teacher, the ones you didn't keep a copy of, are being denied. The only ones they are admitting to are the ones you kept copies of—hard evidence. And any meetings in person or over the phone are also being denied, as there is no hard copy evidence of them."

"But they know the truth." Anna's heart raced.

"Again," the retired judge sounded as though he were a teacher repeating an elementary lesson for the umpteenth time, "the defense's function is to acquit their client, period—regardless of the truth or their knowledge of it. They will do that by any means, true or otherwise. That's just their job. It's how our system works. All we care about is *what a jury can be made to believe*. Not the truth. I told you. If you're looking for justice, you've come to the wrong place." He couldn't help rolling his eyes and began tapping his foot impatiently.

"A teacher noticed the bullying and sent the kid out of class a week before Daniel died, but he was allowed to come back in the very next day. That was against their school policy. That teacher knew," Anna spoke emphatically.

"Well, yes, and I know there is testimony that his friends reported the bullying to the teachers and testimony that Daniel told his friends he was asking the teachers and coaches for help, but you see, teachers and coaches, well, they don't really rise to the level of management, you know?"

What in the world did that mean? Anna thought. *Are the teachers and coaches like the prophetic monkeys? See no evil, hear no evil, speak no evil?* They had entrusted their child to the teachers' care every day, just like millions of other parents across the country, and had assumed that those teachers they handed their children over to had the authority and the obligation to speak up when they saw something happening that should not be. They assumed that part of any teacher's professional and moral responsibility was to address something as serious as constant harassment or any such problem that could be threatening to the health and safety of a student. Was that really too much to ask?

The mediator continued speaking. "The cognitive behavior therapist said in his deposition that he knew Daniel was suicidal and that he had told you about it."

"That's interesting." Anna looked at him calmly, a slight smile on her lips. "His own documented medical notes contradict that. If that were true, why doesn't it appear in any of his written notes he kept, memorializing his meetings with Daniel and with us, and documenting all of his recommendations. He makes comments like 'patient is doing well' all the way up to his last meeting with our son. He even assured us that Daniel's worrisome e-mail was completely normal and that we were overreacting to it. Now he has the nerve to say he knew it all along? Check the records."

"Do any of the doctors claim that there were problems within the household or the family unit that could possibly have led to the death?" Tom pressed.

"No," the mediator had to concede to that one.

"But none of the therapists admit to remembering anything about bullying. In fact, bullying only appears in one of the therapists' notes. The other two don't make mention of it."

Danny stood up outraged. "Of course they don't make mention of it. That's the point! No one took it seriously. And now they're all afraid of their own liability. My wife and I told each one of his therapists at the initial meetings that he had been *mercilessly* bullied. Daniel himself told them. Written notes from one of his doctors specifically state how Daniel himself gave him that background information. In the doctor's initial intake notes, it specifically stated that Daniel was bullied mercilessly in school and that he reported the bullies and was ostracized by the entire school. It's in my wife's intake notes as well. The notes clearly state he regretted reporting them, that it was the biggest mistake of his life."

Danny could feel the anger in every part of his body. His face was hot, his palms drenched. He fought to keep his voice steady as he went on.

"The subsequent doctors all received copies of those reports. They were required, by law, to review them before treating our son. So they can try to deny anything we told them verbally, but they can't deny what's in writing and what they read and wrote. The cognitive behavior doctor stated he specifically remembered Daniel telling him he was being bullied. He sent us an e-mail confirming that fact. He used that word and it's in writing. They can't deny that. It's in the records. *Hard evidence*, as you put it."

"In addition," Anna picked up where her husband left off, "there's written record that Daniel made statements to his doctors such as, 'School is a war zone. Kill or be killed. Make fun of or be made fun of. I wish I had been raised in a ghetto so I would know how to street fight. I wish I knew how to say comebacks when people talk crap to me. People treat me like crap all the time because they know they can and that I won't do anything about it.' How much clearer could my son possibly have been?"

"Ah, but he doesn't specifically state in writing, 'I am currently being bullied, and I need help.' Therefore, there is a gap in your evidence, and I believe a jury will not find in your favor," the mediator casually replied back.

"The autopsy showed cuts and bruising on his face and body." Danny wasn't about to stop. "Many kids witnessed the altercation only an hour before his death. How much more 'causation' do you need?"

The mediator didn't miss a beat. "Ah, but the school is saying your son threw the first punch. So you see the weakness in your case. Your son was just as much at fault."

"Yes, only after *years* of being physically and mentally harassed!" The father was trying hard to maintain control. "What's the definition of the words *first punch*? Do we measure the events only in twenty-four-hour periods, and then the slate is wiped clean? Do we ignore the prior years of abuse? Is that logical?"

Anna clasped her fingers together. "A pastor called us days after our son died and said one of the bully's parents was very remorseful for the role his son played in the bullying. They all know what happened."

"Yes, I know about that. But that actually violates clergy/parishioner confidentiality. The pastor will not be able to admit to that conversation in a court of law. Unless you received something in writing that confirms that. Did you?"

Clergy/parishioner confidentiality? They were family friends, for crying out loud. That's why the confession had been made and offered to the Mendezes. Not from a clergy/parishioner relationship. Anna felt a twinge of regret for refusing the apology offered by Phil Jensen's father days after Daniel's death.

Danny continued, "We have teachers who have contacted our attorney and are offering to testify on our behalf. They have seen bullying occur in this district, and they are instructed to ignore it. They are offering to testify to that."

There it was. Finally, the mediator didn't have a quick response to throw back. His expression froze for a second; then his eyes shot over to Tom Dunn.

"Well, they must be retired teachers because they would never be allowed to keep their jobs if they aren't. Are they admitting they actually saw Daniel being bullied?"

"These particular teachers are from other schools within the district. They aren't saying they witnessed Daniel being bullied, but they've witnessed bullying of other students and want to testify as to how they're instructed to ignore bullying by the district."

"That won't count. They have to be able to have witnessed Daniel's actual bullying. Any other bullying they may have witnessed will be ignored." The mediator was back in business.

"Why doesn't it count?" Anna felt like she had entered another world as she spoke. A world where reason and logic played no role. "It proves this district enabled the bullying by creating a hostile environment where bullying was purposefully ignored and therefore allowed to flourish and directly resulted in my son's death."

"No. In my opinion, your case is very weak." The retired judge looked at his watch. "I'm sorry, but my next case is starting. Time is money, you know. I need to leave now so I just need your answer. So what do you say, in or out?" The mediator's grin was wide.

"We aren't interested in settling," Danny announced. The meeting was over.

CHAPTER
THIRTY-FOUR

Better to be half Mexican than none at all.

—Daniel DiPronio Mendez

Danny was holding a picture of his son, remembering the day it had been taken. It had been Christmas, and Daniel had insisted on buying a giant, blow up Santa to put in the front yard. But the Santa wouldn't stand up straight, and Daniel was struggling to straighten the figure. Just as he had one side secured, the Santa would lean over to the other side, and Daniel would run over to the other side. Danny was inside with his wife and daughter baking cookies and sipping eggnog. They could see Daniel through their big picture window in the living room. They slid the cookies into the oven and glanced out to see what progress Daniel was making. He was now leaning backward under a giant Santa face, boxing it with both his fists as the Santa bobbed up and down on top of him. How they had all laughed hard that day.

His phone rang, jolting him back to the present. Tom Dunn was on the other end. Danny put him on speaker phone so his wife could participate.

"I've been receiving several calls from parents within the district who state that their children are being bullied and the administration is doing nothing about it. They learned about me through our lawsuit, and they want me to help them. Unfortunately, if there are no damages to claim, it's difficult to file a lawsuit."

"What do you mean?" Anna was perplexed.

"Well, your child died, so we have damages. But mental distress is very difficult to prove. So I hate to say it, but if their child hasn't died, there's really very little the legal system can do for these parents. I'm surprised this bullying problem is so pervasive in that district. I just hung up with yet another distraught mother."

The parents shook their heads. It was a broken system that didn't work well even after a bullied child was driven to his own demise.

"The bullying is in all districts, Tom. What's the poor child being bullied for?" Anna wanted to know more.

"This complaint sounds similar to Daniel's. They're calling him racial slurs, socio-economic biases. I just can't believe this is happening in an area as diverse as southern California."

They had no sooner hung up with Dunn when the telephone rang again. Anna picked it up.

"Is this Mrs. Mendez?" asked a frightened voice on the other end.

"Yes," replied Anna. "Can I help you?"

The woman on the other end began to sob.

"I hope so because it seems that no one else can. My son is being bullied. He's coming home every day in tears. Kids are ganging up on him, calling him names, and now they're kicking him. Yesterday, they broke his glasses. We've talked to the school, but they won't do anything. We've put in an application to get him transferred to another school, but it's been denied. We don't know what to do. We're so afraid. Can you please help?"

Anna listened attentively as the woman explained her situation and then offered some advice.

"Get everything in writing," she told the distraught mother. "Don't rely on the thought that face-to-face meetings are more effective. Those can actually be denied in court. Send e-mails to the school, print out hard copies and get any meeting notes in writing. Have you spoken to a therapist? Make sure the therapist comprehends and addresses the anxiety and depression that can result from bullying. Make sure your son understands this is not his fault. It's the bullies' own problems driving them. Your son has done nothing wrong. He needs to know that."

After speaking for hours, the two women hung up and Anna turned to her husband.

"The system is failing not just the children who are victims but the bullies as well. If someone doesn't help correct their behavior now, their actions will only become more serious in the future. And the problem is just perpetuated."

As more calls continued coming to her from distraught parents, Anna began to feel a responsibility to provide a solution. It may have been too late for her son, but there was time for the tortured children who were still desperately hanging on to life. She walked out to her garage and looked down at the spray painted outline of a skateboard on the concrete floor. It was there. It comforted her.

"What time is it?" Dean Hathaway glanced up from his computer screen and looked quizzically at Harold Bart, who had just entered his office. It was dark outside, and Dean was preparing for his commute home.

"I was hoping I could grab a moment of your attention," began Harold apprehensively. He was glad that Dean had noticed the late hour, hoping he would be given some credit for working late when everyone else had abandoned their offices to get home to things like dinners with their families. That should earn him some points.

"What can I do for you?" asked Dean. "I don't have much time. It's my anniversary, and I promised Rebecca I would take her out for dinner tonight."

"I know the meeting with the examiners didn't go as we would have liked," began Harold. "I just keep thinking about their statement that, although we've laid off a high number of employees, they were all at lower levels and we're now top heavy in management structure."

Dean smiled, obviously amused. "Are you offering to accommodate us?" He enjoyed watching Harold squirm. He knew he could play with Harold's mind and enjoyed each time he did it.

"Well, I'm just thinking that Anna's position and mine are basically redundant. She reports to me, and I have no other areas of control under my scope of authority. So, if we eliminate her position, I could take over her functions directly, and the company would suffer no consequences. And we would be accommodating the examiners' most recent criticism of us. We would be eliminating a high-level position."

Dean looked at Harold, hand rubbing his chin.

"I don't know," pondered Dean. "She's our chief lending officer. It's a position that's required by the regulators to be maintained at all times. And your resume doesn't show adequate lending experience to fill that role."

"Dean, you know what a pain she's become. She's always speaking up at meetings, saying things that she doesn't agree with that we're doing. Yeah, she's cut our loan losses, but we want to open credit up again. She keeps saying we're going to make the same mistake we made years ago that got us into the mess to begin with, and she won't let it happen on her watch. I'm so sick of hearing that. We need to start producing loans again, and I think she'll stand in our way. She keeps saying it's her professional reputation at stake and she won't allow it. I don't feel like she's my subordinate sometimes. She doesn't act like it anyway."

"But she says she can increase our new loan production without increasing our credit risk exposure," Dean challenged Harold. "Her resume shows that she's done exactly that at other places."

"Not possible. If we want to make more loans, we have to take more risk. Lower the credit scores that we'll accept. Approve higher monthly payments for borrowers to be obligated to. Stop asking for income verification so much. We've swung the pendulum too much on the conservative side with all of our lending requirements. It's time to bring it back the other way. It's the only way." Harold wouldn't give up.

"The credit risk controls she put in place are on auto pilot now. They can run themselves. And she's hired some strong managers that report to her. I don't need her. I just need the team she's put together and the systems she's built."

Harold could see that Dean was listening with interest.

"And now with her son dead, I hate to say it, but I just don't think she's as effective as before."

"I know what you mean." Dean nodded. "Jeannie and I talked about that. We were afraid she might want to file for disability benefits after her son died. Jeannie saved us a ton of money on that one. But I know what you mean, about her becoming a liability and all…"

"The board likes her though." Dean had already bought into the idea long before Harold had brought it up to him. He had now started to contemplate his obstacles to execution.

"I'll have some convincing to do with them, but I think it could work." Dean got up and slapped Harold on the back.

"Glad to see you stepping up to the plate, my man. Any vacation plans soon? What are you and the family doing?" Harold walked with Dean to his office door.

"We'll probably go skiing as soon as the snow appears again. Have to make sure we get the same exclusive ski-in ski-out resort that we had in Aspen last time. My kids aren't used to roughing it. They saw skiers loading up on shuttles one day and said 'Dad, what are those people doing?' They can't fathom anything less than first class. It's another world to them."

Both men laughed and shook hands.

Harold had a pleased smile on his face as he left his boss's office. Okay. The way he figured, with Anna gone, he had guaranteed his job for at least another couple of years.

CHAPTER
THIRTY-FIVE

Look not mournfully into the past. It comes not back again. Wisely improve the present. It is thine.

—Henry Wadsworth Longfellow

Through Lisa and Aiden's leadership, the Cool to Be Kind kids decided they wanted to host an anti-bullying week. The idea was simple. Tie blue ribbons everywhere and promote anti-bullying education.

Aiden, Lisa, and the rest of the Cool To Be Kind leaders approached the city council. The city council members were receptive to the idea, and they were more than willing to work with the club to get the first annual anti-bullying week in motion. The week was chosen as the week of Daniel's birthday, February 7. When Monday rolled around, blue ribbons were tied everywhere, covering the school grounds and spilling out to the downtown streets. It wasn't just at the school anymore. It was the entire community that the club was reaching. There was fanfare as local merchants participated with donations and promotions. The mayor came to the campus and commended the Cool To Be Kind kids and SV High for their drive and initiative in addressing such a critical topic head-on—another huge success for the Cool To Be Kind club.

———◦•◦———

Successes began materializing in other ways as well. The Mendezes had just begun to clear the dinner dishes when they received a call from their attorney.

"Try as they may, the district was not able to get the case dismissed by the courts due to lack of evidence. The district is offering to settle. So are the kids being sued."

"Okay, let's hear it." Danny pressed the speaker phone button as he motioned for his wife to join him.

"I need to let you know that some school board members are taking this lawsuit very personally." Mr. Dunn prefaced the settlement details.

"Sorry if we hurt their feelings." Danny couldn't contain the sarcasm. "But we lost a child. It's personal to us as well."

"I know it sounds ridiculous," continued Dunn. "It's because of a recent recall election. Two members in particular have taken your lawsuit very personally and want to win at all costs. They want to send a clear message to other parents to never try to sue the district again for bullying. They absolutely have to position this in the public eye as a loss for you." The attorney paused before continuing.

"Go on," said Danny.

"They'll spend millions to defend the claim rather than pay you anything of any significance. What they really want is for the courts to dismiss the case due to lack of evidence, but they don't think they can get that now, so they're willing to settle."

"Tom, that's all we wanted from the onset. It's never been about money for us. It's been about changing paradigms. We don't care about their money. We never wanted their money to begin with and we made that clear from the start," Anna continued. "This lawsuit didn't have to happen if they had just done the right thing from the start. The lawsuit got their attention, and progress began."

"I know, and you're right," Dunn was upbeat. "Since Daniel's death, you've told us how the district has stepped up anti-bullying education and awareness programs. You told us about all of the progress made by the Cool To Be Kind club. They're even spreading to other schools."

"What happens if we don't take the settlement offers and we go all the way to trial?"

"Well, they'll begin deposing the other boys. They'll try to crack anyone who opposes them. It'll be particularly painful for Daniel's friends. They'll continue to discredit your son and your family, along with Daniel's friends. Many of them are already in a fragile state, so we need to think about that. You've personally experienced the lengths the attorneys will go to in order to discredit the witnesses. And the costs will continue to rise for you. If you go to trial and lose, you would potentially be looking at bankruptcy. And for what? You wanted a settlement rather than a dismissal. They're ready to give it to us."

Anna paused. She was curious.

"Tom, can I ask you a question? You knew that money was never what we were after, and we made that clear from the start. But what motivated you to take the case if you knew the chances of being paid anything significant in these types of cases were slim?"

"It was just the right thing to do," Dunn said slowly. "And besides, I love a good fight with those district guys."

"So we should be celebrating." Danny sounded more excited than he had been in a long time.

"Yes, I'm pleased. You accomplished what you wanted, and you can continue on with your mission without the burden of us lawyers stifling your every word or slowing your progress."

"Yes, you have done that." Danny laughed. "No, we don't legislate through the courts. The purpose of the lawsuit was to send the school systems the message that families of victims aren't afraid to claim their legal rights of action and to prompt change within the system. Some change has occurred. I think the administration has gotten the message loud and clear. We'll accept their settlement offers."

The Mendezes, friends, and relatives were pleased as well. Another milestone had been accomplished.

Within hours of accepting the settlement offers, a local newspaper ran the story.

"Family of Bullied Victim Settles"

"Victim Had Identity Issues"

"He Didn't Die Because of Bullying. He Died Because of 'Untreated Depression'"

"Parents Failed to Put Him on Medication"

"Family Settled with Little Paid to Them for Damages"

As promised, the message had to be positioned in such a way that it would seem to be a win for the school district. And they stopped at nothing to do just that. Daniel's e-mail to his therapist had been reprinted in the article.

Danny picked up the phone, paper in hand, waiting for Tom Dunn to pick up on the other end.

"Why would the paper print such a slanted version? Who fed them this crap?"

"That's to be expected. Opposing counsel's law firm has a very tight relationship with that particular publication. They spend a lot of their marketing dollars on advertising in it. Opposing counsel is trying to get their last hurrah. Because they couldn't get the case dismissed, they needed to make their final PR campaign on behalf of their client and any possible new clients who read the story. Their future contracts depend upon it." Tom was matter of fact.

"But why reprint the private e-mail from our son to his doctor? Where are Daniel's rights to privacy?"

"When someone dies, all of their rights die with them. They have no protection from slander or libel and no protection from invasion of privacy. They have no more rights," Tom explained. "Some media organizations have an internal code of ethics of sorts to protect a dead child's privacy because doing otherwise would be in poor taste. I guess this newspaper doesn't. And their client must have insisted that it be printed or they would pull their marketing dollars. Again, part of their strategy to punish you and come out on top. Remember, it's political jockeying."

"Haven't they hurt us enough? Our child is gone."

"You should consider yourselves lucky. Most parents who file these types of lawsuits come out with a lot of hurtful information that's aired about them. This was the best they could do with you."

In their typical point, counter-point style, the paper had included a short unedited quote from a sociologist. "It was obvious by reading the e-mail that the child was being bullied." Upon its publication, the article brought a huge public outpouring of support for the family.

"It's horrible what they did to him."

"Good for you."

"We know it must have been painful, but you did it."

"It needed to be done."

"Only the reputation of someone who lived a life like Daniel had could have withstood the battery of assaults."

"Much has been accomplished now."

If it had been a last hurrah the school district counsel was looking for, their strategy had failed miserably.

CHAPTER
THIRTY-SIX

Do not look back in anger, or forward in fear, but around in awareness.

—James Thurber

Victoria was preparing to attend the SV High school orientation. Two years had passed since her brother's passing, and after much debate and a steady dose of persistence, she had prevailed in the discussion with her parents as to which high school to attend. Her mother accompanied her to the freshmen boot camp. As Anna stepped onto the high school grounds, a wave of memories flooded her, almost crippling her as she made her way toward the entry of the school campus. She saw flashes of Daniel walking down the hallway, waving at her, Daniel coming off the field in his football gear, smiling proudly. She tried to remain enthusiastic for Victoria's sake but struggled to stay focused on the moment.

Anna took her daughter to the multi-purpose room where all the other freshmen kids were crowded and then made her way to the gymnasium for the parent assembly. The same room she had sat in with her son by her side only a few short years before. She entered the crowded room to see the principal on the stage. He was in the middle of his welcoming speech. This time, out of the courtroom and on the school stage, the principal didn't look embarrassed or frightened. He looked flushed and excited as he spoke. This was his territory, and he was in his element.

"I want to welcome you all here today! I just finished talking to your children in the other building, and I'm so happy to see such a large turnout of parents! The California Code of

Education requires the principals as well as teachers to act in the capacity of '*in loco parentis.*' Yes, these are complicated words, but I'll explain their meaning. They mean that we are required to act in the place of parents while your children are on our campus—to care for, guard, and protect your children just as a parent would. And that's exactly what we do. This is your school, and we act in your place. So I want to lead you in a chant today. Repeat after me, 'This is my school! This is my school!'"

The principal pumped his fist in the air as he chanted the words over and over. The parents obediently began to follow his cue. Surrounded by chanting adults, Anna's mind was swimming. *In loco parentis.* Where was that Latin phrase when Daniel needed it? *The principal as well as teachers are required to guard and care for your children.* Were they really? Her mind flashed to the mediator.

"*Yes, the teachers were told about the bullying, but that doesn't really rise to the level of management.*"

Her mind flashed back to the sworn depositions.

"*I don't recall.*"

"*I don't recall.*"

In loco parentis. To care for, guard, and protect your children. Well, perhaps one day. We can hope.

CHAPTER
THIRTY-SEVEN

If all of this suffering does not help us broaden our horizon, to attain a greater humanity by shedding all trifling and irrelevant issues, then it will all have been for nothing.

—Etty Hillesum

In the beginning of my book, I said what was really important was how my story was going to end. The good news is that it's never going to end really.

My death was senseless and never should have happened. In a moment of incomprehensible pain, I did the unthinkable because in my tormented mind, there was no other way out. Sure, I could have handled things a million different ways, but for you to really understand the pain and humiliation I was going through, you would have had to experience being beaten down physically and emotionally day after day, month after month, and year after year. It slowly builds up on you until the weight of it's too much to handle. I didn't even realize the damage that was being done, how it was changing the way I thought about myself and those I loved. I just couldn't make sense of anything, of why the torment kept happening to me and why nothing I did could stop it.

I think what made everything so hopeless for me was not only that I was being trash canned, made fun of, and relentlessly harassed every day that I went to school, but that the people who were supposed to be in charge, the people who were supposed to protect me, turned their heads and looked the other way. Even when I asked for help, they did nothing. I lost faith in the system and maybe even in humanity.

I wondered at what point had we started hating our brothers. When did we begin envying what the other guy had and hating him for who he might be? This wasn't the world my parents had prepared me for. Everything my mom had taught me all my life from the time I could remember about the human spirit, about loving your neighbor, about being godly in your actions, about turning the other cheek—none of it seemed to be true. Had it all been a lie? I only saw dog-eat-dog, violence, no soul, no compassion, no virtues or moral values. Was humankind no better than lowly animals?

While I was sitting at my desk listening to ugly voices calling out, "faggot," "half-breed," "dirty Mexican," or while I was crumpled in the trash can and listening to the snickers of other kids as they passed, that's when I would realize that I was never going to get away from all the crap, ever. And I wanted no part of it. Once I got far enough from the school though, I would start to feel a little hopeful. When I would walk into my house and see my mom's smile, hear my sister's laugh or smell my Nonna's pasta, I would start to think I was okay. Daniel at school and Daniel at home weren't the same person, and that's why nobody got it.

In that incomprehensible moment, I forgot everything. I lost myself. For anyone being harassed out there, know one thing: it's not your fault. What's happening to you is real, and it's painful, and it's not okay. No, you shouldn't have to learn to cope with it. It can really mess you up if you don't get help. Tell everyone, and don't stop talking until someone gets it.

Too many amazing and innocent people have suffered because of my death, and for that I'm truly sorry. I thought I could handle it. I thought I could make all those guys like me if I just held my ground and didn't fight back. I was wrong. But I'm fighting back now. My family and friends are fighting back with everything they have to bring more awareness to this crisis.

To my friends, those who fought and continue to fight for justice in my name both publicly and privately, I always knew how awesome you all were. You know who you are. You stepped up and took a huge risk by speaking out, each in your own personal way. You did it, and you continue to do it. Thanks for being there.

Aiden, thanks for trying to save me from the downward spiral. I love you too, man. It was just bigger than both of us. But now with more people fighting for change, there's hope.

Three months before I died, I wrote a letter to the Deangelo Hall Foundation, asking if I could work at one of their charity events some-day. Deangelo Hall is one of my football heroes. His foundation recognizes that teen violence is a major problem in our society, and I wrote in the letter about how I had personally experienced teen violence and wanted to help fight it. Two years after my death, the Cool To Be Kind club was presented the "Ambassadors of Peace" award by a local anti-violence government entity. You guys are awesome. The work I never had a chance to complete continues on through organizations like the Cool To Be Kind movement. For that, I'm forever grateful, because I've always believed that in the midst of tragedy, there'll always be good that can prevail. But that's just me.

EPILOGUE

We've learned to fly the air like birds, we've learned to
swim the seas like fish, and yet we haven't learned to walk
the earth as brothers and sisters.

—Dr. Martin Luther King, Jr.

The studies noted in the prologue reveal the full and long-lasting
extent of the psychiatric injury, trauma, PTSD (post traumatic
stress disorder), and suicide caused by bullying at school.

The psychological injury from bullying does not result only
after a singular extreme attack but can also result from a prolonged accumulation of everyday insults. These are the child victims most often failed by the system as the attacks are not per-
ceived by society to be as devastating as the more horrific singular
ones. Yet both can result in severe psychological injury. The effects
of PTSD can last long after the bullying has stopped, sometimes
a lifetime, causing some parents to be at a loss when their child
eventually takes his life and never realize why.

Often the symptoms of the psychological damage are erro-
neously chalked up to common teenage issues with no known
cause. They are dismissed as symptomatic of the child's phobias
and low self-esteem. This is a common defense strategy of bullies
and their attorneys: inflict psychological injury then blame the
psychological injury when the victim takes his life.

Under our current system, linking the psychological damage to the prolonged bullying post mortem becomes almost an
impossibility. This is why bullying cases are often not brought to
trial, with many settling out of court. Unless the bullying is wit-

nessed by a large group of bystanders that are not afraid to come forward and speak, is violent in nature and occurs only hours before the death, a lawsuit against the bullies will very likely be dismissed by the courts due to lack of evidence. Any settlement of any kind regardless of amount is considered a win on the part of the victims and their families.

Schools and their legal teams know this and are often not as concerned about legal action by the victims or their families as they are with legal action from the bullies. Until recent media attention, social pressures, and an escalation of legal action, the bullying issue has been a low priority for the school districts to address.

Unlike employers being required to provide harassment-free work environments for their employees, our legal and social systems have not provided a similar standard for our schools and students.

A society is judged by the manner in which it treats its elderly, its sick, and its children. Yes, bullying has been around forever. So have slavery, sexual harassment, and discrimination. Yet laws have been enacted to eradicate those injustices. In the past, the child suicides resulting from bullying have typically been swept under the rug with parents unable to understand what would motivate a child to do something so inconceivable. Now, with the recent spotlight on this national issue and documented medical evidence proving that bullying does cause depression that does lead to suicide, we as a society are finally beginning to understand the ramifications of allowing this type of abuse to continue. Our children desperately need to be given the same rights of protection under the laws that adults have today. Every day, many of our children walk into an environment of dog-eat-dog and might-is-right, where danger lurks around every hall corner. They have become the forgotten group in our society who have yet to be afforded the rights to dignity and a chance to work with pride unaffected by bigotry, abuse, or persecution. Notwithstanding all of the medical evidence that links suicide to bullying and the rash of recent bullying related suicides, schools continue to dispute the evidence. As a society, we must face the brutal facts before we can restore human goodness to humankind.

....

Almost four years after their son's death, the family continues to receive messages from students who had witnessed Daniel's prolonged bullying and the final beating, and are still emotionally struggling that they did not do more to stop it. The ripple effect from the damages of bullying continues to affect many.

Since Daniel's death, Danny and Anna Mendez have begun the National Association of People Against Bullying (NAPAB), a non-profit foundation founded in memory of their son that advocates for victims of bullying (www.napab.org). Victoria Mendez has succeeded to president of the Cool To Be Kind Club in San Clemente, and other school chapters of the club have started across the country. She is a regular speaker on the topic of bullying. Since Daniel's death and other bullying / suicide cases, law enforcement officials have now begun to take into account other bullying events that may have led to the suicide in order to establish a bullying trend and cause of death, rather than to acknowledge only the last event as the only probable cause. The U.S. Department of Justice has also become involved and U.S. attorneys across the country are beginning to raise awareness of the phenomenon within their districts. The new leadership of the school district for Daniel's high school has committed support to the Cool To Be Kind program and dedicated resources to end bullying in the district. More districts need to follow suit with support from legislators, parents, teachers and medical communities.

ENDNOTES

1   Reuters September 8, 2009
2   *The International Journal of Adolescent Mental Health*, 7/2008
3   *Bullyonline.org*
4   *GLSEN Executive Director Dr. Eliza Byard*
5   source: http://www.msnbc.msn.com/id/39758956/ns/
    health-kids_and_parenting/
6   *School Bullying: Tools for Avoiding Harm and Liability*, Mary
    Jo McGrath
7   *Bullyonline.org*
8   *School Bullying: Tools for Avoiding Harm and Liability*, Mary
    Jo McGrath

PHOTOS

Daniel Mendez
You may be gone,
but you're never over.